TRUE CATHOLIC WOMANHOOD

NORTHERN ILLINOIS UNIVERSITY PRESS DEKALB

TRUE CATHOLIC WOMANHOOD

GENDER IDEOLOGY IN FRANCO'S SPAIN

Aurora G. Morcillo

© 2000, 2008 by Northern Illinois University Press

Published by the Northern Illinois University Press, DeKalb, Illinois 60115

Manufactured in the United States using acid-free paper

First printing in paperback, 2008

ISBN: 978-0-87580-997-7

All Rights Reserved

Design by Julia Fauci

Publication of this volume has been supported in part by a subvention from the Program for Cultural Cooperation between Spain's Ministry of Education and Culture and United States' Universities.

Library of Congress Cataloging-in-Publication Data

Morcillo, Aurora G.

True Catholic womanhood : gender ideology in Franco's Spain / Aurora G. Morcillo

    p.   cm.

Includes bibliographical references and index.

ISBN 0-87580-256-7 (alk. paper)

1. Women—Government policy—Spain—History—20th century. 2. Women—Spain—Social conditions—20th century. 3. Catholic women—Spain—History—20th century. I. Title.

HQ1236.5.S7M667   1999

305.42'0946—dc2199-22907

CIP

For Chuck and Carlos

CONTENTS

ACKNOWLEDGMENTS

This book is the culmination of several years of study and research in Spain and the United States and was only possible with the assistance and support from family, friends, scholars, and institutions.

My research was funded by the Instituto de la Mujer, Ministerio de Asuntos Sociales in Spain; the Program for Cultural Cooperation between Spain's Ministry of Culture and United States' Universities at the University of Minnesota; and the University of New Mexico's Graduate Achievement Award.

I wish to thank a number of scholars in the United States and Spain who helped me through this endeavor. I benefited from the support and insightful comments of Robert Kern, Linda Hall, Joseph Sánchez, Victoria Enders, Pamela Radcliff, Stanley Payne, and William Callahan. In Spain, special recognition goes to Isabel de Torres and Octavio Ruiz Manjón. Thanks go to the editors of Northern Illinois University Press, especially Martin Johnson and Susan Bean.

Finally, I thank Manuel Morcillo and Aurora Gómez, my parents, José Manuel Morcillo and Emilia Morcillo, my brother and sister, and Chuck Bleiker, my husband, for their encouragement and inspiration through this process.

TRUE CATHOLIC WOMANHOOD

INTRODUCTION

True Catholic Womanhood

From the ascendancy of Francisco Franco in 1939 to his death in 1975, dictatorial power in Spain rested on the establishment and continuous modification of a Catholic nationalist platform. In maintaining this foundation, Franco's regime looked back with nostalgia to Spain's birth as a nation, to 1492 and the Columbian discovery, and to the Spanish Empire and its Catholic crusades. As it did in the glorious past, Catholicism would constitute the spiritual axis around which nationhood would be drawn. The same Church that blessed the empire would bless Franco's campaign against those twentieth-century infidels, "the Reds."

Franco's state also viewed women as indispensable in nation building. It put institutions in place and passed laws to regulate women's performance of their duties as mothers and daughters of the fatherland. The official arbiters of these duties, the Catholic Church and the women's cadre of the Falange, known as the Women's Section, dictated that women were to serve the *patria* with self-denial, dedicated to the common good.[1]

To untangle the Francoist nationalization of women and the power dynamics that such nationalization entailed, I explore in this study the official discourse on femininity, which I call "true Catholic womanhood," and the ways different Catholic women's organizations responded to that discourse with their own definitions of Catholic femininity. In particular, I examine how the regime articulated opportunities, curricula, occupations, and spiritual beliefs via educational and national legislation and the promotion of Catholic doctrine.

The 1950s were particularly significant for the development of the regime's gender ideology. During this decade Francoism achieved international credibility as a new member of the United Nations and as a good ally against Communism. This international rehabilitation of the regime validated Franco's power at home. In addition, the 1950s witnessed the development of two discourses of femininity promoted by the regime: one valorizing the reproductive/productive woman of the self-sufficient economic postwar model of the autarchy, and the other based upon the Western capitalist/consumer female ideal, established with the arrival of U.S. capital and the regime's enactment of the Stabilization Plan of 1959, inaugurating the era of development.

According to Juan Linz, Francoism fell into the category of authoritarian regimes and was rooted not in an elaborate ideology but rather in distinctive mentalities that are difficult to define.[2] It is my contention, however, that the relationship of the sexes in Franco's Spain revolved around the ideology of the Catholic nationalist platform, which combined religious and political principles and has been labeled National-Catholicism. At its origins, Franco's regime confronted the reconstruction of the country after a brutal civil war (1936–1939). The new regime aspired to restore a new order, based on Catholicism and traditions that had been threatened with destruction by the forces of secularization and modernity during the Second Republic (1931–1939). National-Catholicism unified the right-wing forces led by Franco, fusing the national agenda of the Falange Española with Catholic doctrine. Gender difference was a crucial element in this national enterprise.

The Francoist recovery of tradition sought to revive true Catholic womanhood by emphasizing precepts prescribed in Renaissance treatises by Juan Luis Vives (*Instrucción de la mujer cristiana* [The instruction of the Christian woman], 1523) and Fray Luis de León (*La perfecta casada* [The perfect married lady], 1583); by popularizing female figures such as Saint Teresa de Avila, patroness of several Catholic women's organizations; and through the Sección Femenina de Falange (the Women's Section). True Catholic womanhood rested upon the Christian principles set forth in these texts, which served as guideposts for women's education policy in Franco's Spain. The stereotype of the domestic woman was a crucial element of traditional Catholic Spain that the Francoist order intended to restore. But with the liberalization of the economy in the 1950s, the regime had to redefine its discourse on true Catholic womanhood to effect a transition from the 1940s reproductive female model to the consumer-housewife model of the next two decades.

Guided by the Women's Section of the Falange, Spanish women were to cultivate Catholic virtues under the consumer society as much as they did during the postwar autarchy. In the 1950s, school curricula for girls emphasized domestic training facilitated by the Women's Section's instructors. The

Francoist Catholic version of femininity stressed women's asexuality, exalting either virginity or motherhood, and called for different forms of subordinate behavior. The Francoist educational system in general became the instrument by which the state perpetuated its patriarchal politics. The university was a male realm, a site of state power where the political elites were educated and where scholasticism stood inimical to femininity.

To look for women in the academic realm means to employ gender as a category of analysis in a male (public and political) terrain. Joan W. Scott has pointed out how "gender and 'politics' are antithetical neither to one another nor to the recovery of the female subject." Moreover, gender and politics, broadly defined, dissolve the distinctions between public and private. This view of historical agency affects my research regarding changes in legal policy and symbolic representations by implying a social rather than a biological basis of gender relations. By endorsing the true Catholic womanhood of Church doctrine, the state expected women to fulfill their motherly destiny rather than to become professionals. National-Catholic discourse did not deprive women of a national purpose; on the contrary, their agency resided, paradoxically, in their active political withdrawal. Becoming mothers and wives constituted women's contribution to the national endeavor. Probing into legal texts and statistical data reveals how the regime defined the identity of the university individual and how this subjectivity was irreconcilable with the official meaning of Spanish femininity. The main goal of the Spanish university was to inculcate morality and patriotism, revitalizing the ideals of *hispanidad* along with tradition and Catholicism. The official discourse of National-Catholic womanhood permeated the definition of the college woman's subjectivity.[3] The Catholic Church's doctrine pervaded the *University Regulatory Law* of 1943, which regulated higher education until 1970, institutionalizing the ideals of true Catholic womanhood.

The university lies at the crossroads of power and knowledge. As Michel Foucault has pointed out, since the seventeenth century the knowledge of the order and control of things has been central to state power. The art of government and the empirical knowledge of the state's resources and condition (its statistics) together formed the major components of a new political rationality that Foucault calls "bio-power." Bio-power brought life and its mechanisms into the realm of explicit calculations and made binomial knowledge-power a means for transforming human life. Totalitarian regimes represent the clearest example of bio-power. For the modern state, scientific categories such as population or fertility, rather than juridical ones, became the object of systematic, sustained political attention and intervention.

The other aspect of bio-power is the human body. The body was approached in its biological dimension (particularly in the case of women) and also as an object to be manipulated and controlled. Motherhood turned into a political issue, and biology determined women's destiny. A new set of operations and procedures come together around the objectification of the body.

They form what Foucault calls "disciplinary technologies" employed by the state apparatus to organize its subjects around a norm. The aim of disciplinary technologies such as workshops, schools, and prisons is to "forge a docile body that may be subjected, used, transformed and improved."[4] The university is the institution chosen in this study to decode the power dynamics of the Francoist state in its nationalization of women.

In modern politics, the goal of good government is the correct disposition of things. The state apparatus achieves this by skillfully defining both a national and an individual identity. In Franco's Spain, national identity was explicitly shaped through an educational system that served the purposes of unity and uniformity. Through the promotion of a single language, a single history, and a single religion, the Francoist educational system inculcated, on a grand scale, a sense of individual duty to the National-Catholic agenda.[5] Duty was defined differently for men and women. As the regime (and the Catholic Church) saw it, gender difference constituted the very essence of selfhood; it provided stability and social order to the nation and clarity of purpose to the individual. In Franco's Spain, gender difference was central to the problem of government. The state organized political and social relations by using gender as a signifying element of normalization. The state's powers were inherently masculine. The formulation of laws, statistics, and definitions of normalcy and deviance guaranteed and perpetuated the masculine power of the state. Analysis of the Francoist educational discourse shows the inherent masculinity and the dynamics of power in the nationalization of Spanish women.

As a gender ideology, true Catholic womanhood was far from monolithic or fixed. On the contrary, the women and organizations examined in this book used different versions of the same language system, which divided the world of Catholic womanhood and gave it meaning in different ways. Language encodes competing discourses, or competing ways of giving meaning to the world, and as such is a site of political struggle, a site of power.[6]

It is also important to listen to the personal experiences during the 1950s of leaders and officials of various Catholic women's organizations: the Teresian Institute, the Catholic Student Youth Section (Juventudes de Estudiantes Católicos) within Catholic Action, and the Association of Spanish University Women. These organizations' internal correspondence, their minutes of meetings and conferences, and the oral testimonies of their members illustrate their contribution to the Francoist redefinition of true Catholic womanhood during the transition from autarchy to consumerism. Their definitions of Christian femininity constitute the competing discourses to the official ideology of Catholic womanhood imposed by the regime. The use of oral testimony enlarges the scope of historical analysis to include the subjective hopes, dreams, and interpretations of those who are the subjects of history.[7] Analyzing the life stories of the women of these Catholic organizations helps us to decipher not only how they related to power institutions (such as the university) but also how their beliefs became a source of empowerment.

This study also reveals the significance of gender for right-wing definitions of womanhood. The insights of right-wing women into relationships of power, the relevance of gender difference, and the suitability of equality coincide with the insights of cultural or "difference" feminists. According to Karen Offen, difference feminism (or what she calls "relational feminism") values sexual complementarity in a societal framework, and such complementarity implies difference. Right-wing women also celebrate the distinction between the sexes, but whereas cultural feminists challenge patriarchal privilege, right-wing women call themselves antifeminist and seek protection within patriarchy.[8]

This work explores the mechanisms by which the Women's Section of the Falange, the Teresian Institute, Catholic Action, and the Association of Spanish University Women redefined Catholic femininity and created a variety of female public personae. It is important to understand how gender difference constituted a source of empowerment for these organizations as well as how, in a chaotic world, gender difference represented a basic personal reminder of the order of nature. These Catholic organizations' definitions of femininity demonstrate that gender was central to the Franco regime's transition to modernity and reveal distinct notions of equality and difference within the gender ideology of modern Spain.

CHAPTER ONE

MODERNITY AND
THE WOMAN QUESTION

"Fortunata wanted to learn, but neither her patience nor her concentration was an aid in that effort to acquire some calligraphic skill. Her fingers had become too tough for such delicate operations. Working since childhood had caused her pretty hands to become robust, as coarse as a laborer's, though not steady enough to write. The ink stained her fingers and she perspired profusely, running out of breath and then making a comely little trumpet of her mouth just as she was about to make a stroke." —Benito Pérez Galdós, *Fortunata and Jacinta*, 1886

Being born female in Spain at the turn of the century implied a life of ignorance regardless of one's social status. Benito Pérez Galdós's novel *Fortunata and Jacinta*, published in 1886, captured this reality. The lives of Fortunata and Jacinta were marked by the fact that the former was seduced and then abandoned by Juanito Santa Cruz, who later married Jacinta. Fortunata later met Maximiliano, a small, weak, and sickly bourgeois student, who assumed the responsibility of turning her into an honest woman by marrying her. Although upper-class women such as Jacinta often learned to read and write, their destiny was to become good mothers and wives. In the case of lower-class women such as Fortunata, going to school was not encouraged because in order to survive they had to work, beginning in childhood, in addition to rearing children and running the household when they became adults. In this age of progress, urbanization, and expansion of the railroad, Spain's illiteracy rate remained high, with 56 percent of men and 71 percent of women illiterate in 1900.[1] Progressive Spanish thinkers believed it was imperative to raise the cultural level of Spaniards in order to enter the new century, the modern era. Certainly more equal gender roles would be crucial to the articulation of a progressive educational system.

In Spain, the educational system served as an ideological battlefield in which the forces of secularization and modernization engaged the forces of Catholic tradition. Education became central to the conflict between continuity and change at the turn of the century and continued throughout the century. The forces of tradition confronted the forces of change in a fierce civil war in the late 1930s, from which the National-Catholic Francoist state emerged victorious. With regard to gender roles, progressives and conservatives conceived two different ideal models of women, and they fostered those models through their educational systems. The "new woman" model of the new Francoist state prevailed after the Nationalist victory in 1939. This new woman model was rooted in traditional Catholic values of femininity.

NINETEENTH-CENTURY HERITAGE

According to nineteenth-century progressive thinkers, Spain could not modernize until the level of education was raised. By the end of the century, and within the context of the pedagogical conferences held in the 1890s, gender became a pivotal element of the modernization debate. But equality of the sexes was nothing but a utopian proposal. As Mary Nash points out, "the fragility of the liberal state and the deep conservatism of the Spanish ruling class throughout the nineteenth century strengthened the conservative nature of existing social structures and, where women were concerned, reinforced traditional mores and values."[2]

Since the eighteenth century, enlightened Spanish thinkers had looked to secular education to redeem the country from backwardness and religious superstition and to bring it closer to the rest of modern Europe. Such men as Gaspar Melchor de Jovellanos (1744–1811) believed in the power of education to successfully regenerate the country. In 1809, during the Spanish War for Independence against the Napoleonic invasion, Jovellanos presented his report to the revolutionary governing body Junta Central, entitled *Bases para la formación de un plan general de instrucción pública* (Guidelines for a plan for public instruction). He pointed out the obligation of the state to provide education for all citizens. Later, in 1812 during the assembly of the Cortes de Cádiz, representative Manuel José Quintana presented another report (1813) to the Cortes for educational reform. This report recalled Jovellanos's ideals:

education for all citizens, respect for religious creeds, academic freedom, and limitation of the Catholic Church's influence on the learning process. Such educational projects were rooted in the liberal spirit that inspired the drafting of the Constitution of 1812 in Cádiz.

Secular notions, however, did not go uncontested. Traditionalists and the self-proclaimed neo-Catholics protested any effort to diminish their influence in education, viewing reform as a threat to the Spanish heritage.[3] The restoration to the throne of the Bourbon dynasty in the person of Fernando VII in 1814 after the War for Independence inaugurated a decade of absolute rule by the Catholic monarchy and ended any liberal attempt at modernization until well into the 1830s.

Spain's secular movement again gained momentum with the introduction of the ideas of Karl Christian Friedrick Krause (1781–1832), an obscure German philosopher. Krausism spread in Spain in the mid–nineteenth century through Julián Sanz del Río, a professor at the University of Madrid who in the early 1840s endorsed the work of Krause. Krausists rejected faith as the guiding norm for human knowledge and therefore refused the involvement of the Church in the learning process. Spanish interest in the Krausist ideals led to the founding of the Free Institution of Learning (FIL, Institución Libre de Enseñanza, ILE) in 1876.[4]

By contrast, traditionalists and neo-Catholics embodied the antithesis of Krausism. Their belief in the greatness of Spanish history and religious orthodoxy constituted the main component of traditional thought. Neo-Catholics insisted that Spain's historical mission was to revitalize the Christian doctrine that had originally inspired its forging as a nation.[5] The essence of Spanishness drew upon the principles of unity, hierarchy, and militant Catholicism, which had to be preserved against foreign secular models.

Liberals established themselves in power with the Royal Statute of 1834, which initiated the reign of Isabel II, the daughter of Fernando VII, after his death. Spanish liberals had to fight a series of dynastic wars—Carlist Wars—against the supporters of Don Carlos's ultra-Catholic pretender to the throne, his niece Isabel II. Finally, Spanish liberalism moved toward an increasing radicalism that translated into the Revolution of 1868, which ended the reign of Isabel II and led to the proclamation of a liberal constitution in 1869. The Constitution of 1869 became at the time the last of several constitutions in nineteenth-century Spanish political history. Beginning with the already mentioned Constitution of 1812 in Cadiz, all of them responded to the tension between continuity and change, between traditional Spanish values and foreign modernizing ideals.[6]

The Krausists pursued their ideals for a secular educational system. Their drive to educate women began after the Revolution of 1868 with a series of "Sunday Lectures" about the education of Spanish women, organized under the auspices of Fernando de Castro, president of the Universidad Central in Madrid. Women's education was intended to enhance natural feminine qualities such as purity, piety, domesticity, and subordination. Some attempts to educate Spanish women followed. Founded with private funds on 1 October 1870, the Association for Women's Education gave Spanish women access to higher education within different schools: the School of Governesses, the School of Commerce, and the School of Postal and Telegraph Services. Unfortunately, only upper- and middle-class women benefited from these educational options, which offered better-quality education than the normal schools, the official alternative.[7]

The Bourbon dynasty was replaced by the ephemeral reign (1871–1873) of an Italian candidate, King Amadeo de Saboya, but his rule ended abruptly with a *pronunciamiento,* or coup d' état, that proclaimed the Spanish First Republic on 11 February 1873. The new radical liberal government of the Spanish First Republic needed well-educated mothers to strengthen its republicanism. The concept of educating mothers was not new to political discourse. The ideology of "republican motherhood" was forged during the American War for Independence as part of the debate around citizenship and political rights. The republican mother concept was a variant of the argument for improved education of women that activists such as Judith Sargent Murray and Mary Wollstonecraft had demanded. It defended education for women not only for their autonomy and self-realization, but also to make them better wives and mothers for the next generation of virtuous republican citizens—especially sons. The ideology of "republican motherhood" seemed to accomplish what the Enlightenment had not done by identifying the intersection of the woman's private domain and the public order. As Linda Kerber points out, the idea that a mother can perform a political function represents the recognition that the citizen's political socialization takes place at an early age, that the family is a basic part of the system of political communication, and that patterns of family authority influence the general political culture.[8]

The First Republic, born after the Revolution of 1868 in the spirit of the French Commune, lasted only two years. In the first five months of the new republic's life, five changes of government took place and two presidents took office. This instability led to a conservative coup d'état and the establishment of the conservative republic of 1874, inspired by the French Third Republic and the regime of General MacMahon in that neighboring country. The conservative republic of 1874 eased the transition from the authentic republicanism of 1873 to the Bourbon monarchy with another *pronunciamiento* by General Martinez Campos in December 1874. This event restored the throne to the Bourbons in the person of Alfonso XII, son of Isabel II, after she officially abdicated. Martinez Campos's *pronunciamiento* instated a new system of government known as the Restoration (1874–1902) and a new constitution in 1876. Antonio Cánovas del Castillo (1828–1897), head of the conservative liberal party, constructed a new political system, which dominated Spanish politics well into the third decade of the twentieth century.

According to historian José María Jover Zamora, the First Republic did not destroy the foundations of traditional power in Spain; on the contrary, a traditional ideology of proud lineage persisted among the elite in power as well as among the emerging middle classes.[9] After the Revolution of 1868 and the republican experiment of 1873, these elites identified revolution and democracy with anarchy. Their fear of political chaos led them to support a return to the traditional Catholic monarchy, an essential pillar of authentic Spanish politics, in their view. The army and the Catholic Church were also fervent supporters of the new system. For the Spanish aristocratic army, the revolution and the republican experiment had gone too far: they felt compelled to save the nation from anarchy and disorder. For members of the Catholic hierarchy in Spain, the Restoration reaffirmed their allegiance to the Bourbons, since the Concordat of 1851 favored Church involvement in education and sanctioned a sacralization of the established social order. It is also significant that the Spanish Church had accepted the antiliberal, antisocialist, antirevolutionary ideology of Pope Pius IX's documents.

According to Jover Zamora, the new political system of the Restoration fits the model of the southern European parliamentary regimes in the period of imperialism.[10] This was a predominantly urban phenomenon in an overwhelmingly rural Spain, in which the patronage structure—*caciquismo*—ruled the electoral process, guaranteeing an alternation between the conservative and the liberal parties. Under the new Constitution of 1876, the two parties in power reached a compromise in order to better fight the Carlist threat and the Cuban insurrection. During the 1880s, with the liberals in power, there occurred the most thorough legislative reform program of the Restoration period. They revived the democratic demands of 1868 but retained respect for the new monarchical order. Some of the changes included a law of free association and press (1887), a reform of the penal and civil codes (1889), and the reestablishment of male universal suffrage (1890). Nonetheless, in a society where gender roles were deeply defined by Roman Catholic values, these democratic advances did not improve women's legal and social status.

As Mary Nash points out, the complex political system of the Restoration hampered any attempt to question the foundations of the establishment. Therefore, the political structure in Spain at the turn of the century thwarted the development of liberal political feminism. In the words of Emilia Pardo Bazán, a prominent writer and feminist pioneer of the period, "Freedom to teach, freedom to worship, the right to hold meetings, suffrage, and parliamentarism have been used [by men] so that half of society gains in strength and activities at the expense of the female half."[11]

The 1890s were a turning point in Spanish history. In the international context, this decade represented the height of imperialist expansion, which replaced the historical Eurocentric colonization by a new, authentically global colonialism. But Spain was not able to continue the imperialist race. Throughout the 1890s, Spain fought colonial wars in North Africa (Melilla,

1893) as well as in Cuba and the Philippines (1895), ending with the Spanish-American War in 1898, which resulted in the loss of all the remaining colonies to the United States, a new international power. The year 1898 was called "el Desastre" and lent its name to the "Generation of 98" of new writers and thinkers. After the defeat in the Spanish-American War, disillusionment became the general tone, along with a desperate search for solutions. Spain needed to be reconstructed, reimagined. The body of the Spanish nation suffered from a severe illness and needed urgent care. The Disaster led Spanish intellectuals not only to mourn the loss of the last colonies, but also to reevaluate and reinvent Spain's essence and historical purpose as a nation. The forces of tradition confronted the forces of change, and each side proposed its own solution to ease Spain into modern times and the new century. The Disaster and its ensuing crisis at the close of the century had been in the making for quite some time. For most western European countries, the nineteenth century meant development and progress. In the case of Spain, the nineteenth century witnessed a succession of wars, inaugurated with the Napoleonic invasion of 1808, which led to the War for Independence and ended with the Spanish-American War in 1898.

A new movement called Regeneracionismo emerged as a synonym of reform and modernization. It was a critical response to the sociopolitical crisis of the 1890s. Joaquín Costa was the major proponent of the regenerationist philosophy, which attracted the intellectual elite, business entrepreneurs in Catalonia, and some politicians inside and outside the system, who agreed on the need to reform the Spanish political and economic system. For Ortega y Gasset, one of the most important philosophers at the beginning of the twentieth century, the word *regeneración* meant Europeanization. Spanish traditionalism was regarded as the problem and adopting European ways as the solution. *Regeneracionistas* viewed the school and the reform of the educational system as key to accomplishing social justice and achieving modernity.

In this context, the Spanish Catholic Church felt compelled to modernize its maxims with regard to social conventions within industrial society. Leo XIII's encyclical *Rerum Novarum* (1891) inaugurated social Catholicism. In this document the Pope emphasized the responsibility of the Church to provide for the religious and economic welfare of the working class, and he made education the instrument to accomplish those goals. There were two immediate effects of the *Rerum Novarum* dictum in Spain: the growth of Catholic Workers' Circles both in urban areas and in the countryside and the celebration of six National Catholic Conferences. These labor organizations first appeared in Spain in 1877 by the initiative of Ceferino González, bishop of Córdoba. The mission of the Catholic Workers' Circles was to counter the influence of socialist and anarchist trade unions and the loss of religiosity among the lower classes. It was two years after the *Rerum Novarum* that a national coordinating body was founded.[12] Wealthy patrons directed the circles with a paternalistic mentality, and membership was divided into the "protected" and the "protectors."

The goal of the National Catholic Conferences was to guide Catholics in their attitudes toward modernization and to re-Christianize society through a firm control of education. The proposed educational model reaffirmed the absolute leadership of the Church in this matter with the assistance of the family.[13] It was precisely within the family realm that education of females was articulated. In order to fight the increasing secularization of the times, Catholics proposed the instruction of girls in the Christian values to prepare them to become wives and mothers. The aim was not to educate women for their own good, but rather so that they could render their services to modern society as the first educators of children. To accomplish this task, a variety of religious congregations of women flourished during the nineteenth century, among them the Society of the Sacred Heart of Jesus, the Ursulines, the Congregation of Jesus and Mary, the Company of Saint Teresa de Jesús, and the Company of Mary. These institutions educated the daughters of the middle and upper classes.

The other area of contention with secular ideals of education had to do with coeducation. The view of the Church may be expressed in the words of Jesuit Father Ramón Ruiz Amado (1861–1934):

> Coeducation produces the slow ruin of society because little by little it destroys family values, making both girls and boys almost asexual. In other words, it minimizes in each of them the particular qualities proper to their sex. Coeducation does not train women in the feminine, but rather it creates a hermaphrodite being; a mannish woman, something a thousand leagues away from the image we are used to seeing in our mothers and would want in our wives and daughters.[14]

Toward the end of the nineteenth century, the educational debate also involved other social forces: an active socialist and anarchist proletariat and regionalistic movements, particularly in Catalonia. The labor movement developed the *ateneos* (cultural forums) to educate the working class. Very few women could attend, though, because the gender-based division of labor gave them prime responsibility for the housework and the rearing of the children. There were some efforts to direct lectures and classes only to women, for example in the schools for girls organized by the Catalan Ateneo of the working class, established as early as 1872.[15] It was in the context of the regional and anarchist movement, nonetheless, that women gained political consciousness and participated in popular uprisings.

THE WOMAN QUESTION AT THE TURN OF THE CENTURY

Discussions on education at the turn of the century revolved around two important issues: the propriety of coeducation, and women's access to higher education and professional training. The "woman question" began to be considered in the 1870s in the context of the educational debate raised by American Protestant educational missions, which established the International Institute for Girls in Madrid and the FIL. These institutions, embodying secular ideals, had to confront Spanish Catholic conservatism.

The International Institute for Girls had a great impact on Spanish women's access to education. In the United States, the New England Second Great Awakening had fostered strong sentiments in favor of women's right to higher education and led to the establishment of the Woman's Board of Missions in 1869. Alice Gordon-Gulick, a graduate of Mount Holyoke College, and her husband, William H. Gulick, educated at Andover Seminary, were the first American missionaries of the Board of Missions to arrive in Spain in the late 1870s. The International Institute opened its doors in 1877, initiating a long-lasting exchange of women college students between the United States and Spain. Although the institute was linked to the FIL, it survived throughout Franco's regime and is still functioning in Madrid.[16]

Because there was no organized women's movement in the manner of the United States and Great Britain, the Spanish debate on the woman question in the 1880s remained limited to the elite circles of the FIL and the writings of a few educated women such as Concepción Arenal (1820–1893) and Emilia Pardo Bazán (1852–1921). In the mid-1840s, the former entered the university, disguised as a man, to study law; the latter became one of the most important writers of the turn of the century. The combined efforts of the Protestant missionaries, the Krausists, the FIL, and a few extraordinary women led to official reforms by the late 1870s. A revision in 1877 of the *Law of Public Instruction* of 1857 recommended the creation of normal schools in each province to improve the education of Spanish girls.

Pedagogical conferences became a forum where women's rights and social status were the center of attention. The first national pedagogical conference, held in Madrid in 1882, concluded that teachers had the full responsibility of educating children outside the home and led to the official enactment, in 1882, of the *Albareda Law,* which granted women teachers the right to practice their profession. Ten years later, in 1892, a second conference took place in Madrid, the Hispanic-Portuguese and American Pedagogical Conference. Important topics of discussion were the right of women to obtain a higher education and professional training and the importance of coeducation. A total of 446 women participated in this conference, most of them members of the teaching profession. Concepción Arenal and Emilia Pardo Bazán spoke in defense of women. Arenal was one of the intellectual elite who favored Regeneracionismo. She conceived of education as the most effective means to reform the ills of Spanish society. For Arenal, women's education was part of the social reform: women must be taught what their social and national duties were, their role in the family and civil society. In a report on women's education, she stated, "It is a serious mistake, and one of the most pernicious, to impress on a woman that her only mission is that of wife and mother; this is the same as telling her she is nothing on her own, and destroying her moral and intellectual being." Pardo Bazán presented a paper entitled "Relaciones y diferencias entre la educación de la mujer y la del hombre" (Similarities and differences between men's and women's education), in which she asserted:

> The first conclusion that I submit for discussion and vote is theoretical: I hope that you will recognize that a woman has her own destiny and that her happiness and dignity must be the essence of her culture, and therefore she has the same right as the man to be educated. The second conclusion is practical: I propose that all nations, and particularly Spain, give women free access to official education and allow them to practice their careers.[17]

Nevertheless, very few women had access to a college education by the end of the nineteenth century. Those few who studied were able to receive a certificate of attendance but never a formal diploma. Not until 1881 did a woman obtain a bachelor's degree in a Spanish university. The next year Martina Castells Ballespí was the first woman to receive a doctoral degree in medicine and surgery. She died as a result of a difficult pregnancy, and antifeminists exploited this to promote their conviction that education was pernicious for women, whose main goal, according to social convention, should be maternity.[18]

Those opposed to women's rights to education had strong supporters in the conference of 1892. Their arguments made biological determinism the unquestionable reason to exclude women from the classroom. Dr. Fernando Calatraveño argued in his speech that only a female elite could escape women's "natural destiny," mediocrity:

> [A woman] will never be anything but mediocre. Her nervous system dominates the rest of the organism; her periodical disorders, pregnancy, and nursing, her special organs, uterus, breast, and ovaries, make her constitution completely different from that of the opposite sex. Besides differences purely physical, . . . her brain weight is a hundred grams less than the male brain. . . . a fact of extreme importance and significance if added to the differences mentioned above.[19]

At the end of the conference, the proponents of continuity and those of change tried to reach a compromise. The conference report concluded that the principle of equality in the learning process was valid for men and women but was not valid in relation to their professional aptitude. Therefore, Spanish women were given the right to gain an education but they were not allowed to practice their careers. There was no reason to fear the crumbling of the gender status quo. At the turn of the century, the illiteracy rate was alarming: in 1900, 63.8 percent of the population was illiterate; the rate for men was 55.8 percent, and the rate for women 71.5 percent. Benito Pérez Galdós describes the ignorance of the Spanish lower classes when he tells us about some of the things Fortunata had to learn.

> She also learned such important things as the order of the months of the year (which she didn't know) and which months have thirty and which have thirty-one days. It may be hard to believe, but this gap is a typical one in Spanish ignorance, found more in cities than in towns, and more among women than men.[20]

During the first three decades of the twentieth century, women benefited from the turn-of-the-century debates on education. The royal decree of 26 October 1901 extended the curriculum for the girls' schools, and the law of 23 June 1909 made primary education compulsory until age twelve. The new subjects taught to girls were Christian doctrine and Church history; Castilian Spanish (reading, writing, and grammar); algebra and geometry; geography and history; rudiments of law; physics, chemistry, and biology; physiology and hygiene; arts and crafts; and physical exercise and sewing. By 1930, the illiteracy rate among women had dropped to 47.5 percent, whereas male illiteracy was 36.9 percent; 52.6 percent of all Spanish girls attended primary schools, compared to 54.3 percent of the boys. There were 37,642 women students at the secondary level or in professional training. The university, though, was a realm less populated by Spanish women, with a total of only 1,724 women college students.[21]

The beginning of the twentieth century witnessed some coeducational initiatives in Spain. The FIL and the anarchist Modern School of Francisco Ferrer Guardia promoted coeducation in contrast to the Catholic Church prescription of segregated schools. Coeducation was an offense to morality, according to Catholic doctrine. The fact that it was part of the curricula of the liberal FIL and the anarchist schools of Ferrer Guardia made both institutions, from the Catholic point of view, hotbeds of rebellion and anticlericalism.

It was also in the 1880s that the working-class movement blossomed, with both socialist and anarchist branches. It had a bigger impact on the Spanish working class than the Catholic Workers' Circles, its counterpart at that time. The emergence of the working-class movement is another urban phenomenon of the period.

Those anarchist ideals were the context of Ferrer Guardia's pedagogical program, which sought global emancipation of the individual. He developed his revolutionary program in the Modern School of Barcelona, inaugurated in 1901. Following the precepts of a rational secular school, Ferrer Guardia proposed consistent coeducation in order to achieve the equality of the sexes and make women true companions of men. The coeducational experience was an essential part of the Modern School from its inauguration. To disseminate his pedagogical methods, the Modern School published the *Modern School Bulletin* and created its own press to provide textbooks for its classes. But this anarchist experiment did not last very long in the existing climate of opinion, which was shaped by the anticlericalism of the labor movement, mixed with the unpopular policies of the monarchy's renewed colonialism in northern Africa and the memory of the defeat of 1898. On 12 October 1909, Ferrer Guardia was executed in the Montjuich Fortress at Barcelona after a military council found him guilty of being "head of the insurrection" that had, a few months before, lit the flame of civil war in the city during the Tragic Week, a period of popular riots in Barcelona in 1909 that protested government colonial policies.[22]

Meanwhile, the FIL founders emphasized secular schools, coeducation, and the instruction of women. In the public arena, women's access to education was encouraged by members of the FIL who belonged to such institutions as the Students' Residence and Institute, the Women's Residence, the Council of Public Instruction, and the Committee for Post-Graduate Studies. In 1909 the Normal School for Higher Education was founded to produce well-trained teachers. A year later the Students' Residence opened its doors, and in 1915 the Women's Residence was established under the direction of María de Maeztu; they shared facilities, including dormitories for young college men and women.[23]

The Schools of the Ave-María, founded by Father Andrés Manjón (1846–1923) in the late nineteenth century represent the best example of the Catholic response to the turn-of-the-century liberal and anarchist pedagogical experiments. Manjón founded the first schools for girls in Granada, in the poorest part of town, known as Sacromonte, where gypsies lived. He conceived of these schools as the best means to fight illiteracy, marginalization, and social injustice. In 1905 he started the Teacher Seminary as well as a newsletter, *Hojas del Ave-María*, to promote the school's methods and Christian values. Both curriculum and pedagogical methods in Manjón's schools followed modern approaches to learning. The active impulse of the child was to be respected: experimental rather than rote learning was emphasized, and physical education was employed as a means of intellectual, moral, and aesthetic development. Manjonian pedagogy is profoundly Catholic. The Ave-María schools were segregated by gender, and in the seminary the teachers were trained to become totally devoted to their work. According to Manjón,

> the married male teacher is not bad, but the female teacher, *virgin, is even better.* Why? because to make vows of having no other children but those she educates and to devote herself completely to them, means to celebrate the pedagogical marriage between virginity and fecundity.[24]

As in other women's organizations, the "virgin teacher" was viewed as a social rather than a biological mother, the closest to the Marian ideal dyad virgin/mother.

By the 1920s, a variety of historical circumstances on the international scene favored a return to domesticity: the need to eliminate the female workforce after World War I, the enactment of postwar birthrate policies, the rise of totalitarian regimes, and finally, the simultaneous crisis of parliamentarism and liberal feminism. In addition, the Western world plunged into an economic depression on the eve of the 1930s, which sharpened demands for a return to the old-fashioned languid and domestic model of femininity. Demands for women's higher education seemed futile in this context. Even before the full force of these events was felt in Spain, Margarita Nelken, of German Jewish descent and a member of the Spanish Socialist Party, published in 1919 a collection of essays on the social status of Spanish women, entitled *La condición social de la mujer en España* (The social condition of women in Spain). She was trying to counteract the antifeminist mood of the times. In her essay on the realities that faced college-educated women, she lamented: "The worst thing that can happen to a studious woman is what is happening here [in Spain] to all women students: to be an *exception*."

Feminism had not taken root in Spain, and during the 1920s and 1930s, some Spanish intellectuals initiated a debate on the comparison of the sexes that tried to explain male/female differences in "scientific" terms. The discourse that emphasized the differences between the sexes, understood in terms of inferior versus superior, was revived throughout Europe in the first third of the twentieth century. New psychological and sociological arguments revitalized the already stale notion of biological determinism. The ideas of Freud, Simmel, and Nietzsche influenced such Spanish thinkers as Gregorio Marañón and José Ortega y Gasset to argue that men and women were different not only physically but psychologically as well. Marañón, a liberal-minded physician, argued for political equality of men and women and for access of women to public office; in regard to family matters, he favored the availability of contraception and divorce. In light of those views, Marañón's pronouncements about motherhood are surprising. "Women," he affirmed, "must be only mothers, even to the oblivion of any other interest of their own. Marriage was not conceived for the self-satisfaction of the spouses but rather to bring children into the world."[25]

Spanish intellectuals agreed with Freud that women's character was basically passive and self-effacing. They proclaimed motherhood/obedience as the only possible means for fulfillment for the woman. This reductionist essentialism led Ortega y Gasset to write: "If the male is the rational persona, the female is the irrational. Women offer men the magic opportunity to deal with a being without reason."[26] In this context, women's access to higher education and the opportunity to practice their professions were out of the question. Those who insisted on educating themselves were regarded as abnormal and could only anticipate a life of misery without love.

Catholicism and the rise of fascism further thwarted Spanish women's move toward emancipation. Beginning in 1923, Spanish politics became very unstable. Alfonso XIII, the posthumous son and successor of Alfonso XII since 1902, supported General Miguel Primo de Rivera's dictatorship, which began in September 1923 with a nineteenth-century-style *pronunciamiento*. The difference this time was in the ideological nature of this dictatorship. Some of the regenerationist axioms permeated right-wing ideology—in particular, as Sebastián Balfour points out, "the idea of Spain's spiritual mission, the distrust of parliamentary politics, and the belief in an essential, as opposed to plural, Spain whose roots lay in Castile and Catholicism."[27] Although Spain remained neutral in World War I, Primo de Rivera's regime proved unable to resolve the economic and political crisis that the country faced after the war. As a result, when free elections finally were held on 14 April 1931, male Spanish voters, hostile to political corruption and totalitarianism, rejected the monarchy, an act that led to the proclamation of the Second Republic.

The Spanish parliamentary system, sanctioned by plebiscite, became an anachronism among the totalitarian states of Europe. Spanish fascism, a latecomer to the European scene, did not emerge until 1933. At that time, even as the Second Republic reforms were occurring, Falange Española was born. On 29 October 1933, José Antonio Primo de Rivera (son of the dictator), Julio Ruíz de Alda, and Alfonso García Valdecasas met at the Teatro de la Comedia in Madrid and formally constituted the new party. Four months later they merged with another fascist group, Juntas de Ofensiva Nacional Sindicalistas (JONS), which had been in existence since 1931, to form the Falange Española Tradicionalista y de las JONS (FET de las JONS). Initially, the Falange did not have substantial social support because Catholic conservatism of the Coalition of the Spanish Right (Coalición Española de Derechas Autónomas, CEDA) occupied the ideological domain later usurped by the Falangists.[28] Ultraconservative Spanish political forces, such as CEDA, became very active during the early years of the Republic and won the elections of November 1933 because CEDA voiced the political demands of conservative Catholicism and landowners.

The progressive spirit of the Second Republic had materialized in the Constitution of 1931, which declared the secular nature of the state and repudiated the Catholic Church's role in political matters. In addition, the first government of the new republic tackled two secular problems: agrarian reform and army reform. The agrarian reform provoked deep unrest among owners of large amounts of land, for it aimed to redistribute land among the poor peasants. The intention of the reform of the army was to reduce the inflated number of officers and their potential threat to political stability.

The Republican constitution also granted Spanish women the right to vote and fostered progressive legislation on family and educational issues. Article 36 stated that "the citizens of both sexes, twenty-three years and older, will have the same electoral rights in accordance with the law."[29] After a long debate, the article was approved by the Parliament. Clara Campoamor, a member of the Radical Party, was a chief defender of women's suffrage. She argued that the democratic spirit of the Second Republic could not afford to deny this right to women, but progressive and left-wing parties saw it as a threat because of the strong influence of the Catholic Church over Spanish women.[30] Along with women's suffrage, some legislation was passed on family issues. A law of 9 September 1931 protected working mothers between the ages of sixteen and fifty years. The state recognized the validity of civil marriage and the equality of legitimate and illegitimate children; and in March 1932, divorce was legalized.

The Second Republic also sought to reform the educational system, putting into practice the secular ideals of the FIL and reaching the proletarian masses. Article 48 of the constitution, for example, established that education was entirely the responsibility of the state and not of the Catholic Church. The touchstone of the Republican legislation was the secularization of schools by the law of 6 June 1933, which granted state public institutional control over the educational system, excluding the Catholic Church from the process. Republican educational policy aspired to eradicate illiteracy for both sexes. This law never took effect, however, because of the shortage of public schools and the rise to power of the conservative CEDA in 1933. But the Republic's desire to educate the Spanish people was not entirely fruitless: women's access to and opportunities in higher education greatly improved during the Republican years.[31] The presence of women in college grew slowly, and although small, this growth was indicative of the official interest in education. Such progress abruptly came to an end with the outbreak of the Civil War and the victory of conservative Catholic forces. During the three years of conflict, the Republican school system began to be dismantled on the nationalist side, and the Francoist educational apparatus began to take shape.

THE SPANISH CIVIL WAR (1936–1939)

In Spain the clash between fascism and antifascism was particularly violent, lighting the flame of a cruel civil war. Again, the forces of tradition and modernization fought to control the country's destiny. Between 1936 and 1939, two political powers coexisted. On one hand, the legitimately elected Republican government of the Popular Front incorporated liberal and working-class parties. On the other, the rebel government of the self-proclaimed Nationalists united a variety of conservative elements, such as the army, the Catholic Church, landowners and financiers, Falangists, and monarchists, under the aegis of General Francisco Franco. Each side in the conflict used education as a means of war propaganda. Nationalists' texts, speeches, and documents stressed traditional Catholicism, imperialistic nationalism, and hierarchical order, whereas Republican propaganda emphasized democracy and a social revolution based on the notion of secular society.[32]

Even though the Republican government moved to Valencia and struggled to retain control over provincial juntas, it continued to follow its educational ideals. The Republican central government created 5,413 elementary schools between 1936 and 1938. In addition, the government maintained 75 high schools, enrolling 25,000 students at the beginning of 1937. One of its most progressive actions, representing the Republican zeal to educate the masses, was to establish high schools for workers; they could attend four shortened semesters a year for two years. The most important educational endeavor of the Republican government was the creation of the Misiones Pedagógicas (Cultural Missions). Teams of teachers were formed to reach both soldiers and civilians in an attempt to eradicate illiteracy, which was the Republican government's main goal. The Ministry of Public Instruction issued an antifascist school certificate to those who learned to read under the Cultural Missions program. In the central region, between May 1937 and August 1938, 167 soldiers' homes were created, at which some 75,000 soldiers benefited from the literacy campaigns.[33] These campaigns were also a good propaganda tool for Republican ideals.

It was also under the Republic that, for the first time, a woman headed a ministry. The anarchist Federica Montseny was appointed minister of health in September 1936. Women organized women's branches of the Communist and Anarchist Parties; but the two political organizations disagreed about the best strategy to win the war, and this halted progress in women's rights. For the Communists, the proletarian revolution would take place after the conflict was over, whereas anarchists considered war and social revolution to be parallel tasks. In the context of the Civil War, women's demands for emancipation became a secondary issue.

The most important Communist female organization was the Antifascist Women's Association, created in 1933. Its activities included raising funds and collecting clothing for the soldiers, establishing kindergartens and shelters, and filling the jobs men had left behind when they went to the front. The Communist propaganda, voiced by party members such as Dolores Ibárruri, fostered the traditional feminine nurturing qualities and duties of mothers and caretakers, whose place was on the home front.[34]

Of the anarchist women's organizations, Free Women was the most significant. Founded in 1936 by Lucía Sánchez Saornil and Mercedes Comaposada, this organization disappeared with the end of the war in 1939. Free Women acknowledged the double struggle of working-class women as workers and as women. Sánchez Saornil wrote in 1935: "I believe it is not the place of men to establish the role of women in society, however elevated that might be. The anarchist way is to let the woman act on her own freedom, without either guides or enforcement; to let her move in the direction that her inclinations and abilities direct."[35] Free Women treated women's subordination as part of a larger system of hierarchies within an anarchist framework, whereas focusing on the specific gender consequences of those inequalities differentiated women's subordination from the mainstream of the movement.

For these libertarian women, education provided the key to emancipation. To this end they developed a set of programs with two separate but related goals: *capacitación,* introducing women to anarchist principles, and *captación,* actively recruiting new women members. This dual orientation was explicit in the statement of purpose of Free Women:

> (a) to create a conscientious and responsible female force [originally a "revolutionary force"] that can act as a vanguard of progress; and (b) to this end, to establish schools, institutes, conferences, special courses, etc., designed to empower women and emancipate them from the triple enslavement to which they have been, and continue to be, subject, the enslavement of ignorance, enslavement as a woman, and enslavement as a worker.

At the Libertarian Institutes, anarchist women began trying to overcome illiteracy, but their classes also taught a new understanding of what it meant to be a woman: a woman had to take the initiative and seek her independence. Literacy courses were supplemented with classes in mechanical skills, child care, and nursing and medical assistance. All of these were useful later in the war effort as women substituted for men at the workplace and served as nurses in hospitals at the front or in their hometowns. Free Women also showed deep concern for birth control education and what they called self-conscious motherhood. "What we wanted," said Mercedes Comaposada, "at the least, were self-conscious mothers *[madres conscientes]*. People should be able to choose whether and when and how to have children and to know how to raise them . . . and they shouldn't have to be one's own children—there is need to take care of other people's children, of orphans and the like."[36]

Good mothering, then, was central to the Free Women project of women's emancipation. They wanted to educate women to be more than "dolls." In the eyes of these anarchist women, traditional women's education and socialization did not foster good mothering. With the Republicans (particularly in Catalonia, where the government resided), Spanish women benefited from liberal legislation on abortion, marriage, and divorce. But the Nationalist victory in 1939 put an end to these opportunities.

On the Nationalist side, a militarized society was imposed from the very start of the conflict. Nationalists regarded the Civil War as a crusade against atheist Spain. Those individuals without God were the genuine enemies of the fatherland. Hierarchical order and Catholicism constituted the boundaries within which social relations operated. The state apparatus used Catholicism as an omniscient and exclusive category of analysis for the political and social reality. Any other ideological dimension of Spanish politics was anathema. The Nationalists proclaimed themselves as the true Spaniards, guardians of the nation's tradition and Catholicism, which was equated with the Spanish identity. An official National-Catholic discourse surfaced from the beginning of the war, with the support of the Catholic hierarchy's writings. Pla i Daniel, bishop of Salamanca, claimed in his pastoral letter "Two Cities" (30 September 1936) that "Communists and Anarchists [were] the offspring of Cain." Other churchmen, such as Fray Ignacio G. Menéndez Reigada, declared that "the Spanish soul is by nature Christian. . . . there is hardly any distinction between our Spanish and Christian identities."[37] The most important feature of this discourse is that, far from being new, it had roots in nineteenth-century traditionalism.

The Nationalist military junta of Burgos began to dismantle Republican educational policy right from the start of the war. An order of 19 August 1936 stipulated that the schools that were opened on 1 September must use a curriculum in accordance with national demands. An order of 4 September 1936 abolished lay coeducation and made mandatory the subjects of religion and Christian heritage. The Nationalist state organized two-week courses to prepare teachers on matters of "religion and nationhood." It also created the Cultural and Educational Committee of the Technical Junta and the Rectorates to administer elementary education, which lasted until 1938. That same year the Ministry of National Education was founded and more elaborate schemes emerged. The law of secondary education enacted in 1938 by the ministry aimed to tear down the Republican educational apparatus, which it considered responsible for the erosion of traditional Spanish values. Its main goal was to restore a "Christian civilization."[38] Finally, in higher education, the newly created Institute of Spain began to conduct scientific studies and initiatives to offset the Republican Junta of Post-Graduate Studies.

Women on the Nationalist side were organized by the Sección Femenina de FET y de las JONS (the Women's Section of the Falange), founded in 1934. At the start, its hierarchical structure was carefully articulated. The national secretary, Pilar Primo de Rivera (sister of José Antonio), and seven other university women came to the Falange through the university union, Spanish University Student Union (Sindicato Español Universitario, known as SEU). In a sense, the Women's Section was created by college women who truly believed in the principles of José Antonio: abnegation and sacrifice for the fatherland. By September 1936, the Falange Española had 320,000 members, of which 80,000 were women.[39] During the Civil War, the Women's Section grew even more significant. The organization's objective was to create a population of women subservient to the regime's needs.

During the conflict, the Women's Section's social and cultural functions were crucial for the new state's indoctrination of the Spanish people. The duties performed by Falangist women during the war consisted mainly of assisting the wounded and children and creating sewing workshops, as well as forming a new service called Laundresses of the Front, which organized groups of women who followed the soldiers to the front to wash and mend their clothes. In October 1936, the Nationalist government created Winter Help (a replica of the German Winterhilfe) to manage all welfare services. Two months later, the National Committee of Winter Help was established under the direct supervision of the Women's Section. Eventually, Winter Help was renamed Social Help, which became the most important welfare apparatus of the Francoist regime. The war situation demanded a well-organized war relief system, so by the decree of 7 October 1937, Spanish women were required to serve the state for six months in the Social Service, a community/front service organization. "The imposition of a Social Service for Spanish women will serve the purpose of applying feminine capacity to alleviate the pain in the present struggle and the social anguish of the postwar."[40]

The Women's Section thus secured for itself a certain amount of power, since its long-term task, once the war was over, was to direct the state social services. By using a discourse of abnegation and sacrifice in line with that of the Catholic Church, the state found its social services covered free of charge.[41] Decree 378 of 28 November 1937 officially regulated the Social Service as a national duty for all Spanish women between seventeen and thirty-five years of age, to reconstruct the fatherland. The legislation demanded complete cooperation. Only married or disabled women could exempt themselves from this national obligation. All other women had to show a document issued by the Women's Section certifying completion of the service in order to obtain any professional diploma, to practice a career, or to hold a public office. There were two different types of certificates: one was issued for employment and career practice, and the other simply indicated the completion of the service.

The decree of 1937 was the first step toward the nationalization of Spanish women. But the official discourse contained inherent contradictions. On the one hand, women were expected to participate in the public sphere through the Social Service, and they were encouraged to join the Women's Section of the Falange. On the other hand, their work was defined explicitly as secondary to the masculine task of the state; they were to be mothers and wives, preserving the sanctity of the home. The creed for the Women's Section illustrates this subaltern role:

1. At dawn raise your heart to God and think of a new day for the fatherland.
2. Be disciplined, disciplined, disciplined.
3. Do not comment on any order; obey without hesitation.
4. Never, under any circumstance, excuse yourself from an act of service.
5. Action is not yours; encourage others to act.
6. Let the man in your life be the best patriot.
7. Do not forget that your mission is to educate your children for the good of the nation.
8. Compensate for the anguish of your woman's heart with the serenity that you are helping to save Spain.
9. Work with joy and without hesitation.
10. Obey, and by your example teach others to obey.
11. Try always to be the wheel of the cart and let the one guiding it be in control.
12. Do not stand out; help someone else to excel.

13. Love Spain over everything else, so as to be able to inculcate in others your love.

14. Do not expect any reward for your efforts except your own satisfaction.

15. Let the Falangist bundle of sticks be rooted in a common individual yearning.

16. Whatever you do, improve yourself doing it.

17. Your strength will encourage the victory.

18. There is no glory comparable to the glory of having given everything for the fatherland.[42]

. . .

The nineteenth-century contest between tradition and change was dramatically resolved by a ferocious civil war in the next century, in which traditional Spain proclaimed its victory. Both sides viewed education as the means to incorporate the country into the modern international scene. Gender was central to the debate of modern versus traditional visions of Spain. Education was instrumental in articulating Spanish women's destiny throughout the nineteenth century as well as during the Civil War. Both left- and right-wing discourses emphasized nurturing female qualities such as good mothering in a time of despair and chaos. The Republican side, however, did not seek women's war (and social) contribution through the state apparatus, but rather through the women's branch of each left-wing party and trade union. Ultimately, disunity on the left prevented the articulation of a unitary program for women's national role.

By contrast, the self-proclaimed Nationalists' acknowledgment of the importance of the Women's Section of the Falange in the war effort since 1937 shows that conservatives had a clearer notion of how they wanted to nationalize women and demonstrates that gender policy was more central to and explicit in their national project. With the end of the war, the new state-institutionalized Women's Section of the Falange was entrusted with the task of creating the Francoist new woman, whose Christian virtues came to be essential to the reconstruction of Spain.

CHAPTER TWO

THE FRANCOIST RECOVERY
OF TRADITION

"Today, with the Red Army captive and disarmed, our victorious
troops have achieved their final military objectives. The war is over."

—Francisco Franco's Last War Bulletin, 1 April 1939

The new regime regarded 1939 as the year of the triumph
of good over evil. Every official document recorded that date as the "year of
victory." Four basic conflicts of Spanish political history in the nineteenth and
early twentieth centuries clashed in the Civil War: monarchy versus republicanism, clericalism versus anticlericalism, central government versus regional
autonomy, and the propertied classes versus the proletariat.[1] With the end of
the Civil War, the quest for the secularization and modernization of Spain initiated during the Enlightenment collapsed, and Franco legitimated himself
and his regime by appealing to tradition, Catholicism, and the authentic
Spanish ethos.

Nowhere in Europe were conservative Catholics so dominant and politi-
cally influential as they were in Spain. According to William Callahan, Spain
had "an ecclesiastical mentality deeply rooted in a quasi-medieval scholastic
interpretation of social organization that had long dominated clerical think-
ing."[2] Francoist recovery of tradition was grounded in a National-Catholic
discourse that included gender as an essential element in defining the new
state's concept of nationhood.

To establish a sound political consensus, the Francoist regime used the educational system as a means of indoctrination in the new National-Catholic ideals. Coeducation was proscribed, and the younger generation was educated in gender-segregated schools that thwarted the later encounter of men and women at the university level. In the official propaganda, college education for women was regarded as an assault on their authentic feminine destiny: to become wives and mothers under the new state.

NATIONAL-CATHOLICISM

From its inauguration in 1939, the regime sought to fuse Catholicism with the concept of fatherland and national identity. It aspired to restore what it considered Spanish tradition, to revive the imperial spirit of the Catholic monarchs of five centuries earlier. José Pemartín, a monarchist-turned-Falangist, proclaimed the Nationalist movement to be founded on "sixteenth-century Spanish Catholicism, because our national identity forged itself in that historical moment, incarnating the Catholic ideal of our Military Monarchy." Fragmented and demoralized after the Civil War, Spain needed reconstruction that consisted of achieving national unity, but only through the restoration of her glorious "imperial Catholic past." Franco, the Caudillo, became "the medieval warrior-crusader, defender of the faith and restorer of Spanish national greatness, with his relationship to the Church as an important plank in the theatrical panoply." Approval came from the Catholic Church without delay. On 2 April 1939, the daily *ABC* published a telegram from Pope Pius XII congratulating Franco on his victory:

> Raising our heart to the Lord, we sincerely thank Your Excellency, [for] the desired Catholic victory [in] Spain. We pray for this dearest country, that once peace is reached, it may revive with new strength its old Christian traditions, which made it so great. We send effusively to Your Excellency deep feelings, and our apostolic blessing to the noble Spanish people.[3]

There is acute disagreement among scholars about the ideological nature of the Francoist regime. Some scholars, following official propaganda, proposed different descriptions of the regime throughout its existence: "totalitarian state"; "nationalist totalitarian-authoritarian state"; "national-syndicalist regime"; "Catholic, social, and representative state"; and "organic democracy." The political opposition defined it simply as "fascist." In 1939, as Stanley Payne indicates, a fascist style predominated, with ritualistic apparatus and salute, as well as praise to the Caudillo, with invocations of "Franco, Franco, Franco." Two elements connect Francoism in its origins to other European totalitarian regimes in the 1930s: first, the use of violence in acquiring power (in the Spanish case, a civil war) and a repressive system articulated after the Nationalist victory; and second, the establishment of a single party, the unique FET y de las JONS.[4]

Like the Nazis and the Italian Fascists, Falangists used violence to gain political power. In the Spanish case, there were three elements in the process. The first was the totalitarian assault on the power of the democratic government of the Second Republic. The second was the different nature of the repression in both zones during the Civil War: on the Francoist side the violence was directed from the state apparatus, while in the Republican zone it was the result of the political disorder and anarchy. The former was violence a priori, the latter a posteriori. The third element was the justification throughout Francoism of the repression during the Civil War.[5] The Falange was the party authorized to indoctrinate the Spanish people with its twenty-six National-syndicalist principles. Those principles, reprinted in 1949 by the press of the Movimiento, corroborate the fascist tones of FET y de las JONS doctrine.

The Civil War offered the Falange an opportunity to run a single-party state that provided the military dictatorship with an ideological cloak. Official Francoist discourse fused the Falangist Nationalist agenda to traditional Catholicism. The Francoist state apparatus thus rested upon Spanish medieval institutions that provided an illusion of democratic structure by the end of World War II. In 1943, a legislative assembly, the Cortes, was established to give the appearance of a certain freedom, but in reality, the political function remained within the Procrustean confines of the Francoist system. Once the war was over, the differences among the right-wing forces that had supported the uprising resurfaced. Each group (Falangists, Monarchists, landowners, Carlists, and Catholics) sought to promote its own agenda. Those rivalries allowed Franco to continue playing, in peacetime, his wartime role as common denominator and provider of unity by distributing power among the different "political families." By allowing these divisions, Franco remained indispensable to political stability. Only after the defeat of the Axis powers in 1945 did Franco's regime begin to adopt a more popular constitutional legitimacy. The Caudillo relegated the Falange to the political second rank, dismissed his pro-Axis brother-in-law and minister of interior, Ramón Serrano Suñer, and promulgated the Spaniards' Charter, a document that defined the rights of all Spanish people, posited on each person's acceptance of the regime. Article 35 stipulated that articles 12 through 18 could be temporarily suspended by decree. Ironically, these articles guaranteed the protection of freedom of speech, association, and secrecy of correspondence; banned trespassing; and forbade holding an individual in prison for more than seventy-two hours without being formally charged.[6]

Catholics benefited immeasurably from the political realignment of 1945 because their ideology conferred historical and divine sanction upon Francoism. In addition, National-Catholicism made the regime malleable in the changing political circumstances of the Cold War. Western democracies condemned Franco's regime in 1946 but made it clear they would not intervene to accelerate the return of liberal democracy. National-Catholicism became the ideological substratum of Francoism, making it distinct from other totalitarian regimes in Europe. In the late 1960s, Juan Linz defined the Spanish regime as "authoritarian," a description that became the model for analyzing Francoism's ideological nature.

Authoritarian regimes "are political systems," Linz says,

> with limited, not responsible pluralism: without elaborate and guiding ideology (but with distinctive mentalities); without intensive nor extensive political mobilization (except at some points in their development); and in which a leader (or occasionally a small group) exercises power within formally ill-defined limits but actually quite predictable ones.[7]

The main criticism of this categorization from Spanish scholars focuses on the semantic opposition of ideology/mentality. Some of its critics consider that the mentalities are a reflection of the ideology. Ideology and mentality, far from being opposites, reveal distinct degrees of elaboration and origin. In the ideological realm there are unsystematic and diffuse discourses as well as systematized ones. The former would be described as mentalities, the latter as ideologies. Nonetheless, both are ideologies. It is easier to identify the intellectualized discourses, because the traditional mentalities are hidden behind everyday customs and relations. The Francoist Catholic values, or mentalities, prescribed, imposed, and ultimately permeated the "modus vivendi" of Spaniards, just like any formal ideology. Hence, Linz's model leads us to consider Franco's regime as lacking a formalized ideology, or dominant discourse, but embodying instead a conglomerate of mentalities or competing discourses.

A second point of debate with regard to Linz's model has to do with the notion of "limited pluralism." The fact that there existed different interest groups disputing the extent of their power did not make the regime representative, since none of the political factions constituted a threat to the regime. All of them could survive only as long as the regime did. By the same token, the regime's survival depended on its ability to create a balanced distribution of power among these groups. Thus, there existed a symbiotic relationship between the state body and its members. They joined in the common goal of frightening away "inorganic democracy."[8]

National-Catholic discourse endowed the new state with a chameleonlike quality that allowed Franco to stay in power for four decades without changing the regime's totalitarian/authoritarian foundations. Several aspects of the discourse specially favored Franco's lifelong authority. The religious establishment acquired supreme rank among the competing political factions and was key to the concept of Spanish nationhood. National-Catholicism articulated and perpetuated a secular dichotomized vision of the Spanish historical reality: the two Spains, continuity versus change, good versus evil, order versus chaos. And finally, this dichotomized historical vision proved to be essential in legitimating the absolute power of the Caudillo and, therefore, in repressing any dissidence. Franco sought the support of the different political factions, using a policy of divide and rule. "The need to tamper with reality," says Paul Preston, "which is revealed by Franco's tinkering with his own past was indicative of considerable insecurity . . . creating for himself successive personae," and maintaining an ambiguous public facade: "Franco is a man who says things and unsays them, who draws near and slips away, he vanishes and trickles away; always vague and never clear or categoric."[9]

Franco brought the policy of divide and rule with him as political baggage acquired during his military career in Africa; he would carry it through the rest of his life. He associated government and administration with the constant intimidation of the ruled. Implicit was the patronizing colonial notion that the colonized were like children (or women) who needed a firm paternal hand. He considered the political left as the enemy to be eradicated by repression and terror. The paternal element became central to his own perception of his rule over Spain as a strong and magnanimous father figure.

The *Law of Succession* on 31 March 1947 proclaimed Franco as head of the state for as long as he lived. Franco had decided that the ultimate definition of the Spanish state over which he presided would thenceforth be a kingdom, and "one day" he would choose a prince of royal blood to reign in Spain. In the meantime, Franco appointed the members of the Council of the Realm himself. He also designated a Council of Regency, which would take his place in the event that he died without naming a successor. By proclaiming Spain a kingdom, he legitimated the new state historically and projected it into the future for the survival of Francoism after Franco.

To justify and recognize Franco's concept of himself, the savior chosen by God, the regime considered it crucial to remember the fateful past history of Spanish Communism. The raison d'être for the new Spain was the preservation of the old Spanish essence forged in the sixteenth and seventeenth centuries. Even those areas of Spanish life that would be modernized rested much upon the restoration of old Catholic traditions. These would be the parameters regulating social relations that were articulated around the dichotomization of the two politics (Francoist/anti-Francoist) and the gender roles (male/female).

Gender ideology itself became crucial in defining the state, its territory, and its authority. Spiritual/Catholic values, authority, and discipline were to govern an important institution: the family. Social and gender relations blended in the family, and women—as mothers—represented an essential element in the reconstruction of the fatherland. The preamble to the Spaniards' Charter (Fuero de los Españoles) defined the new state as the guardian of Catholic doctrine, and article 6 declared state protection for the practicing of the Catholic religion, tolerating no other public religious expressions. Article 22 of the law declared the state's recognition and protection of the family as a natural institution and pillar of society, with rights and obligations superior to human law. The same article proclaimed state support for large families and decreed that marriage was to be indissoluble. Such an arrangement of social relations by the state implicitly followed Catholic Church doctrine.

The participation of Spanish women in the reconstruction of the fatherland, thus, was defined within the discourse of abnegation, one of the Catholic feminine virtues. Spanish women were expected to help those in need, easing their pain and bringing happiness into their lives. The decree of 28 November 1937 defined the self-sacrificing virtues of women as key to the reconstruction of the fatherland.

> Because evidence of virtues and sacrifices does not only consist in the passive and mechanical performance of technical or administrative tasks. It also requires that these responsibilities be infused with fraternity between those Spaniards who suffer and those who help them in their pain.[10]

The Women's Section of the Falange, as institutionalized by the decree of 28 December 1939, became the mediator between the state and Spanish women. In this way, Franco compensated Falangist women for their exemplary war service, which, in his words, did not diminish Spanish women's feminine virtues so much as "it rather surpassed these virtues, as a result of the thorough religious and patriotic education that was a constant preoccupation of the Women's Section in their yearning for the total spiritual instruction of women."[11] Article 1 of the decree entrusted the Women's Section with the mission of teaching Spanish women Falangist political and social values.

In later years, the regime enacted legislation exclusively affecting women and their duties to the fatherland. The Women's Section supervised and controlled the Social Service, which underwent successive changes in the 1940s. Although women were supposed to fulfill their service in their province of residence, national needs during the war required some women to move to other cities to do so. Social Service, thus, facilitated women's mobilization and provided room and board in centers of "absolute moral guarantee." All other expenses had to be covered by their families; there was no compensation for the work, and discipline was strict. Lack of enthusiasm or obedience could be penalized by extension of service by seven days, fifteen days, or a month, depending on the offense, with penalties repeated until performance improved. Three penalties in a month meant denial of the certificate of completion.[12]

The decree of 1941 obligated Spanish women to fulfill the Social Service. To qualify for all public jobs in Spanish society, women had to prove that they had rendered their services to the fatherland. Articles 3 and 4 levied fines of fifty to five thousand pesetas (today five to fifty dollars) to those employers who hired women without a Social Service certificate. The decree of 9 February 1944 made service a prerequisite to obtain a passport or belong to any cultural association (article 2) but gave special dispensation to nuns and to daughters or wives of men of the Nationalist side killed during the war (article 4). The same year, by the decree of 21 November, all women enrolling at a university also had to present the Social Service certificate.[13] Above all, the Social Service was intended to instill domestic values in Spanish women who were bound to be mothers and wives.

In addition to imposing national service on Spanish women, the new state, in its zeal to protect the family, created the Board for the Protection of Women in 1942. Furthermore, sexually related crimes were severely penalized, such as abortion and any kind of contraceptive propaganda (by the law of 24 December 1941), as well as cohabitation outside of marriage and women's adultery (by the law of 11 May 1942). Wartime casualties made it crucial to repopulate the country, and good mothering became a national imperative. Franco's demographic goal was a population of forty million Spaniards. Maternal and infant care received special attention from the Ministry of Health, which by the law of 12 July 1941 reorganized the appropriate institutions. The law was intended to resolve demographic, hygienic, and medical problems. "This law," says article 2, "applies to pregnant and nursing women and those who take care of either their own children or the children of others, as well as to the child from birth to fifteen years old."[14] The law established a web of health centers both in cities and in rural areas to assist mothers and children. The centers were under the supervision of the Ministry of the Interior and the General Commissary of Health with the joint assistance of the Women's Section, Social Help, syndical organizations, and the secretary of welfare. Article 15 established the National School of Infant Care "to train competent personnel of both sexes." Each child under fifteen years of age was issued a health book to record his or her clinical history: vaccinations, illnesses, pathological incidences, and so forth (article 25). At the Institutes and Services of Infant Care, a division called Lactario obtained and kept the mother's milk. To complement this provision of the law of 12 July 1941, the Ministry of the Interior issued an order of 20 December 1941 to educate nursing women on good mothering. This order prescribed that during the first five days of each month, infant care centers were to provide free classes and lectures, which mothers were required to attend (article 3). After four lectures on infant care, health, and hygiene matters, the final session concentrated on the state's demographic policy and needs, addressing topics such as "What Spain Provides for Mother and Child," "Protection for the Working Mother," and "The Danger of Working for Good Mothering." Its motto was "the Caudillo wants forty million Spaniards."[15]

So that women could perform well as mothers and deliver healthy citizens for the new state, the government prevented them from entering the labor force. Instead, they were to stay home and perform their domestic duties. As early as 1938, the Francoist labor system and social order was defined in the Labor Charter (Fuero del Trabajo): "Renewing the Catholic tradition of social justice and human sense that informed the legislation of our glorious past, the state takes the responsibility to guarantee Spaniards Fatherland, Bread, and Justice."[16]

By the order of 9 March 1939, the government made it mandatory to educate workers in the charter's principles. The Spanish Labor Charter followed the Italian Carta di Lavoro (1927), echoing the Catholic social doctrine prescribed in Pius XI's encyclical *Quadragesimo Anno* (1931). Using direct quotations from Leo XIII's encyclical *Rerum Novarum* (1891), Pius XI had reminded Catholics of the social Church doctrine in defense of working men. *Quadragesimo Anno* rejected the class struggle and proposed fraternal cooperation between workers and employers using a corporate structure ruled by religion. The document delineated Christian social relations by recognizing the concept of private property as emanating from the law of nature, and it regarded socialist ownership of the means of production as a "subtle poison" for gullible people. Pius XI's encyclical recommended an equal distribution of capital to allow workers to live with dignity. The right to work was associated with the ability to sustain the family, a task entrusted to men. Women, according to the encyclical, needed protection from the "crime" of having to work:

> Mothers can devote themselves, at their home or close to it, to their chores without neglecting their home. But it is gravest abuse, which must be completely eradicated, that the mother, because of the low salary of the husband, finds herself forced into *lucrative art* [*sic*], abandoning her peculiar duties and chores at home and, above all, the education of the small children.[17]

Thus, working-class women were considered first of all to be mothers, bound—as prescribed by the Catholic Church—to fulfill the only purpose of Christian marriage: reproduction. The Labor Charter prohibited women's and children's labor at night, regulated home labor, and forbade married women to work in factories and workshops. In this context women's national duty remained confined to the home, and to this end, the regime issued a series of laws regulating and protecting women's labor opportunities. The order of 27 December 1938 proposed an increase in male workers' salaries so that they could provide for their families as breadwinners and keep their wives at home (article 3). The order prohibited married women's employment when their husbands' incomes were sufficient (article 4).[18]

The 1940s, known as "the hungry years," made austerity the keystone of a new self-sufficient economic policy called autarchy. A Nationalist program of economics was imposed by circumstances. After the Civil War, Spain faced major reconstruction and redevelopment, stemming from the Depression and World War II. In addition, Franco's cooperation with the Axis powers during the world conflict led to Spain's exclusion from the European Recovery Program (better known as the Marshall Plan) in 1947. But the Nationalist program of economics also responded to Franco's own preferences and the Labor Charter's social Catholic principles. Franco preferred a policy of nationalism and voluntarism that subordinated economic affairs to state policy. On 5 June 1939, therefore, he announced that Spain must carry out re-

construction on the basis of self-sufficiency, or autarchy, which, though foreign models were not invoked, implicitly paralleled the then-current policies
of Italy and Germany.[19] The basic ideas of autarchy were outlined in an extensive document entitled *Guidelines for a Plan of Reform for Our Economy*
that the Caudillo signed on 8 October 1939. The plan laid out a vague ten-
year program to achieve economic modernization and self-sufficiency. It revealed great faith in the economic potential of Spanish society and the ade-
quacy of domestic raw materials, but the effectiveness of statist direction and
control was simply presumed.

The decree of October 1939, creating the *Law for the Protection and Development of National Industry,* initiated autarchist industrialization, providing a wide variety of incentives, tax benefits, and special licensing norms for
the creation of factories. It culminated in the establishment in 1941 of the
National Institute of Industry (Instituto Nacional de Industria), a state investment and holding company created to stimulate industrialization, designed after the Italian Istituto per la Ricostruzione Industriale. The National Institute
of Industry played a significant role especially in the industries of coal, other
fuels, and electric power. From 1942 to 1948, it developed major new enterprises, including the national airline Iberia (1943) and ENASA, which fostered Pegaso, the country's principal producer of trucks and buses. The railroad and telephone systems were nationalized, and a massive program of dam
construction to boost electrical output and to provide water and irrigation
was promoted.[20] Irrigation constituted an important agricultural reform mea-
sure to stimulate productivity. Under the new National Institute of Colonization (1939), the regime encouraged private capital to help place peasants on
untilled land, although with little success; and by the law of April 1946 on local resettlement, land was placed in the hands of a small number of landless
peasants.[21] Nonetheless, scarcity and hunger remained the norm in the countryside, pushing many to migrate to urban centers in search of jobs.

On 4 May 1939, general rationing of certain staples had to be imposed
and remained in place for more than a decade. Food supplies were allocated
through the new General Commissary of Supplies and Transport, which put
into operation a complex web of bureaucratic controls. The new economic
policy of these government controls fostered a widespread *estraperlo* (black
market), operating at nearly all levels of the economy. Corruption quickly became general and led to official intervention with several series of arrests and
even executions. The new agricultural policy was a failure. According to Stanley Payne, during the five years that followed the Civil War, there were at
least two hundred thousand deaths from malnutrition and disease. Even the
Church hierarchy denounced corruption and the delicate economic situation.
In 1950, the pastoral letter "El pan nuestro de cada día dánosle hoy . . ."
(Give us Lord Our Daily Bread . . .) by Don Vicente Enrique y Tarancón,
then bishop of Solsona, decried the precarious economic situation facing the
working class and the illicit enrichment of the elite after the Civil War. The

bishop urged authorities to take proper Christian measures to resolve such a state of affairs.[22] But the government was unable to stop issuing food stamps until 1951, and economic hardship led to strikes in Madrid, Catalonia, and the Basque Country in the 1950s.

In this context, women's national duty remained confined to the home. The decree of 31 March 1944 regulated piecework at home in which an entire family worked for entrepreneurs in a cottage-industry system (article 116). Married women needed their husbands' permission to practice any "trade or industry" (article 132); even if they were separated, the husband's consent was mandatory and his signature was required in his wife's contract (article 133). The key issue in women's access to the labor market was moral protection. A married woman could work only under the supervision of her husband, doing piecework at home. To work in a factory, she needed to obtain his consent, which had its own bureaucratic form. Working at home did not interfere with her duties as a reproductive/productive mother. Articles 166 and 167 of the decree of 1944 guaranteed protection to working mothers who returned to their jobs after a baby was born.

In accordance with Christian principles, the government prohibited night labor by children and women by the decree of 29 July 1948 (ratified on 12 June 1958). Article 3 dictated that "[n]o woman of any age may be employed at night, either at any public or private industry or at any of their branches, the only exception being when the woman works as part of a family enterprise."[23] This prohibition could be suspended only by special government order based on national interests (article 5). The regime promoted a reproductive/productive model of women appropriate to the autarchist program of austerity and self-sacrifice. Through the educational system, the regime imbued in Spanish women the official Francoist Catholic feminine ethos.

THE FOUNDATIONS OF TRUE CATHOLIC WOMANHOOD

The Francoist recovery of tradition involved gender roles as well. Catholicism was inherent to the regime's definition of Spanish femininity. The new educational system aspired to promote true Catholic womanhood by appealing to Spanish historical tradition. First, the regime sought to revive a sixteenth-century devotion to saintly figures—such as Santa Teresa de Jesús or the Virgen del Pilar—and hoped to repopularize Renaissance treatises on the character and proper education of women by Fray Luis de León and Juan Luis Vives. Second, the Francoist official discourse on women rested on the traditional doctrine of the Catholic Church as prescribed in Pius XI's encyclicals *Divini Illius Magistri* (1929) and *Casti Connubii* (1930). Finally, the Women's Section was entrusted with the task of preserving Catholic values among Spanish women.

Giuliana di Febo has studied the regime's manipulation of sacred images. In particular, she points to the importance of Santiago Apostol (Saint James), the Virgen del Pilar, and the Sagrado Corazón (Sacred Heart). An old legend tells how the Virgin appeared to Saint James by the Ebro River in A.D. 40 to encourage him to Christianize Spain. Zaragoza became a pilgrimage center for visiting the shrine of the Virgin. During the Napoleonic invasion in the nineteenth century, she was proclaimed the symbol of national unity. So deep was the devotion to the Virgen del Pilar that the Aragonese troops sang, "The Virgen del Pilar says that / She does not want to be French, / She wants to be captain of the Aragonese troops." The Republican soldiers changed the rhyme during the Civil War to "The Virgen del Pilar says that / She does not want to be fascist, / She wants to be captain of the communist worker." The regime also used the figure of Saint Teresa de Jesús—one of the great mystics, reformer of the Carmelite Order, and founder of new convents throughout Spain in the 1500s—as a role model for Spanish womanhood. Since the 1930s Saint Teresa de Jesús had become the symbol of Christian feminism. Such Christian feminism was more desirable and more genuinely Spanish than the "lay feminism" represented by the progressive and left-wing parties in the context of the Second Republic.[24] After the Civil War, Saint Teresa de Jesús became the patroness of a variety of women's Catholic organizations, such as the Teresian Institute, Women's Catholic Action, and the Women's Section.

The Francoist cult and manipulation of the Teresa de Jesús figure began during the Civil War. The uncorrupted body of Saint Teresa was found two years after she died. In 1585, after the amputation of the left hand of the saint, Father Gracian, provincial of the Carmelite Order, took it from Alba de Tormes, where she was originally buried, to Lisbon. The relic remained there in the convent of the Discalced Carmelites until 1925. That same year the hand was moved to Ronda, where it remained until the Civil War. On 18 February 1937, the daily *ABC* published in Sevilla an article about the occupation of Málaga. It reported that a Nationalist soldier found the uncorrupted left hand of Saint Teresa de Jesús in the suitcase of the Republican Colonel Villalba. Nationalist propaganda argued that the sacred relic constituted a proof of divine assistance in the crusade and confirmed the miraculous nature of the war. Franco became the guardian of the saint's hand, which he kept in the chapel of the Pardo palace, his residence, until he died in 1975. Teresa de Jesús was portrayed as "old Christian," noble, and obedient to the Church dogma against Lutheran threats, and she was later proclaimed "Saint of the Race." Although in 1946 the researcher Narciso Alonso Cortés found documents in Valladolid that demonstrated the Jewish origins of Teresa de Jesús, thus destroying the myth of "Saint of the Race," the discovery was conveniently ignored.[25]

The Catholic tradition of the sixteenth-century empire also experienced a revival in Franco's Spain with the publication in the 1940s and 1950s of Renaissance treatises on the education of Christian women. Juan Luis Vives's *Instruction of the Christian Woman* (La Instrucción de la mujer cristiana), the most comprehensive treatise on women's education of the sixteenth century, appeared originally in 1523. The Spanish princess Catherine of Aragon, who married Henry VIII of England, had appointed Juan Luis Vives to direct the education of her daughter Mary Tudor. His book, written in Latin and translated at the time into Spanish, English, Dutch, French, Italian, and German, thus became the leading work on women's education in any language. For Vives, the purpose of women's education was only to preserve their honesty and chastity, for their lives rotated around the protection of their physical and spiritual virginity. "When women do not know how to protect their chastity," wrote Vives, "they deserve the worst of punishments; paying with their own life is not enough."[26]

Virtue was the product of education. Vives did not deny women's ability to learn, but he considered the main goal in educating a lady to be separating wisdom from lust. The curriculum should be carefully chosen to train the woman's character for life in the "womanly sphere." The readings assigned included the Bible and the writings of the Church fathers, Plato, Cicero, and Seneca. Vives considered educated women to be morally superior to those who did not study. Educated women were believed to be better housewives, more virtuous mothers, and more receptive to their husbands' authoritative "reason."

> The length of time a woman must study I do not believe has to be longer than the time a man studies; I want the man to know more things and be more diverse, for his own benefit and to teach others for the benefit of the republic. A woman must be knowledgeable in those aspects of the doctrine that teach her how to live virtuously and give order in her upbringing and goodness in her life. I want her to learn for the sake of learning, not to let others see her knowledge, because it is good for her to be silent; thus her virtue will speak for her. In a woman nobody seeks eloquence or good rhetoric, neither great wit nor administration of cities, memory or liberality. There is only one thing required in her, and this is her chastity.[27]

Although chastity was the road to absolute perfection for women, marriage represented the ultimate goal for a Christian woman, allowing her to accomplish motherhood. Fray Luis de León published *The Perfect Married Lady* (La perfecta casada) in 1583. He respected the excellence of virginity over marriage but argued that each state was a path to the perfection of the soul in its own way. His treatise, which became a traditional wedding present for brides in Franco's Spain, represented the voice legitimating the glorious past of true Catholic womanhood because it focused on female character, analyzing women's virtues and vices. De León used the sacred Scriptures to define his own theory of a "woman of value," stating that such value resided precisely in the fact that such a woman was more than rare. A *"Woman of value . . .* is difficult to find," he wrote, "and there are very few. Therefore,

the foremost compliment to the good woman is to say that she is a rare thing
. . . because a woman by nature is feebler and weaker than any other animal."
De León spelled out the virtues of the Christian married woman. Spiritual
and physical chastity after marriage was inherent to a woman's identity. Adultery represented the worst of transgressions: "A woman is not laudable for
being chaste, because it would be indecent and abominable if she was not.
Hence, the Holy Spirit does not ask her to be chaste, but assumes she already
is, because breaking her husband's trust is for the stars to lose their light and
the skies to fall, and to violate the laws of her nature."[28]

According to de León, the duty of the perfect married lady stemmed from
two female virtues. First, she had to be neither extravagant nor lavish. Second, she had to be industrious. These were the womanly virtues promoted by
the Francoist regime under autarchy, but this model underwent a revision.
The Catholic model of austerity and the domestic ideal of the reproductive
woman and prolific mother were altered somewhat in the 1950s with the addition of the role of consumer-housewife. Spanish women were to accept
their new role as buyers in the same way they had performed their role as
thrifty homemakers for the good of the fatherland. Obedience and abnegation were the mottoes in both cases.

Silence was another precious virtue of the Christian woman. De León believed that all women should be proud "of being quiet, because for all of
them silence and rare talk is not only a pleasant condition but just virtue."

> Given that nature, as we said and will say, locks women at home, in the same
> way, it forces them to shut their mouth . . . [b]ecause talking is the result of un-
> derstanding, and words are nothing but images or signs of what intelligence con-
> ceives in itself. Nature did not make the honest and good woman to study the
> sciences and difficult things, but for one simple occupation, domesticity; hence it
> limited her understanding, and therefore limited her words and arguments.[29]

A woman's body and appearance became objectified as the paramount
proof of her modesty. Vives's and de León's treatises devoted special attention to the discussion of the female body as a temple. Christian women ought
to avoid wearing any makeup; they should try to present themselves to their
husbands as they "really" were. Those women who enjoyed ornamenting
themselves were not trustworthy.

> Honest women wear only those things that can honor an altar. This means that
> all your dress and embellishment must be holy . . . [any makeup] is an offense
> to God and your soul. . . . Because this is a damage inflicted on their own bod-
> ies, which do not belong to them but to the Holy Spirit, to whom they were
> consecrated through Baptism. And for the same reason a woman's body must
> be treated as a holy temple with honesty and respect. . . . What does the mar-
> ried woman want to embellish herself for? . . . [T]he answer to this resides in

her disorderly self-esteem, insatiable appetite of vain excellence, ugly greed, dishonesty, adultery, prostitution, never-ending offense.[30]

Such austerity became hard to preserve when Spanish women saw the advertisements for makeup, perfume, and luxury products that appeared in Spanish magazines in the late 1950s. Those colorful ads appealed to women's search for eternal youth and beauty.

In *The Instruction of the Christian Woman* and *The Perfect Married Lady*, the identity of a woman emanated from the objectification of her body. These works emphasized the preservation of virginity and then consecrated the female body as the receptacle of human life through motherhood after marriage. The ultimate role model prescribed for women was the Virgin Mary, in whom both virginity and motherhood coincided. In such a way, the discourse established the Catholic binary view of female essence: Mary/Eve; holy/evil. According to Vives and de León, the road to Christian perfection for Catholic women consisted of a struggle against their evil nature to achieve the holy sublimation of either virginity or motherhood. Such redemption was possible only through suffering: suffering for God, the fatherland, their husbands, and their children.

In addition to reclaiming sixteenth-century treatises on female education, Franco's regime also looked to contemporary Church doctrine to reaffirm his agenda. In particular, he heeded two encyclicals of Pius XI: *Divini Illius Magistri* and *Casti Connubii,* which have their foundations in the writings of Leo XIII at the end of the nineteenth century, especially *Arcanum* (1880) and *Rerum Novarum* (1891). These documents laid the foundation for notions of Spanish femininity, notions that would extend well into the 1960s. Reaching the reading public in periodicals such as *Razón y Fe, Ecclesia,* and *Senda,* Church doctrine stressed the biological differences between men and women.[31] It did not deny women the right to be educated, but it argued that they ought to be trained differently and separately from men. Men were to be the soldiers and scholars, women the wives and mothers. Though men and women were educated in separate disciplines and settings, their destinies would converge in marriage and progeny and in their service to the Church and the nation.

Divini Illius Magistri, published in 1929, was an encyclical letter on the Christian education of youth. It proclaimed educators and students to be agents of Catholicism in Christian nations. Education was a social endeavor to be consecrated by the Church, facilitated by the state, and carried out by the family. The Vatican assumed supremacy in questions of education, proclaiming that "only the Church possesses . . . the total moral authority *Omnem Veritatem* that encompasses all the particular truths." Invoking its divine power, the Church presumed to regulate truth and morality in Catholic countries, insisting on its right to watch over public and private institutions of knowledge. The roles of the Church and the family in Christian education superseded that of the state, explained *Divini Illius Magistri,* since both "have this divine and natural right [that] is undeniable, inevitable, [and] uncompromisable."[32] The familial right to educate children prevailed over the right of the state in matters of instruction.

For its part, the state possessed a double function in the educational process: to protect and promote Christian education, but without depriving the family of its primacy in the matter. The state's laws were to secure the family's sacred duty of educating its progeny while at the same time respecting the supernatural rights of the Church. Christian education, according to Pius XI, was directed not only to the soul but to the body as well. The individual in his totality was the subject to be educated. Because of original sin and the feeble nature of humanity, the Church thought it necessary to correct man's disorderly inclinations and cultivate his good ones from childhood on through adulthood. *Divini Illius Magistri* grounded gender differentiations in biological disparity. Physical separation of the sexes became fundamental in achieving their biological destiny. Coeducation, therefore, was not only erroneous but pernicious to Christian learning. It rested on a deplorable misconception of what the legitimate social order ought to be. Based upon a leveling equality, coeducating the sexes would produce a promiscuous human society. "Our Lord," reads the text, "orders and disposes that the perfect coexistence of the sexes must take place within marriage."[33] Nature had made them different not only biologically but also in inclinations and capabilities; therefore there was no need to educate both sexes on equal terms. In this light, and in view of the basic male character of the institution, the presence of women in universities would be seen both as strange and as a transgression of the ideal of Catholic womanhood promoted by the Church and the regime.

Gender relations were further spelled out in 1930. An encyclical letter on the dignity of Christian marriage, *Casti Connubii,* reiterated the principles that Leo XIII had laid out fifty years earlier in his encyclical *Arcanum.* Both documents endorsed four Victorian feminine virtues: piety, purity, submissiveness, and domesticity. *Casti Connubii* ordained that women should submit their very being to men's will, following the "love hierarchy" that "embraces both the supremacy of the man over the woman and children, and *the diligent submission of the woman and her complete obedience,* recommended by the apostle with the following words: 'married women ought to be subjected to their husbands, as they are subjected to the Lord; because the man is the head of the woman as Christ is the head of the Church.'" Educational policy was to segregate the sexes, according to *Divini Illius Magistri,* and *Casti Connubii* legitimated gender relations only in marriage and family, declaring sacred the cooperation between the spouses. It further claimed that the ultimate purpose of marriage was reproduction and permitted sexual activity only for such ends, condemning contraception "because the man who avoids the conception of progeny, even with his own wife, acts illicitly and immodestly."[34] Both spouses were to devote themselves to educating their children. Pius XI asserted that the heroism of motherhood was the pride and glory of the Christian wife, even at the risk of losing her own life. "Who will not admire extraordinarily a mother who gives herself up to a certain death, with heroic strength, to preserve the life in her womb?"[35] Self-sacrifice came to be the motto of a woman's life, and motherhood her unavoidable destiny. Any rebellion condemned her as a sinner.

Feminism was regarded as the most ominous threat to a woman's soul. *Casti Connubii* described women's efforts to achieve equality as debasing and unnatural: "There are many who dare to say, with much audacity, that the servitude of one spouse over another is an indignity, that both spouses have equal rights, defending presumptuously that . . . there ought to be a certain emancipation for the woman."[36] True freedom for the Christian woman resided within the domestic realm, at home. The Church recognized that, as a human being, she deserved the same respect as the man. But in everything else there was to be a certain inequality and moderation, implemented to preserve the welfare of the family and the proper unity and stability of the household. True Catholic womanhood restored Spanish traditional womanly virtues: self-sacrifice, obedience, and strict chastity.

THE FRANCOIST EDUCATIONAL PROJECT

Spain's destiny demanded the cooperation of all Spaniards, especially the younger generation. Hence, education became the new "crusade" for the forces of tradition. The Francoist educational system set about to dismantle the one in existence during the Second Republic. Extremely hostile to secular ideals, Francoist National-Catholic pedagogy presented itself as genuinely antithetical to the FIL's anti-Christian and anti-Spanish postulates.[37] Against democratic materialism and disorder, the new educational system tried to restore an authentic Spanish ethos and spiritual values through authority and discipline.

National-Catholicism laid the foundation of the new school model while, at the same time, the educational apparatus became a means of state propaganda. The Ministry of National Education, created in 1938, included the state services of press and propaganda. The new minister, José Ibáñez Martín (who served from 1939 to 1951), declared that the state's educative action remained at the core of "the policy of the Movement." The new era appeared "as an opportunity," he announced, "to impose eternal Spanish principles." A systematic dismantling of the Republican educational system immediately followed. The prohibition of coeducation and lay instruction preceded the censorship of textbooks and purges of teachers and faculty. The *Law of Elementary Education* of 17 July 1945 reiterated the prohibition of coeducation proclaimed in previous legislation on the grounds of moral decorum and pedagogical efficacy. Article 14 declared, "The state, for moral and pedagogical reasons, prescribes the separation of the sexes and the separate instruction for boys and girls in elementary education."[38]

Religion dictated that the sexes be separated and educated in different environments under the guidance of a priest, who came to embody the purest educator; his classroom symbolized a sanctuary, a temple. The order of 30 March 1939 required the display of the crucifix in the classroom, along with a picture of the Caudillo, the nation's savior. A variety of laws produced the ideological cleansing of the educational system. The *Law of Political Responsibilities* of 9 February 1939 initiated the persecution of those teachers and intellectuals suspected of treason to the new National-Catholic state. In the first years of the regime, it was crucial to be able to prove one's loyalty to the new authoritarian order. The Ministry of Education provided some workshops on religious culture and Spanish history for professors who wanted to keep their positions. In addition, those students who could demonstrate their cooperation with the Nationalist forces during the war or who had been persecuted by the Marxists would obtain a tuition waiver and be exempted, by the order of 20 August 1939, from taking the entrance exam to the university.[39] All these measures had a dual purpose: the re-Christianization and re-nationalization of Spain. The state entrusted the former to the Church and the latter to the Falange.

Schools turned into indoctrination agencies; the new curriculum emphasized religious and patriotic content, disregarding technical and scientific knowledge. The state delegated to the Church the ideological unity and orthodoxy of the educational system. Following the mandate of Pius XI's encyclical *Divini Illius Magistri* on the education of youth, the Francoist regime gave private schools, administered by Catholic orders, the same recognition as public schools. The *Law of Secondary Education* of 20 September 1938, revised in 1953, stressed classical and humanist learning with sound Catholic and patriotic foundations as the highest and purest form of education. Likewise, the inauguration of several institutions of higher learning, such as the National Research Council on 24 November 1939 and the Political Studies Institute on 11 September 1939, was intended to restore religious tradition and preserve the essence of Hispanic knowledge. The same religious zeal inspired the Project for University Regulatory Law, initiated in 1939 and promulgated on 31 July 1943. In a speech before the Cortes, the minister of education, José Ibáñez Martín, defended the Catholic essence of the Spanish university. "The most important thing," he said, "from a political point of view, is to Christianize the state's education, to eradicate secular nonpartisan teaching and scientific creation. . . . The Marxist revolution was incubated during fifty years of lay teaching." Now it was time, according to Ibáñez Martín, to "conquer the young generations' minds and hearts," and to build the future.[40] All Spaniards were expected to devote their minds and hearts to the reconstruction of Spain. To balance reason and faith, the *University Regulatory Law* established the position of University Secretary of Religious Formation.

The Nationalist component was also an essential part of the Francoist educational endeavor. The new state entrusted the Falange with the political instruction of Spaniards to boost patriotic sentiments. The law of 6 December 1940 gave the Youth Front of the Falange the task of indoctrinating young people in the Falangist spirit; patriotic instruction became mandatory in all schools, from primary to higher education, by the orders of 16 October 1941 and 29 March 1944. The *University Regulatory Law* required that faculty and administrators verify their loyalty to Falangist ideals, and students had to join the only student organization allowed until the mid-1960s, the Spanish University Student Union of the Falange.

State zeal to maintain a gender-segregated educational system gave the Women's Section the opportunity to take charge of women's education. *Divini Illius Magistri* emphasized the important role of the family in the educational process and the essential function of the Christian mother in this venture. Article 11 of the *Law of Elementary Education* (17 July 1945) defined the goal of primary education of girls: "Female elementary education will prepare girls especially for the home and for domestic crafts and industries." The education of girls and women was shaped to fit the autarchist concept of the productive/reproductive woman that was necessary during the postwar years. In 1942, José Pemartín, general director of primary and secondary education, proclaimed the need to prevent women from gaining a college education. "In my opinion, we must keep women away from the university. I mean that the place of a woman is at home, and thus Christian and authentic Spanish instruction in higher education must base itself on the premise that very seldom should a woman go to college."[41]

The Women's Section of the Falange directed the instruction of Spanish women within these parameters. Women learned the domestic arts of cooking and infant care through their training in Social Service, in domestic schools, and through institutionalized women's professional instruction. The order of 30 June 1941 made homemaking instruction mandatory for girls in all primary and secondary schools.[42] For domestic instruction, every high school had women teachers, who were appointed by the Ministry of National Education and endorsed by the Women's Section of the Falange. No girl could graduate without passing the courses in home economics, sewing, pattern design, arts and crafts, darning and mending, cooking, and music.

The professional orientation of women also received official attention. The Association for Women's Education, in existence since 1870 and known for its affiliation with FIL, became the target of severe criticism and strict surveillance. The Women's Section revealed the association's religious and patriotic fervor in 1939 in a report to the minister of national education about this liberal institution.

> The classes lack any style. Everything gives the impression of being dead and obsolete, with a total lack of spirit. There are neither portraits of José Antonio and the Caudillo nor the crucifix in any classroom. . . . For all these reasons we hope your Excellency, Mr. Minister of National Education, will be so gracious

as to grant us the Association; thus nobody would be hurt and we could revitalize it, incorporating it into the New Spain. We will establish a Learning Center for women, which will include subjects from Home Economics, to generate real homemakers, to a School for Secretaries to prepare those who find themselves forced to abandon the home to go to work.

> Madrid, 9 November, year of the Victory
> The Provincial Director of Culture
> Glory to José Antonio!
> Salute to Franco!
> Glory to Spain![43]

The domestic orientation of Spanish women's professions was regulated by two legal texts. On 17 November 1943, the government established the Central Junta for the Professional Instruction of Women, and by the decree of 2 March 1945, the Institute for Women's Professional Training was founded. In its introduction the decree proclaimed the essential participation of Spanish women in the national endeavor. "The female sex," it stated, "is entrusted with the task of defending traditional family values and preserving the domestic arts essential to maintain happiness in the home."[44] Although there was no legal exclusion of women from college, the state regulated and channeled them into so-called women's careers. A college woman was a *rara avis*. The regime's propaganda presented a woman's intellectual interests as dangerous to her femininity, especially to her ultimate destiny, motherhood, which constituted women's national responsibility.

As the head of a rigidly hierarchical women's organization, Pilar Primo de Rivera was bound to become the mediator between Spanish women and the state. She employed an openly declared antifeminism as the key to the prominence of the Women's Section throughout Francoism, even after the Falange lost political influence in the regime. Between 1940 and 1950, 624,826 women joined its political ranks, and 1,208,654 performed the mandatory Social Service.[45] Under the auspices of the Women's Section, Spanish women were expected to achieve the ideal Catholic womanhood of the imperial past.

CHAPTER THREE

CATHOLIC WOMANHOOD AND CONSUMERISM

"The woman in Spain, because she is Spanish, is also Catholic. Today, when the world agonizes in a military vortex that dilutes any morality and prudence, it is a joy to count on the *old and always new* image of the reserved, industrious, and discreet Spanish women. We must not be deceived by that other kind of woman that flourishes in the climate of our current versatile society, a woman filled with "snobism" who adores foreign ways and falls for them. Such a female type has nothing to do with the Spanish woman and, at most, is simply a deplorable translation of a model not worthy of imitating."

—Agustín Isern, September 1943

By 1950, the regime had matured and Franco had secured himself in power as the indispensable head of the state. The Caudillo's Nationalist rule continued to foster a unified neotraditional culture that would reanimate Spain's spiritual life and imbue the younger generation with a strong sense of nationalism, religion, and tradition.[1]

The challenge confronted by the regime in the 1950s was how to preserve tradition in the context of unavoidable modernization. In 1953, Spain and the United States signed the military and economic agreements known as the Pact of Madrid, which facilitated the expansion of the Spanish economy in its transition from autarchy to a market economy and consumerism. Consumerism had a tremendous political and social impact on Francoist Spain; it played an increasing role in shaping alternative identities to the official discourse, especially with regard to gender relations. The image of woman-as-consumer (and woman-as-commodity) is regarded as a central character in modern family life, representing the intersection of capitalism and gender. Exploring gender and consumption reveals the functioning of gender and power in Western cultures as well as in this particular dictatorship.[2]

To persuade Spanish women to return to a traditional model of the "domestic woman," the regime glorified domesticity and encouraged women to become mothers and "queens of the home."[3] The fatherland did not need women scientists, doctors, or lawyers. If a woman decided to study and pursue a career, she was expected to also fulfill her motherly obligations. With the Women's Section's aid, the state had facilitated domestic training for women by imposing it in the school curriculum. Its goal was to restore the romantic image of the traditional Christian housewife. But economic realities demanded a revision of this female model to adjust to the free-market society inaugurated in the 1950s. Spanish women were expected to cultivate Catholic virtues in the consumer society as much as under autarchy.

Economic and social changes were prompted by the regime's international rehabilitation. In the context of the Cold War, National-Catholicism provided an impeccable anticommunist facade, and Franco presented himself as the "sentinel of the west."[4] The same year the Pact of Madrid was signed with the United States, a new concordat was settled with the Vatican that reiterated the Catholic nature of the regime.

Internal politics were dominated by two cabinet reorganizations (in 1951 and in 1957), implemented to put an end to the country's economic penury. The autarchist policies proved to be inefficient, and the material hardships of the 1940s continued into the first half of the next decade. American financial aid eased the transition of the Spanish economy from autarchy to consumerism, and the Stabilization Plan of 1959 initiated the period of development. The Spanish population grew from 28 million to 30.6 million between 1950 and 1959. Many people began to migrate from the countryside to the city, particularly to the industrialized urban areas of Madrid, Barcelona, and the Basque Country. The nature of the labor force changed, although agriculture remained the most important sector. In 1950 the agrarian sector represented 47.6 percent of the labor force; the industrial sector, 26.5 percent (divided among construction, chemical, and metallurgical industries); and the service sector, 25.9 percent. By 1960, these percentages changed to 39.7, 33, and 27.3, respectively.[5]

Modernization was unavoidable. The regime intended, nevertheless, to preserve the traditional foundations of Catholic Spain, including gender relations. Feminism was regarded as foreign and as threatening to women's dignity. The official discourse promoted a "Christian femininity" embodied in figures such as Saint Teresa of Avila and Queen Isabel of Castile. True Catholic womanhood had to be preserved in the passage from autarchy to consumerism.

INTERNATIONAL REHABILITATION OF THE REGIME

The defeat of Nazi Germany and Fascist Italy in 1945 did not signal the end of dictatorship in Europe: Franco was to remain in power until 1975. The official discourse of the Francoist regime did have to adjust to the de-fascistation of Europe, though, in order to become part of the international political scene. The regime's emphasis on the Catholic spirit, which guided the crusade against Communism during the Civil War, ameliorated the fascist overtones of the Falange in the 1950s and facilitated the rapprochement between Spain and the United States in the context of the Cold War.

The regime continued to promote an exultant rhetoric that presented Franco as the true leader of all Western civilization and Spain as the spearhead of a worldwide struggle against Communism. After the Civil War, Franco's regime could claim victory over Communism. The Caudillo rejected multiparty regimes that struggled with Communist or socialist opposition, regarding them as morally inferior. This attitude prompted Western European governments to remain more hostile to the regime than Washington, where there was mounting interest in bringing Spain within the defense network of the United States. On 20 December 1948, for example, an article appeared in *Time* magazine that described Franco's dictatorship as transitory and based on Spanish traditions:

> [I]nstead of replacing old institutions and traditions (in particular the Catholic church), [Franco's regime] clings to them. It is not strongly ideological. It does not present itself as an utopian answer to everything, or as an irresistible urge of historical force. Franco himself calls his government "provisional" and speaks of a future return to "normalization."[6]

Franco's regime gained American support because Communism became the threat in the context of the Cold War. Two important events favored the international rehabilitation of the Francoist regime: the signing of the military agreements with the United States and the concordat with the Vatican, both in the late summer of 1953.

By 1951, a regular relationship had been established with the United

States, which evolved rapidly in the context of the Korean War. The exchange of official ambassadors took place in 1951, and the integration of Spain into international organizations followed. Carlton J. H. Hayes, former American ambassador to Spain, said, "Collaboration with Spain requires, of course, an overcoming of democratic scruples about General Franco's government, which is undoubtedly a *kind of dictatorship—a military and anti-communist dictatorship.*" [7] For Hayes, Franco's totalitarian regime was not of the same sort as Hitler's or Stalin's.

Spain and the United States signed on 26 September 1953 the Pact of Madrid, made up of three executive agreements, which provided for mutual defense and military aid to Spain, the American establishment of three air bases and one naval base in Spain for a ten-year period, and military assistance. From this point on, American capital (private and public) flowed into Spain. The U.S. Congress authorized on 1 August 1950 the establishment, through the Import-Export Bank, of a credit to Spain of $62.5 million, and further American economic help after 1953 reached $1.183 million. Foreign capital made imperative the transition from autarchy to a liberal economic system. In addition, this agreement with the United States at the beginning of the 1950s incorporated Spain geographically into the strategic American network. Such an association with the greatest power in the world strengthened the Spanish regime both at home and abroad and increased its stability. As Stanley Payne maintains, "the American pact gave Franco a recognition he had never before possessed; coming on the heels of the new Concordat with the Vatican, it marked the apogee of the regime's rehabilitation." [8]

Within a few years, though, Franco recognized some of the disadvantages of the air base agreement. He complained of the dangers posed by American installations to nearby cities and of the disappointing scale of American economic help. [9] Furthermore, in his role as defender of the faith, Franco became concerned when Cardinal Pedro Segura and the hierarchy complained that a deal with the United States would open up Catholic Spain to the harmful influence of Protestantism.

The Caudillo was careful to cultivate a public image of total identification between himself and the Church. Paul Preston recounts that as a young man, Franco had displayed only conventional piety and had even rejected religion when he was in Africa. In 1936, however, he saw the political utility of the Church endorsement in winning the war and started to play the role of defender of Christianity. In successive years, Franco behaved like a medieval king in public and continued to enter and leave churches under the canopy previously reserved to Spanish kings. The International Eucharistic Congress celebrated in Barcelona in May 1952 represented a step toward international acquiescence. The papal delegate, Cardinal Tedeschini, with the solemn presence of the Caudillo and his wife, doña Carmen Polo de Franco, presided over the religious ceremonies, which were attended by three hundred thousand faithful, twelve cardinals, and three hundred bishops from seventy-seven countries.[10] This event was a step toward the consummation of the concordat, which the Vatican finally signed in August 1953. Negotiations were initiated by Joaquín Ruiz Giménez, Franco's ambassador to the Vatican from 1948 to 1951, and were carried to completion by his successor, Fernando María Castiella.

The concordat provided the fullest recognition by the Church, reaffirmed the confessionality of the state, and confirmed the right of presentation of bishops by the head of the state. The Catholic Church became the moral director of the country. It received supervisory power over education, and the media facilities were placed at its disposal. The clergy were exempted from military service and Church property would not be taxed. Franco's greatest gain from the concordat rested on the Holy See's entering an agreement with him. It also confirmed the ancient privilege of having two Spanish assessors in the Court of the Rota with jurisdiction over cases presented by Spain. Appointments of prelates were made by joint agreement between the head of the state and the Vatican. Finally, the Spanish government had the right to establish the boundaries of dioceses and provinces at will and to make them correspond with those of civil provinces.[11] Coinciding with the American agreement, the Concordat of 1953 marked another major step in the international recognition of Franco's regime. Only two years later, Spain was admitted to the United Nations.

DOMESTIC ADJUSTMENTS TO THE TIMES

The international circumstances prompted a realignment of the regime's political factions. The principal demand by the Western democracies during the period of ostracism had been the elimination of Falange's fascist overtones from Spanish life. However, as Payne points out, the Falange proved indispensable to Franco for several reasons. First, it furnished the necessary cadre of leaders and manpower for the bureaucracy of the regime; second, it provided a modern social doctrine and through the Women's Section had developed most of Spain's social welfare; third, it staffed the press and propaganda system; and finally, it could even serve as "a scapegoat whose nominal downgrading would be evidence of reform and liberalization."[12]

It is worth noting that among the Falangists there was a group called liberal Falangists, represented by writers such as Dionisio Ridruejo, Antonio Tovar, and Pedro Laín Entralgo, who sought to promote a more dynamic and modern culture, largely secular in inspiration. Laín Entralgo, for example, argued in his work *España como problema* (1962) that ever since the sixteenth century in Spain a conflict between modernity and tradition had existed. He proposed that the task of his generation was to resolve this dilemma. For Laín Entralgo, the time of synthesis had arrived, and it was imperative to incorporate Catholicism into the modernization of the country.

The 1950s, however, witnessed the political downturn of Falangism and the accentuation of conservative Catholicism. The main Catholic groups were Catholic Action, the National Association of Catholic Propagandists (NACP), and Editorial Católica, the largest and most influential Catholic publisher in Spain. In addition, a new Catholic organization had acquired significance by the 1950s: Opus Dei (Work of God), a secular institute founded in 1928 within university circles by Monseñor José María Escrivá de Balaguer y Albas (1902–1975). In February of 1947, the Holy See published the apostolic constitution *Provida Mater Ecclesia,* which established the Secular Institutes—Opus Dei being the first of them. Opus Dei's goal was (and still is) "to spread among all the civil classes, and in particular among the intellectuals, the aspiration to Christian perfection in the world." Its mission was the sanctification of the secular world, and this objective was best achieved through key professions such as university teaching, business, finance, and the higher levels of management. Most of its members had careers in those areas, and Opus Dei eventually developed a reputation of elitism. A halo of secrecy shrouded Opus Dei, constituting an essential element of the institute. According to Joan Estruch, the originality of Opus Dei resided in its introduction to Catholic Spain of Protestant values (in the Weberian sense) such as the Calvinist ethic and the development of capitalism. Its members favored the adoption of rational modern capitalism in Spain as well as the monarchy as a form of government. The most vocal group of Opus Dei formed around *Arbor,* a publication of the National Research Council, led by Rafael Calvo Serer and Florentino Pérez Embid. This group—proclaimed to be the Third Force—was known as the "Generation of 48"; it strongly supported an authoritarian Catholic monarchist succession.[13]

The Catholic elements certainly gave the regime a better international image than the old totalitarian national-syndicalist philosophy of the Falange. Under such circumstances, and pressured by economic chaos, the first cabinet change in six years was announced on 18 July 1951, prompted by a need to redefine the Francoist state apparatus and its foundations, as well as an attempt to liberalize economic policy. The new cabinet of 1951 featured continuity more than change, providing some opportunity for Catholic formulas to be applied. Luis Carrero Blanco's position as undersecretary to the president (the closest collaborator to the Caudillo) was upgraded to cabinet rank, and the Catholic layman and former ambassador at the Vatican Joaquín Ruiz Giménez was appointed minister of education. The Vice Secretariat of Popular Culture, in charge of censorship under the Ministry of Education, was now placed under the newly created Ministry of Information and Tourism assigned to the far-right-wing Gabriel Arias Salgado. If the cabinet was backward-looking in political terms, in the economic sphere it marked one of the major turning points of the regime. With the Americans pressing for economic liberalization, Juan Antonio Suanzes, the architect of autarchy, was removed as minister of industry and commerce and replaced by two ministers, Manuel Arburúa in commerce and Joaquín Planell in industry.[14] American support entailed the cancellation of autarchy, a political move that would deepen American friendship and, in the long run, promote economic growth. At this juncture, highly trained experts—technocrats—rather than military men were required to administer the economy.

Most scholars regard the 1940s autarchist formulas as the extension of the Primoriverrista economic doctrine, which sought Spain's modernization through state intervention and military rule. Franco had continued this experiment, but it resulted in material stagnation.[15] He realized that progress was only possible with a liberalization of the economic policy.

During the first half of the 1950s, private investment began to rise, the rationing of basic necessities ended in 1952, and tourism became the major factor in economic expansion. Imports, although subject to restriction, increased during the fifties, in part simply because more food and other consumer items were being purchased, fueling the rising standard of living. As Stanley Payne has noted, industrial production doubled, and the real growth of the GNP, at an annual rate of 7.9 percent from 1951 to 1958, was one of the highest in the world.[16] But this growth encountered major obstacles. Foreign exchange was controlled, and trade was regulated by the state through direct intervention in licensing for exports and imports. The significant investments of the National Institute of Industry had an impact as well. Whereas in the 1940s that institute favored fuels, fertilizers, and electric power, in the 1950s it supported metallurgy and automobiles through large, new industries such as EN-SIDESA and SEAT. American financial aid was an important stimulus to the economic takeoff, but by 1956 further difficulties appeared, including high inflation, a trade deficit, and endemic underemployment.

Franco and Carrero Blanco did not anticipate a major change of economic policy but rather some adjustment and tightening of the existing system. The regime needed better economic leadership; thus, in February 1957, Franco announced a reorganization of the government that incorporated three key experts in economic and state administration, all of whom were members of Opus Dei. Laureano López Rodó, a law professor at the University of Santiago de Compostela, though he did not receive a cabinet position, was appointed to the newly created position of general technical secretary for the undersecretary of the presidency. He was also made head of the Government Secretariat and of the Office of Economic Coordination and Programming (a technical position created especially for him). Alberto Ullastres Calvo, a history of economics professor at the University of Madrid, was appointed minister of commerce, and Mariano Navarro Rubio, a lawyer, directed the Ministry of Finance.

The economic crisis was not the only circumstance prompting the formation of a new government in 1957. As a result of acute labor and student turmoil, Joaquín Ruiz Giménez was replaced in 1956 as the minister of education by Jesús Rubio García Mina, a university professor and former undersecretary of education. Ruiz Giménez, an open-minded Catholic, had initiated a policy of tolerance. Under his administration some liberal Falangists were appointed to key posts in his ministry and the university system. Pedro Laín Entralgo was made rector of the University of Madrid, and Antonio Tovar assumed the rectorship in Salamanca. New legislation on secondary education was passed, and new university regulations established more impersonal and automatic procedures for participation in the qualifying boards for the designation of professorial chairholders, thus eliminating some of the provisions of the *University Regulatory Law* of 1943.

Franco needed to reestablish some political balance. Always faithful to the Falange but conscious of the need to benefit other factions, he executed a double play. On the one hand, he commissioned the general secretary of the Movement, José Luis Arrese, to revise the party statutes and develop three legislative projects: a law of the fundamental principles of the state, an organic law of the movement, and an organizational law of the government. Such action was a vote of confidence for the Falange to develop what came to be considered the constitution of the regime. On the other hand was the reshaping of the cabinet in 1957, which established the presence of the Opus Dei in the government and the application of liberal economic policies, along with the monarchy, as the formula for succession. The cabinet launched two important measures to accommodate the regime to the unavoidable political and economic modernization of the times: first, the *Law of the Fundamental Principles of the State* in 1958, and second, the Stabilization Plan of 1959. Both measures defined political and economic boundaries that would favor the arrival of consumerism.

The three draft projects of the *Law of the Fundamental Principles of the State* elaborated by Arrese's commission made no reference to the monarchy, as prescribed by the *Law of Succession* of 1947. On the contrary, the projects emphasized the Movement's political significance and strengthened the power of the National Council and the general secretary of the FET de las JONS. Both leadership and succession remained vague. Undoubtedly, criticisms came from all fronts: army, Church, and Opus Dei. The non-Falangist members of the cabinet regarded Arrese's proposal as a Falangist coup de main and rejected it entirely. Monarchists objected particularly to the absence of any mention of the crown, and the Church hierarchy declared the proposals "in disagreement with pontifical doctrine," proclaiming that the projects had no roots in "Spanish tradition, but in totalitarian regimes of certain countries after the First World War." At this point, Franco shelved the Falangist proposals and accepted those presented by Laureano López Rodó with the endorsement of Carrero Blanco. López Rodó designed the final document that was approved in the Cortes on 19 May 1958. The new version of the Principles of the Movement was conceived as the constitution of the regime, although the spirit of the 1936 uprising remained. The old twenty-six principles of the Falangist Nationalist Movement were replaced by twelve, fully sanitized of any overtly fascist expression. They affirmed patriotism, unity, peace,

Catholicism, the family as the pillar of society, and representation through the syndicates and the municipalities. Principle 2 defined Spain as one nation, whose unique faith was Catholicism: "It is the core honor of the Spanish Nation to obey God's laws, in accordance with the Roman Catholic Church doctrine, the only true one; such faith is inseparable from the national conscience and inspires our legislation."[17]

In National-Catholic Spain, the family remained the mainstay of social relations, along with the syndicate and municipal authorities. This corporatist social order sustained the "traditional social and representative Catholic monarchy." Political participation was allowed only through the family, the syndicate, and the municipality, and "any other political organizations outside of this representative system [was] considered illegal." The regime enacted an "organic democracy" based on a "limited pluralism," in Linz's words.[18]

Economic hardship led to strikes in Madrid, Barcelona, and the Basque Country in 1951 and again in 1958. Clearly, the autarchy experiment had failed. Prices and the cost of living grew by about 10 percent between 1956 and 1959, whereas the average yearly growth of per capita income was only 5.5 percent. Spain's per capita income was three hundred dollars in 1960, making it the poorest country in Europe twenty years after the Civil War.[19]

Alberto Ullastres and Mariano Navarro Rubio tried to bring some order to the chaotic economy and, with López Rodó, developed a new program of economic liberalization and stabilization. On 20 July 1959, with the regime facing bankruptcy, Ullastres presented the Stabilization Plan. The objectives were to control inflation and immediately liberalize and rationalize the economy. The measures included devaluing the peseta, reducing fiduciary circulation, raising interest rates, liberalizing imports, and reducing government spending.

For the next four years, the prices stabilized, foreign loans and investments were made to Spain, and the devaluation of the peseta allowed the tourist industry to flourish. The social cost, though, was high. Salaries were frozen between 1957 and 1961; the number of unemployed rose from 150,000 to 200,000, and many Spaniards emigrated to other European countries, such as Germany, Great Britain, or France, searching for jobs. Tourism and migration promoted the expansion of an urban culture, to which consumerism was central. But until the 1960s, consumption remained low because of limited productivity and low wages.[20]

Franco continued to distrust liberal economics as much as any aspect of liberalism. He agreed to the Stabilization Plan only when the minister of finance appealed to his patriotism and national pride and portrayed the plan as a new phase in the evolution of the Francoist regime. The technocratic economic shift had been a wise move toward economic recovery and the *desarrollo* (economic prosperity) of the sixties.[21] The technocrats inaugurated a new style and a language full of technical and economic terms. The Catholic component remained central to the regime's political discourse in the service of development. In this context, gender relations underwent an adjustment that served the political evolution of the regime and the times.

THE LURE OF THE CITY

In the 1950s, Francoism continued to foster a return to the nineteenth-century model of traditional Christian womanhood. Family was the central pillar of the social order, and women's patriotic duty was to be rendered within its boundaries. Such a social arrangement had been sanctioned by the Napoleonic *Civil Code* of 1889.[22] Spanish women's social, political, and economic status was shaped by this civil code.

The transitional nature of the 1950s in economic and political terms, however, led to a revision of the legal status of women and therefore to a new delineation of gender relations. The 1950s represented the evolution from a rural to an urbanized society, from autarchy to capitalism, from the reproductive/productive model of women of postwar autarchy economy to the consumer-housewife of the new market economy of the development era. Modern times demanded a new social role for women. They were needed in the labor market and as consumers. Nevertheless, their presence in the public sphere had to maintain the Christian virtues prescribed by the regime. They were expected to bring moral values into the modern, dechristianized industrial world.

The regime's active role in preserving Christian gender relations was translated into law with the reform of the *Civil Code,* enacted in April 1958 under the auspices of the Institute of Political Studies. This reform was followed by the *Law of Political, Professional, and Labor Rights of Women* in 1961. With the reform of 1958 and the law of professional rights for women—sponsored by the Women's Section of the Falange—gender relations were redefined by the state in the context of a transitional political and economic period. Yet both documents sought to preserve the Catholic family and domestic values by endorsing true Catholic womanhood.

Economic recovery favored the rapid urbanization of the country, and some aspects of that phenomenon produced a change in the social relationship of the sexes. First, there was a transfer of population from the rural areas to the cities because of the lure of job opportunities, recreation facilities—cinemas, ballrooms, cafés—and the opening of department stores such as *Galerías Preciados.* Second, a change in mentality was facilitated by contact with other cultures through tourism and the emigration of Spanish workers to other European countries. Finally, the mass media, especially magazines and Hollywood movies, had a great impact on Spanish female identities, because they proposed an alternative to the official discourse on womanhood.

Madrid became a big city during the fifties: it grew from 1.5 million in 1950 to 2 million in 1959. Shantytowns began to appear in the city's outskirts, prompting government intervention by the National Institute of

Housing, which had become a ministry in 1957. This ministry financed construction of housing for low-income groups on a national scale. In 1960, though, seventy thousand flats in Madrid remained empty because most Spanish families could not afford them.[23] Thus, wage raises were granted not only as a response to the disruptive strikes in 1951 and 1958 but also to enable demand to meet supply.

The city's appearance underwent a significant transformation with the construction of new residential neighborhoods and skyscrapers such as the Edificio España and the Tower of Madrid in the downtown area. Department stores offered credit to consumers, allowing many families to buy their first television set—a step upward from the radio. In 1956, when the State Broadcasting Company's RTVE began broadcasting regular television programming, there were only six hundred television sets in the country. Two years later, the number of sets had increased to forty thousand. As a Marconi ad stated in 1962, television had won over Spanish homes. By 1959, along with radios and television sets, middle-class Spanish housewives could enjoy new AEG appliances, Bru washing machines, and Edesa vacuum cleaners, which were advertised in colorful magazines (see fig. 1). Such devices mechanized housework and turned it into a scientific enterprise with the aim of achieving maximum cleanliness efficiently. Choosing the right detergent guaranteed success, as an Omo detergent ad remarked: "Of course my laundry is whiter. I changed to Omo."[24] When many middle-class families purchased their first cars, town councils began to regulate traffic. The most popular model was the SEAT 600, a small, two-door vehicle that many women drove in the sixties.

The autarchy's austerity philosophy became hard to preserve when Spanish women were exposed to the advertisements for makeup, perfume, fashion, and luxury products appearing in Spanish magazines such as *Blanco y Negro* in the 1950s and 1960s, and the consumption of luxury articles such as watches, Chanel perfume, and high-fashion clothing became more common by the end of the 1950s. The colorful ads appealed to women's search for eternal youth and beauty. Pond's promised to enhance female beauty (see fig. 2), and Dermaluz's ad proclaimed, "Ser joven y bonita es maravilloso" (Being young and beautiful is wonderful). A new woman-as-commodity to appeal to woman-as-consumer was manufactured in the shopper culture. The ideal of beauty turned transnational, as a Cutex ad claimed, "Cutex contributes to beauty in more than a hundred countries." The message of such advertisements contradicted the treatises from the 1500s that had been promoted by Franco's regime, for example, de León's assertion in *La perfecta Casada:* "Honest women wear only those things that can honor an altar. This means that all your dress and embellishment must be holy . . . [any makeup] is an offense to God and your soul."[25]

The new ads in the press urged Spanish women to remake themselves. They could now purchase a new identity, a sense of self-worth based on physical appearance rather than spiritual value. This opportunity to "perform

Figure 1. "Of course my laundry is whiter. I switched to Omo." Advertisements such as this were an essential part of economic modernization in Spain, promising women admiration and greater self-esteem if they purchased the right products: "You will be so proud when everybody admires how white your clothes are when you wash them with Omo." *(Blanco y Negro,* 16 June 1962, Hemeroteca Facultad de Filosofia y Letras, Universidad de Granada, Spain)

Figure 2. "With Pond's she enhanced her beauty." With the advent of consumerism Spanish women were continually urged to remake themselves. They could now purchase a new identity based on physical rather than spiritual beauty. *(Blanco y Negro,* 15 March 1958, Hemeroteca Facultad Filosofia y Letras, Universidad de Granada, Spain)

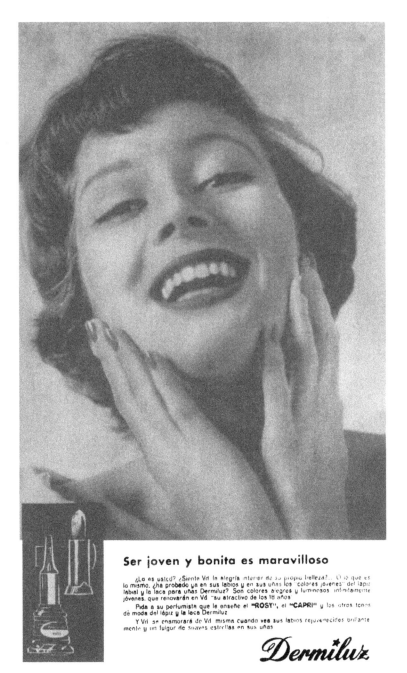

Ser joven y bonita es maravilloso

¿Lo es usted? ¿Siente Vd. la alegría interior de su propia belleza?... O lo que es lo mismo, ¿ha probado ya en sus labios y en sus uñas los "colores jóvenes" del lápiz labial y la laca para uñas Dermiluz? Son colores alegres y luminosos, infinitamente jóvenes, que renovarán en Vd. "su atractivo de los 18 años"

Pida a su perfumista que le enseñe el **"ROSY"**, el **"CAPRI"** y los otros tonos de moda del lápiz y la laca Dermiluz

Y Vd. se enamorará de Vd. misma cuando vea sus labios rejuvenecidos brillantemente y un fulgor de suaves estrellas en sus uñas

Dermiluz

Figure 3. "Youth and beauty is marvelous." The sensuality implicit in promises of eternal youth and beauty through make-up conflicted with the National Catholic emphasis upon chastity and modesty. The challenge was to remain a chaste woman behind the mask of make-up. *(Blanco y Negro,* 13 July 1957, Hemeroteca Facultad Filosofía y Letras, Universidad de Granada, Spain)

Beba Coca-Cola ¡Verá qué rica es!

Si le ofrecen Coca-Cola, lo harán con una sonrisa porque
Coca-Cola es lo mejor para la sed. Recuerde que, en todo
momento, en cualquier sitio, como refresco no tiene igual.
Su sabor delicioso y único, es conocido en el mundo entero.
Beba una hoy mismo, verá qué rica es.

EMBOTELLADA POR LOS CONCESIONARIOS DE COCA-COLA

Figure 4. "Drink Coca-Cola. You'll see how great it tastes!" Large quantities of American products first entered the Spanish market in the 1950s. That smiling, young women could enjoy such things helped to erode the spirit of thrift that dominated the lives of most Spanish families during the period of autarchy. Little by little, going to the movies or drinking Coca-Cola was no longer frivolous. (*Blanco y Negro,* 20 July 1957, Hemeroteca Filosofia y Letras, Universidad de Granada, Spain)

Figure 5. "Enjoy the summer with Lambretta." This image of a mobile and independent young woman contradicted the sheltered and virginal model of Catholic womanhood promoted by the Francoist regime. (*Blanco y Negro,* 10 August 1957, Hemeroteca Facultad de Filosofía y Letras, Universidad de Granada, Spain)

Figure 6. "Cooking, a delicious game for the housewife." Modernity confronted middle-class housewives with new choices, identities, and pastimes. These stoves presented on a chessboard await the young woman's next move in the "delicious cooking game." *(Blanco y Negro,* 26 September 1959. Hemeroteca Filosofía y Letras Universidad de Granada, Spain)

identity," to buy beauty, became a promising means to do better in National-Catholic Spain's marriage market. The challenge was to remain a chaste lady behind the makeup mask.

Fashion complemented makeup. One ad read, "Mujer sin medias, pájaro sin plumas" (A woman without stockings is like a bird without feathers), making this piece of clothing a must in all women's wardrobes (see fig. 3). Christian Dior's hourglass female figure was popularized in 1947. Women all over the world wore large flare skirts and showed a voluptuous bosom, following Hollywood actresses such as Marilyn Monroe, Jayne Mansfield, and Mamie Van Doren. Barbara J. Coleman, in her study of American women's images through the analysis of ads for Maidenform bras, interprets the new Dior effigy as a metaphor of the Cold War containment policies. "In the scramble to reshape the feminine form," she says, "women, in their large Dior skirts, began to resemble the nose cone of a rocket." Spanish magazines also popularized this turn in women's fashions, an eroticization of the female body that further distanced women from motherhood. In America, Coleman points out,

> [t]he breast, as other parts of the body, became sculpted objects subject to the confines of elasticized rubber, wire stays, and clever stitching. In the fashion world, breasts became decorative, sexual, and symbolic—not functional. It seems to be no coincidence that during the 1950s, breast feeding of infants dropped from 60 percent before 1950 to only 38 percent by 1961. In the 1950s, breast connoted sex appeal, not maternity.

Victoria de Grazia's study of the Italian situation shows that "Hollywood stars had made the whole body, not merely the face, the vehicle of physical expression, influencing the way Italian women had of sitting, getting up, walking, pausing, and turning."[26] The influence of foreign models of female beauty imported from France and the United States certainly had a great impact on shaping the modern female body. A new cult of beauty emerged. Women's bodies became more than vessels of motherhood. With the eroticization of female bodies shown in magazines and movies, the Francoist regime's virginal ideal as prescribed in de León's and Vives's 1500s treatises became only a parallel discourse on female identity.

The images of beautiful women popularized in the media also altered the relation between the sexes. Marriage and motherhood were the ultimate destiny for Spanish women; unless she entered a convent, the single woman suffered the disapproval of society. The problem was that men and women were a mystery to each other because they were educated in separate worlds. Writer Carmen Martín Gaite's analysis of Spanish women's magazines reveals that the code of courtship required a woman who wanted to get married to avoid being critical, to avoid analyzing things, and to fail not to smile on a regular basis. Men disliked serious or sad women who showed no femininity. There was also a rift between love and sex. Men rarely arrived at marriage as virgins, whereas virginity for women was a must. The moral double standard was redefined with the urbanization of the country. It was a commonplace in the 1950s to distinguish between the *señorita* (a young lady) who lived in the city and the *fulana* (a hooker) who lived in the outskirts of the metropolitan areas. Young working-class women helped *señoritos* (middle-to-upper-class young men) preserve their masculinity and the virginity of their fiancées. Historian Rafael Abella mentions also the figure of the sexually repressed male as a product of the official control of gender relations in sexual and love matters. This was a man whose sexual fantasies were not fulfilled by his own wife or his visits to the brothel. As some women were not able to enjoy their sexuality in the name of motherhood and purity, this man, not being able to enjoy his fantasies, turned also into an oppressed sexual being.[27]

The city offered men and women the opportunity to encounter each other in informal social settings other than the Church or family gatherings. Movie theaters, for example, proliferated. Each film was preceded by one of the official state newsreels, NO-DO, showing Franco's latest hunting trip or the inauguration of some public works project. At the movies, the Spanish population became acquainted with the American way of life. To protect Christian moral conventions, government censorship and Catholic groups developed a grading chart of sorts and took special care, when dubbing films, to strip American sound tracks of any moral or political intemperance.[28]

In addition to movies, other social entertainment emerged. The traditional café gave way to gourmet coffeehouses, as well as bars and nightclubs, where people enjoyed American products such as Coca-Cola and Winston or Camel cigarettes. The spirit of thrift that dominated the lives of most Spanish families during autarchy began to fade, and little by little, things that would have been considered superfluous, such as going to the movies or drinking Coca-Cola in a café, became indispensable (see fig. 4). The images of women smoking (see fig. 5) or riding a motorcycle (see fig. 6) contradicted the prudish model of Catholic womanhood that the regime wanted to preserve. The new eroticized depiction of women (woman-as-commodity) in the media constituted a transgression of Christian purity and Francoist's prescribed gender relations. The images of "femme fatale" or "desirable beauty" were as powerful as they were inaccessible both for Spanish men and most Spanish women. As Mary Louise Roberts points out, "these images of female bodies exist only to be looked at and desired."[29]

Social and gender relations were further affected by the emigration of workers to other countries and the explosion of tourism. Contact with other cultures expedited a change in social relations. With wages frozen between 1957 and 1960 during the first phase of the Stabilization Plan, some of the surplus Spanish labor moved into industrial and service jobs in France, Germany, Belgium, and Switzerland. This favored the expansion of employment in Spain, and at the same time, the remittances of migrant workers provided a further source of international exchange.[30]

A new phenomenon, tourism, infiltrated Spanish society and also led to sociological changes. In 1951, 1.3 million foreign visitors entered Spain; by 1960, the number rose to 6.1 million. Tourism stimulated consumption and economic growth. According to Manuel Fraga Iribarne, minister of tourism in the early 1960s, "foreign tourism constituted the most important means of financing Spanish development and industrial modernization." Tourism facilitated the creation of jobs in the service sector, particularly on the coast (Costa del Sol, Costa Brava, and the Canary and Balearic Islands), where many found seasonal work in the hotel industry and in restaurants, as well as in construction.[31] Thousands of apartment complexes, hotels, and houses were built to accommodate the outpouring of visitors.

Tourism served a very important political purpose as well. The regime wanted to show the world the permanence of Spanish eternal traditional values: order, family, and Catholicism. "Those who visit us," asserted Fraga Iribarne, "have the opportunity to get in touch with a country that offers an original vision of its common values and is loyal to its singularity."[32] He considered that the most precious feature of Spanish society was the preservation of family values and the atmosphere of Christian morality that was part of social relations.

Franco embodied the best example of Catholic family values. But his fatherly image and family-oriented life experienced an important turn in the 1950s when his dear and only child, Carmen (or "Nenuca"), was married on 10 April 1950 to Dr. Cristóbal Martínez Bordiu, soon to be Marques de Villaverde. Martínez Bordiu, a minor playboy from Jaén, took advantage of his relationship with the dictator's family to initiate a series of business ventures. He made a fortune with the acquisition of the exclusive license to import Vespa motor scooters from Italy. His extravagant way of life, driving a series of Chrysler and Packard convertibles, gained him the nickname of Marqués de *Vayavida* (what a life), or *Vespaverde*.[33] While the Caudillo pushed for austerity and a simple lifestyle, his son-in-law exemplified the consumer mode of the times. Nevertheless, Nenuca's marriage changed Franco's life and image in a positive way. Between 1951 and 1964, she bore seven grandchildren, to whom the dictator devoted the kind of affection absent from his military-like life until then. Franco's new image of loving grandfather softened that of the dictator both internationally and at home.

Of course, in the new consumer era, the changes in society also affected women's role, image, and status. The new economic demands opened to people the possibility of entering the public space by joining the workforce and of becoming buyers rather than merely producers and savers. Nonetheless, family values were to be preserved. On entering the labor force, women would occupy those areas that required some nurturing or motherly qualities, such as nursing, elementary teaching, or serving as a flight attendant. Although modernity broadened their horizons, they continued to be valued for the same virtues. Francoist nationalization of the potential of the female population became even more evident, for modern industrialized society needed feminine care and nourishment. The woman was the heart of the family and society. A series of ads for Far Stoves published in *Blanco y Negro* illustrates the woman's destiny in the modernized society. Spanish little girls dreamed of becoming housewives (or "queens of the home," as one ad defined them). So internalized was this duty in Spanish women that cooking ended up, in the words of another ad, being just a delightful game.

FRANCOIST REGULATION OF GENDER RELATIONS

The social changes brought about by the new consumer culture prompted the regime's regulation of women's status and participation in the National-Catholic state of the development era. Francoist legislation had always conformed to the Catholic parameters prescribed for gender relations. As early as 12 March 1938, the regime reestablished the *Civil Code* of 1889. Under this code, single women enjoyed a certain freedom after reaching their *mayoría de edad* (legal adulthood). But article 321 prohibited them from leaving their parental home without their father's permission unless they were getting married or entering a convent or one of the parents remarried. The legal status of a married woman was equal to that of a minor; her guardian was her husband. She had neither custody rights over their children nor economic or legal independence.[34]

The economic and political changes of the 1950s required a revision of women's legal status as prescribed by the *Civil Code* of 1889. At the national Conference of Justice and Law, held in Madrid in 1952, distinguished lawyers discussed the issue of women's legal status within the family and concluded that it was necessary to reform the *Civil Code*. A year later, lawyer and writer Mercedes Formica published an article in the daily *ABC* entitled "El domicilio conyugal" (The conjugal home) in which she addressed domestic violence. Formica discussed the death of a wife stabbed by her husband and pointed out that, legally, the family residence was considered the husband's home, and this situation left women unprotected from an abusive spouse.[35] Formica's piece initiated a series of articles in the pages of *ABC* that discussed the issue. In addition, the Academy of Jurisprudence and the College of Law organized a cycle of lectures in 1953–1954 and 1956–1957 about the legal status of women. As a result, the General Commission of Codification prepared a draft to reform the *Civil Code*.

The new cabinet of 1957 that endorsed the economic liberalization of the country also sponsored the revision of the *Civil Code*, and Franco's regime announced the changes on 24 April 1958. The new law did not abolish certain limitations resulting from biological distinctions. It continued to support different minimum ages for marriage—twelve years for women and fourteen for men if married in court, fourteen and sixteen years, respectively, in the case of a canonical marriage. A widow was obliged to wait 301 days after the death of her husband before remarrying, in order to assure the paternity of her deceased husband in case she was pregnant. Single women could not abandon the parental household before they were twenty-five years of age unless they married or entered a convent. Although these limitations were kept, others from the *Civil Code* of 1889 were cautiously removed. Under the new code of 1958, single women could be testamentary witnesses, but a male continued to be preferred. A married woman could be a guardian, an executrix, or a testamentary witness with her husband's permission. In addition, the household was now considered *hogar conyugal* (a conjugal home) rather than *casa del marido* (the husband's household). In the case of a nullification of the marriage, a woman could keep half of the joint possessions and properties, and she would have the complete administration of whatever belonged to her. Adultery was a cause for separation for both men and women. The most important reform was that of article 1.413, which prescribed that husbands needed their wives' permission to administer their *bienes gananciales* (shared possessions). The state recognized only canonical marriage, allowing civil marriage only when one of the spouses was non-Catholic. Finally, any Spanish woman marrying a foreigner could keep her own nationality if she did not acquire her husband's.[36] Although Spanish women gained certain legal leeway, they remained subject to their husbands' and fathers' authority, since the family continued to be the axis around which social relations revolved in the late 1950s.

Further reforms took place when, in 1961, the government enacted the *Law of Political, Professional, and Labor Rights of Women*. The Women's Section endorsed this legislation, which represented a legal sanction of the economic and social transformation that had already taken place in the country. Many men had migrated to Germany, France, or Great Britain, and this outflow of manpower pushed women into the labor market.[37] Although the Labor Charter of 1938 was intended to liberate married women from factory work, the reality proved quite different. Spanish men were not able to fulfill their masculine duty as breadwinners in a depressed economy and had to either migrate or allow their wives to work. Women's presence in the labor force was a fact by the end of the fifties, and thus the law of 1961 sanctioned de jure a de facto situation. The *Law of Political, Professional, and Labor Rights of Women* was discussed in the Cortes on 15 July 1961 and published ten days later in the government organ *Boletín Oficial del Estado*. Pilar Primo de Rivera, head of the Women's Section, and Fernando Herrero Tejedor, general secretary of the Movement, each defended the law with a speech at the Cortes assembly.

Herrero Tejedor began his speech by insisting on the necessity to confront women's issues from a social point of view. He proposed an approach rooted in religious principles that avoided "following the easy demagoguery of the absolute equality of rights and responsibilities between men and women." He said the economic transformation of Spanish society demanded a redefinition of women's patriotic role. They had to help their husbands financially by entering the labor force but without forgetting the ethical religious principles of the regime. The implementation of this reform, he emphasized, was of the greatest importance. "We cannot be carried away by hollow attitudes that call themselves feminist or antifeminist. It is extraordinarily important that this legal project is taken up by the government based on a legal proposition elaborated precisely by the Women's Section."[38]

Herrero Tejedor's words clearly illustrate the state's paramount interest in the nationalization of the female population and the firm delimitation of gender relations. The state's goal was to accommodate its legislation to what he called the "real human dignity of women," assuming their virtues and allowing them to develop their inherent abnegation. Spanish women were expected to render their traditional self-denying service either by devoting themselves with love to the family and home or by contributing to the national venture by joining the labor force. The official discourse on female individuality continued to be based on the virtues of pure Catholic womanhood. Women's empowerment rested upon the acceptance of their weakness as a divine gift. Although the state was opening the door of the public realm to them, they would enter it only as an extension of their domestic duties. They were supposed to support their husbands and the national endeavors without asking any questions.

> Family and children demand the presence of women at home, and we wish to facilitate this dedication for them, because women are the center of the unity and love that bind all the components of the family. That is the requirement of our Christian beliefs and our political doctrine, which make the family the basic structure of the community.[39]

Herrero Tejedor affirmed the significance of Church doctrine on family and marriage in Spanish legislation and declared the natural superiority of the husband within matrimony as the encyclical *Casti Conubii* ordained. He did not consider the legal reform as threatening to the National-Catholic principles that had ruled gender relations in Spain since 1939. By sanctioning the law's draft presented by the Women's Section of the Falange, the state entrusted that organization once again with the task of guiding Spanish women into the country's new consumer venture.

Pilar Primo de Rivera's speech at the Cortes in defense of the law began by making it very clear that the Women's Section did not intend to make men and women equal. "In some ways we want to make men and women equal beings; they will never be equals by nature or by the ways they live their lives, but we do ask that in the same work, they have equal rights." She emphasized that if women were entering the labor force, it was out of necessity and not because it represented one of their rights. The law was not a feminist text; on the contrary, it declared masculine patronage over the "weaker female sex." The Women's Section also was concerned about preserving married life: "For us," asserted Primo de Rivera, "Divine laws are sacred, and we always have had the Church support in our endeavors." Hence, educating Spanish women in Catholic doctrine remained the Women's Section's preoccupation and major task.

> We are convinced that in protecting women's access to work and learning, we do not violate the laws. An educated, refined, and sensitive woman—precisely for that reason—is a better educator of her children and a better companion for her husband. In the Women's Section, we have thousands of cases of university women who are married and whose families are a model of compassion and harmony. According to José Antonio, a woman cannot limit herself to being a "foolish recipient of compliments." Abnegation, her essential virtue, is much more consciously and efficiently developed if she has an education.[40]

In the spirit of *La perfecta casada* and *La instrucción de la mujer cristiana*, education helped to prepare conscientious mothers for the service of the fatherland, and it served a higher purpose: the nationalization of motherhood.

The *Law of Political, Professional, and Labor Rights of Women* is short, consisting of a preamble, five articles, and two brief provisions. The preamble alludes to the principles of the Spaniards' Charter, which guaranteed the access of all Spaniards to public offices and their right to perform any valuable social activity. The objective of the law of professional rights of women was to "develop and apply effectively such principles, suppressing restrictions and discriminations based on sociological circumstances that belong to the past and are not compatible either with the preparation and capability of Spanish women or with their evident promotion to posts and offices of responsibility."[41]

When regulating women's legal status, the law asserted the need to consider both women's gender and their marital status. The former was based on biological differences; the latter made married women a distinct legal entity subject to their husbands' will. "Nature, religion, and history endow the husband with the authority in marriage. It is still the supreme norm of the Spanish State to free married women from the workshop and the factory, as stated in the second declaration of the Fuero del Trabajo [Labor Charter]."[42]

Although the law granted "equal rights" to men and women, it still acknowledged certain limitations exclusively for women. Article 5 maintained the husband's authority, for a married woman still needed his permission to work. Article 3 granted women access to all levels of education, but certain careers were to remain closed to them:

a) The Army, the Air Force, and the Navy, except by special permission to perform specific services.

b) The armed forces and services and careers that normally imply the use of arms as part of their duty.

c) Administration of Justice in the positions of judge, magistrate, and public prosecutor, except in the jurisdictions of labor and guardianship of minors.

d) Qualified personnel of the Merchant Navy, except the sanitary services.[43]

Education continued to be the means by which the regime shaped distinct gender roles. The legislation produced in the 1950s by the Ministry of National Education had established two separate identities for men and women within the educational realm, and the *Law of Political, Professional, and Labor Rights of Women* only confirmed this trend.

Both the reform of the *Civil Code* in 1958 and the law of 1961 represent the official discourse on traditional Christian femininity. These laws were based on the Francoist recovery of traditional Catholic femininity. Although gender relations were revised as a result of the economic and political changes that the regime confronted in the fifties, Catholicism remained central to the social relationship of the sexes, and true Catholic womanhood prevailed in the transition from autarchy to consumerism.

THE NEW SPANISH WOMAN OF THE 1950S

The Women's Section of the Falange promoted the legal reforms of 1958 and 1961 regarding the status of women and conducted studies and surveys on the legal and economic status of Spanish women at the end of the 1950s. These surveys were intended to discover the real character and psychology of the Spanish woman. Although she was becoming an active member of the new consumer society, deep inside she still respected the importance of the family and male superiority. According to a report produced by the organization entitled *La mujer española* (The Spanish woman), there were five hundred thousand affiliates of the Women's Section in 1959.[44] This study provided statistical data about the sociopolitical situation of Spanish women for the year 1950. The Women's Section's officials acknowledged in the report the significant economic and social evolution of the country. Their survey showed that many young women had begun to enter the labor market and to acquire higher education, but they maintained their devotion to the family, their respect for male superiority, and their dedication to domestic duties. This feminine zeal was considered to be rooted in the psychological character of Spanish women:

> Spanish women, due to their psychology and preparation, devote themselves to marriage and domestic life as their only vocation. When they take professional positions, traditionally in the hands of men, they do it with femininity and without traces of feminism.

With regard to psychological characteristics, there exists some homogeneity. . . . The Spanish woman, in general, possesses a deep Christian religious sentiment, and her morality stems entirely from the concept of virtue prescribed by the Catholic Church.[45]

The modernization of the country could not do away with traditional Spanish Catholic womanhood, and it was to this end that the Women's Section devoted its efforts. The study pointed out that although Spanish women had begun to work, they also relinquished such a possibility when they needed to devote themselves to their family and children. Motherhood, thus, remained the highest patriotic offering to the fatherland, because good mothering was crucial to the maintenance of an orderly society.

In Spain there is neither juvenile delinquency, as such, nor the "teddy boy." There are not even suicides, a real plague in other countries. Perhaps this is because the constant care of a mother from the cradle is all that is necessary and sufficient to resolve the problems of adolescence and youth.

After the war, women became mothers to provide the demographic recovery the fatherland needed. In the 1950s, however, the fertility rate did not show a significant increase. The birthrate was 20.1 per 1,000 population in 1950; that dropped to 19.8 in 1954. By 1960, the birthrate rose to 21.6. Thus, although female patriotism was expressed in biological and ideological terms as reproducers of the regime, during the 1950s the fertility rate did not experience a significant growth. With regard to marriages, the vital statistics show in 1950 15.0 marriages per 1,000 population versus 15.6 marriages ten years later.[46] The state, the Church, and the Women's Section had prevented any access to public life by Spanish women in order to encourage the fulfillment of the prescribed Catholic womanhood. The Women's Section's task in the 1950s faced a contradictory reality. On the one hand, true Catholic womanhood had to remain untouched; on the other hand, economic development required the incorporation of women into the labor force and, to a certain extent, a betrayal of domestic life.

In 1950, the total female population was 14.5 million, of which 7.7 million were single, 5.3 million married, and 1.5 million widows. The women's labor force for the same year was 1.7 million, although only about 114,000 were professionals who had earned an academic degree. Sixty-two percent of Spanish women devoted themselves to domestic life, what was called *sus labores*. Of these, 422,000 worked as artisans or day laborers and 578,000 as domestic servants. Young country girls who moved to the city easily found jobs as servants. In addition to a salary, a servant girl received room and board, and to a certain extent, a special relation existed between the master and the young woman servant that was considered an extension of parental guardianship. "The relation between the master and the servant is 'sui generis,'" maintained the Women's Section's report, "since in Spain this is considered an extension of the family ties. Given that the servant lives under a family's roof, this relationship is not regarded as one of employer/employee."[47]

The Stabilization Plan of 1959 concluded the autarchy period, and on 28 December 1963, the government approved the First Development Plan, which took effect between 1964 and 1967. On the eve of the approval of the plan, the Women's Section conducted another survey under the title *Realidad laboral de la mujer* (The labor status of women), which focused on the condition of women in the labor market. The main purpose of the survey was to establish a strategy to prepare Spanish women to enter a professional life in accordance with the *Law of Political, Professional, and Labor Rights of Women* of 1961, "to force the educational institutions to open their doors to women, eliminating any barriers or obstacles in the centers for industrial promotion and qualification."[48]

By 1960, the female population had grown to 15.7 million. During the 1950s, the total labor force amounted to 11.6 million, of which 2.1 million were women. The total labor force—both men and women—increased from 12.4 to 16.6 percent of the population, and the percentage of women in the labor force rose between 1950 and 1960 from 8.9 percent of the total labor force to 13.4 percent. By 1957, women held 50.7 percent of the jobs in the service sector, 25 percent of those in industry, and 24.3 percent of the agricultural jobs. According to the study, "economic independence was one of the main motivations for women to enter the labor market," but women's work outside the home also augmented the family income as the country ventured into consumerism. Economic demands required a change of mentality, a certain acceptance of female autonomy within well-established limits. The Women's Section's report stated that "outside the home, in society, a woman continued to be a mother, an educator, and a guardian of her children. Her tenderness, sensibility, and maternal instinct were the most valuable things society needed from her."[49]

When women entered the labor market, they worked mainly in the service sector and the areas of the industry left open by men who had emigrated to other European countries. A woman worked only if her husband's salary was insufficient, because she made only 70 to 80 percent of a man's salary. Women therefore constituted a secondary workforce. *Teresa,* one of the Women's Section's magazines, published an article in March 1954 entitled "El salario femenino" (The women's salary) by José Montero Alonso, based on the author's interviews with three men: Mariano González Rothvoss, general inspector of labor; Pepín Fernández, director of the major Spanish department store Galerías Preciados; and Eugenio Pérez Botija, a university professor of labor law. For González Rothvoss, the phenomenon of the lower value of women's work and the resulting higher salary for men was due to women's weakness: they held their jobs for a shorter period of time because of "physiological" reasons that led them to marriage; and besides, they did not have the responsibility of sustaining a family. He believed that to deserve equal pay, women had to perform with equal perfection. Pérez Botija considered that biological differences justified different pay. Fernández's reason for the difference in pay was that women's true vocation was marriage, not working outside the home. He based his opinion on the fact that most of his female employees left their jobs after marriage. But Fernández failed to mention in his interview the "marriage prize," a compensation paid to those women who renounced their jobs and any future work when they got married.[50]

The Women's Section's zeal to preserve a domestic femininity within a changing economic reality led to the development of a guide to feminine occupations. There were two different types: intellectual or university occupations and those that required some kind of technical training. The most recommended of the latter type included nursing, social work, technical positions within the movie industry such as script or film cutter, journalism, tourist guide, and teacher, either in elementary or high school.

In 1954, *Teresa* began including a section entitled "Las mujeres quieren trabajar" (Women want to work). The objective was to inform Spanish women of their occupational options, particularly in careers *de tipo medio* (middle careers) that did not require a college diploma. The issues of *Teresa* published between 1954 and 1961 advertised the proper careers for the new Spanish woman of the fifties. For example, several issues explored the idea of studying languages so that women could become teachers, tourist guides, or secretaries. Women could also study at the School for Research Assistants, created in 1941 under the direction of the National Research Council. At this school they learned, in a three-year curriculum, to be first-class secretaries, laboratory assistants, archivists, or librarians and to develop their natural sense of tidiness and order. "Once the documents are restored," reads the article, "they are hung to dry, just like the laundry. This type of work seems especially created for women."[51]

Some careers were particularly suitable to the assumed innate, artistic qualities of women. For example, at the School of Fashion Designers in Madrid, women had the opportunity to develop their feminine "good taste" by designing clothing. The cinema industry and television opened new professions for women as actresses and anchorwomen, both of which required them to be pretty and photogenic. Physical appearance was less important for a scriptwriter or a journalist. The latter required a diploma from the Official School of Journalism. Journalism was regarded as a very appropriate career for women because of "their ability to observe and their wittiness, very important qualities for such a profession."[52] At the Institute for Professional Training for Women, women could learn to be administrative assistants or arts and crafts teachers in only three years.

The most popular career for women was nursing. The main training institution, the National School of Nursing, was directed by the Women's

Section. In May 1959, there were fifteen thousand nurses in Spain. That same year, more than six hundred nurses from all over the country met at the First National Assembly of Nurses, organized by the Women's Section and the Nurses Syndicate in Madrid, to discuss their professional status, rights, and obligations. Although the meeting's objective was to demand recognition of nurses' rights and professionalism—especially those who had worked during the Civil War—Pilar Primo de Rivera reiterated the Women's Section's antifeminism: "The Women's Section of Falange, the organizer of this assembly, as on many other occasions has promoted this meeting to discuss the improvement of women's status, but without a hint of feminism, which repels us." Primo de Rivera gave a speech in the closing session that underlined the feminine qualities of the nursing profession and recapitulated the characteristics of a good nurse.

> What your profession and your personal dignity demand from you, above all, is authentic religious training, a clear conscience, morality, abnegation, patience, a sense of responsibility to be in touch with those who are dying and those confronting eternity at their doorstep, whose happiness might depend many times on your strength and diligence. . . . The acceptance of their misfortune might be easier if they find in you humane and compassionate treatment instead of tiredness and brusqueness. Be always polite and clean. Cleanliness, always important, is even more vital in your profession. Be compassionate with all of those who work with you, to avoid unpleasant confrontations, and [finally]— you certainly know this—show *absolute subjection to the doctors.*[53]

The professions listed in the special section of *Teresa* were related to the social origins of the readers. Those professions directed to middle-class women required certain formal schooling and the knowledge of a foreign language, although no diploma was necessary. They could aspire to become nurses, language teachers, secretaries, librarians, research assistants, opticians, tourist guides, and even international bureaucrats. Working-class girls could become skilled cooks, maids, nannies, or hairdressers. A pretentious technical language colored these articles, creating an illusion of professionalism hitherto absent in such occupations. Cooks, maids, and hairdressers now needed a professional diploma. Improving the economy required qualified workers, but women's contribution to the reconstruction of the chaotic economy had to remain domestic, as evidenced by the professions advertised in *Teresa* that emphasized domestic and family duties. Hence, the official discourse directed to them did not change; in essence, it only gave old tasks new names and new social value. The Women's Section sponsored courses to prepare nannies and social workers and created the School of Domestic Service, which offered training courses for cooks and maids.

> In these courses, organized by the School of Domestic Service of Madrid, cooks

learn in detail not only the preparation of the most difficult recipes but also the arrangement of the plates, preparation of appetizers, and fine pastry making. Maids learn how to serve guests at the table, manners, ironing, cleaning of delicate porcelain, and the use of stain-removers, as well as the functioning of modern electric utensils for the home. The mandatory practical training allows them to get familiar with these new utensils and use them naturally.[54]

Stress was placed upon the mechanization of chores with the arrival of new appliances in the middle-class home; servants had to prepare themselves for such innovations. In addition, the availability of manufactured products that could replace domestic production added a new responsibility to the middle-class housewife now in charge of buying. The new consumer housewife, mostly of upper- and middle-class status, had to learn how to use her husband's salary wisely, making purchases that were appropriate to the family income.

The Women's Section contributed actively to the forging of the "new woman" within the parameters of a National-Catholic agenda. It drew its strength from its reiterated antifeminist discourse, glorifying submissiveness and sacrifice as the patriotic traits of the new woman. A hierarchical concept of the world was the essence of their discourse. National syndicalism divided the world into three hierarchical realms: the *natural order*, which included the family, the municipality, and the syndicate; the *historical order*, which was the fatherland; and the *supernatural order*, facilitated by religion.[55]

Pilar Primo de Rivera, in a circular letter of 1 December 1955, proposed that the "rethinking of problems" was necessary to adjust the organization to the changing international and national political reality. She declared: "A new orientation in political instruction is appropriate, not in essence, but in form, in accordance with the evolution taking place in the world since the last world war." The new order of things was discussed in the XVIII Consejo Nacional, held in Málaga in January 1956. The main concern was to unify the Falangist family during the time of crisis.[56] Women's political influence was limited to their duties as mothers and wives within the family. They had the responsibility to mold the consciences of their children as future citizens. The family represented the microcosm of the Francoist regime, with ultimate authority resting in the father. Franco embodied the fatherly figure; his authority was divinely sanctioned to guide the country into its unavoidable imperial destiny, and every Spanish family had to mirror the Francoist sociopolitical order.

The preservation of public morality in line with Catholic Church doctrine remained a crucial concern for the state. The Board for the Protection of Women was reorganized in 1952, ten years after it was created. The board was part of the Ministry of Justice, and its objective was to "protect public morality and in particular women's." Article 4 described the dual purpose of the institution: first, to protect women's morality; and second, to punish prostitution, publication of pornographic material or information on contraception and abortion, and any activity "against Catholic doctrine." Provincial boards were established to enforce this legislation. The law ordained the boards to be chaired by two men assisted by other members of both sexes. Prostitution, though it was one of the concerns of the Board for the Protection of Women in 1952, was not officially outlawed until 3 March 1956, when it was declared illegal and all brothels were closed. Article 5 prescribed that prostitutes would be reeducated in institutions directed by the Board.[57]

The strict moral code that regulated the relation between the sexes had to change with the arrival of tourism and the emigration of workers to other countries in the second half of the 1950s. Urbanization affected the definition and boundaries of the family unit, and consumerism became an essential part of it. The rationalization and mechanization of the public sphere reached the private realm as well. Domestic appliances facilitated and rationalized housework, allowing women time for other matters. María Laffitte acknowledged in 1964 that young Spanish women had begun to seek companionship rather than authority in marriage, and they believed that gaining an education was the way to be better friends of their husbands.[58]

In order to confront unavoidable modernization, Franco's regime attempted to accommodate economic and social changes through the Fundamental Principles of the State in 1958 and the Stabilization Plan of 1959. With regard to gender roles, the regime tried to preserve Catholic values in the context of the new market economy with reform of the *Civil Code* in 1958 and with the *Law of Political, Professional, and Labor Rights of Women* in 1961. The Francoist state sought to preserve domesticity and true Catholic womanhood in the passage from autarchy to consumerism. The legal reforms did not eradicate traditional gender definitions and roles, but rather they represented the state's means to reconcile modernity with Catholicism. Central to the project of "modern" identity assumed by the Francoist state during the 1950s were its attempts to square Christian motherhood with women's paid employment and consumption and to produce a "new woman" capable of bringing feminine virtues into industrialized society.

Consumerism, however, transformed notions of self and collective identity. Just as advertisement messages conflicted with the cult of true Catholic womanhood fostered by the National-Catholic state, so the advent of consumer culture in the 1950s challenged the foundations of Franco's authoritarian state.

CHAPTER FOUR

KNOWLEDGE AND POWER IN THE FRANCOIST UNIVERSITY

"Tell me, Mario, why should a woman study? What would she gain from it? She would just become a mannish woman, because a university girl is a girl with no femininity; don't twist it around. For me, a girl that goes to college is a girl with no sex appeal. Studying is not proper for her." —Miguel DeLibes, *Cinco horas con Mario,* 1966

The preservation of Catholic family values remained one of the main aspirations of the regime in the 1950s. By adopting Catholic doctrine as part of the regime's political discourse, Franco not only gained divine sanction for his authority but also courted international approval of the regime in the context of the Cold War and created a sense of stability at home.

The state's task in this transitional period consisted of adjusting the definition of nationhood—fought for during the Civil War—to the new capitalist demands of the times. On both national and individual levels, National-Catholic ideology lent cohesion to Franco's regime and legitimated its existence. Perpetuation of Franco's power necessitated a considerable degree of sustained popular support—a national consensus of sorts—which the regime sought to forge through its system of education.[1]

THE FRANCOIST UNIVERSITY

Education served the forces of unity and uniformity. It was the process by which the individual related to the concept of nation. Through the promotion of a single language, a single history, and a single religion, the Francoist educational system inculcated, on a grand scale, a sense of individual duty to the National-Catholic agenda.[2] But duty was defined differently for men than for women. As the regime (and the Catholic Church) saw it, gender constituted the very essence of selfhood; gender differences provided stability and social order to the nation and clarity of purpose to the individual. Changes in the 1950s necessitated the official redefinition of national and individual principles, and pressure by the intellectual community reflected discontent with the regime's foundations and goals.

A new generation of students and writers appeared on the cultural scene. They were children of the war, who now experienced a longing for reconciliation, a sense of responsibility that necessarily led them to anti-Francoist dissidence. Although gender relations were not the primary concern for the new generation of intellectuals, by the end of the decade their progressivism led them to question the social relations of the sexes.[3]

One dimension of the relationship between the Francoist state and the women of the population was set forth in the arenas of school and university. Analysis of the institutional discourse on gender relations as prescribed by educational legislation and revealed in government statistical data shows the degree to which true Catholic womanhood permeated the definition of Spanish femininity and Spanish women's national duties. The spirit of the encyclicals *Casti Connubii* (1930) and *Divini Illius Magistri* (1929) inspired Francoist educational legislation, particularly the *University Regulatory Law* (*URL,* Ley de Ordenación Universitaria) of 1943, which regulated higher education until 1970.

Yet Franco's regime presented a central paradox in the 1950s, when analyzed from a gender point of view. There was a contradiction between the forces creating the conditions for anti-Francoist political dissidence and the prevailing cultural conservatism. Statistical analysis of the presence of women in the Francoist university reveals this paradox. Another contradiction arose from the economic changes the country confronted. Material conditions pulled women into the public sphere and caused them to accommodate to the consumer society, but official discourse proclaimed the sanctity of family values and the importance of staying at home. Thus, significant power dynamics were brought into play during the 1950s.

Foucault defines power as

> The multiplicity of force relations in the sphere in which they operate and which constitute their own organization; as the process which through ceaseless struggles and confrontations, transforms, strengthens or reverses them; as the support that these force relations find in one another, thus forming a chain or a

system, or on the contrary the disjunctions and contradictions which isolate them from one another; and finally as the strategies in which they take effect, whose general design or institutional crystallization is embodied in the state apparatus, in the formulation of the law, in the various social hegemonies.[4]

Foucaldian theory looks to historically specific discursive relations and social practices. The official National-Catholic discourse on education and true Catholic womanhood during this transitional decade was met by counterdiscourses of dissidence, and the tension between the two sets of discourses and meanings formed a system of disjunctions and contradictions. Paradoxically, such tension and contradiction between official and dissident discourses made the two possible; their struggle revealed the power dynamics of the Francoist regime when it was confronted with modernization and the demands of the market economy.

The advent of consumerism in the mid-1950s generated tension between the centralizing official discourse on femininity, orchestrated through new legislation, and what Victoria de Grazia calls the "new centrifugal pressures"[5] of the mass media messages that contributed to fostering alternative female identities. The question here is whether the official discourse of the 1950s shaped a femininity inimical to the definition of a scholar and how this oppositional discourse affected the actual educational experience of Spanish women in this period.

Gender difference continued to be central to the problem of government in the 1950s. The Francoist political and social relations used gender to signify normalcy in every facet of life. All the laws, statistics, and definitions of normalcy and deviance guaranteed and perpetuated the masculine power of the state. Foucault argues that the "power of the state to produce an increasingly totalizing web of control is intertwined with and dependent on its ability to produce an increasing specification of individuality."[6] The stability of Franco's power depended on his ability to juggle the political weight of each of the factions (Falangists, Monarchists, the Catholic Church, and Opus Dei) in the play of power. Such juggling was particularly obvious in the 1950s when he sought international approval and had to liberalize the economy and ostracize the Falange from the government. But the dissident intellectual elite also presented a challenge to the regime to rethink its foundations and adjust to the changing times in order to survive.

The Francoist educational legislation, including especially the language and meanings that emanated from it, reveals the official efforts to build individual gender identities (subjectivities). The language of the *URL* of 1943 and the legislation enacted by the Ministry of Education to regulate secondary education established the state Catholic version of femininity that stressed asexuality, exalting either virginity or motherhood, and called for different forms of subordinate behavior. At the same time, Spanish women were subject not only to the alternative messages on femininity coined by the media but also to alternative definitions and discourses on true Catholic womanhood that came from women's Catholic organizations.

Franco's state viewed women as its indispensable complement in nation building. It established institutions and passed laws to codify women's duties as mothers and daughters of the fatherland. Official arbiters of these duties, the Catholic Church and the Women's Section of the Falange dictated that women were to serve the fatherland with abnegation by dedicating themselves to the common good.[7] As we have seen, true Catholic womanhood was rooted in principles set forth in Catholic encyclicals and treatises dating from the sixteenth century, texts that would serve as guideposts for women's educational policy in Franco's Spain. The educational system in general became the instrument by which the state perpetuated its patriarchal politics. The university, in particular, was a male realm, a site of state power where the political elites were educated, where women were scarce, and where scholasticism stood inimical to femininity.

The main goal of the Spanish university was to inculcate morality and patriotism, revitalizing the ideals of *Hispanidad* along with tradition and Catholicism. This project implied well-defined gender roles. The state expected women to fulfill their motherly destiny rather than to become professionals. National-Catholic discourse in its elaboration of true Catholic womanhood did not deprive women of a national purpose; on the contrary, their agency was based, paradoxically, on their active political withdrawal. Becoming first wives and then mothers constituted women's contribution to the national endeavor. As we learn from the legal texts and the statistical data how the regime defined the identity of the university student, it becomes clear that this subjectivity was irreconcilable with the official meaning of Christian femininity.

As in the rest of Europe, universities emerged in Spain in the thirteenth century. They were originally established at Palencia (1212), Salamanca (1215), and Valladolid (1260). By 1574, about twenty-five universities were founded in Spain. The most important of the medieval universities were those of Salamanca and Alcalá de Henares, the former rivaling Paris and Bologna in its influence.[8]

The Francoist university remained an institution of the past in its structure and apparatus. The zealous preservation of Hispanic idiosyncrasy and tradition constituted its essence and purpose. Its nature and objectives as an institution were always a polemical issue and a focus of discussion for Spanish intellectuals.[9] The university embodied a microcosm of Spanish social and political reality, where the contest between continuity and change was argued and somehow settled. Catholicism was central to the *URL* of 1943, along with Falangist principles. The official discourse ruling academic life rotated around National-Catholicism, which imposed absolute state control over universities.

In structure, the Francoist university followed the Napoleonic model, which made the institution a state's means of power. Napoleon himself had outlined the totalitarian university: "My main goal in establishing an academic body is to institute a means to direct political and moral opinions." By the nineteenth century, there existed twelve university districts, located in Barcelona, Granada, La Laguna, Madrid, Murcia, Oviedo, Salamanca, Santiago, Sevilla, Valencia, Valladolid, and Zaragoza, all of them under the direct control of the government. The Francoist conception of the academic community, according to the Napoleonic model, continued to call for total control by the state, which provided the financial support, organized the curriculum, appointed administrators and faculty, and even prescribed the public morality to be taught to the new generations. The objective was to create a centralized university that supervised secondary education as well and was concerned with the instruction of the political elite. The *Moyano Law* of 1857 established the Napoleonic university model in Spain, and it remained untouched under Francoism. The *URL* of 1943 preserved the centralization ordained by the *Moyano Law* a century earlier and did away with two Republican decrees—one in 1931 and another in 1933—that legislated the self-government of the universities of Madrid and Barcelona.[10] It was not until the 1950s and 1960s that the university again became the focus of attention of intellectuals and politicians, who acknowledged its crisis and demanded a revision of the legislation of 1943, as well as a serious analysis of the social, economic, and political ramifications of the university functions.

By the 1950s, Spain's social and economic circumstances had changed, and the distance was wide between what had been prescribed by the *URL* and what the country needed. Ruiz Giménez's efforts as minister of education to ameliorate the problem and bring the university closer to the Spanish social and political reality evidenced both the emerging intellectual dissidence and the perennial contest between continuity and change.

Several scholars published their concerns about the lamentable state of the university. Antonio Tovar, former rector of the University of Salamanca and member of a group known as liberal Falangists, criticized years later what he considered to be the two major wrongs of the Francoist university: its ultra-conservatism and chronic fear of progress on the one hand, and its anti-intellectualism and phobia of criticism and dissent on the other. According to Tovar, the Spanish educational system prepared young people to lead Spanish society without questioning its foundations. Although he proclaimed that the state needed to articulate an education to better serve the needs of the country, he also believed criticism was crucial for progress and modernization. The Spanish society born after the Stabilization Plan of 1959 needed new experts and specialists, and the role of the university in producing an increasing number of them was critical.

> The results of an education based on old social values have been so damaging that foreign observers arriving in our country since 1960 are shocked by the few experts we have; they see the dissociation between our problems and needs and what our institutions of higher learning teach.

Most scholars emphasized the functional nature of the university to produce experts in technology who could aid progress and modernization. Angel Latorre argued that the new times demanded a university in tune with the needs of society, rather than one closed and isolated from the world.[11]

A number of factors made the university of the 1950s different from the nineteenth-century model established by Francoism. First of all, with more students and graduates, it was no longer the refuge of an educated minority. And this growth presented other tangible problems, such as the construction of more facilities and the hiring of more professors. Second, science and technological advancement became central to society's progress. The new times demanded increasing specialization and training for new professions. The mission of the university was no longer to follow the *Orteguian* ideal. According to Ortega y Gasset, the university should escape "barbaric specialization." Its main goal was to produce culture, understood as a system of living ideas. The university was not simply the depository of knowledge and science but a reproducer of culture. Spanish society, however, demanded a larger number of specialized individuals and researchers to achieve economic development, as did other Western countries. Finally, the new university became an international institution. The university of the nineteenth century had been conceived as an entity removed from the world, but now the university was one of the forces cooperating with society for the common good to produce economic prosperity and scientific and technological progress. The two major tasks of the university, then, were education and the advancement of knowledge.[12] Nevertheless, the Francoist establishment did not revise the *URL* until 1970, after much debate about the need for reform had taken place.

THE UNIVERSITY REGULATORY LAW OF 1943

The Francoist university became one of the state's loci of power, and the *URL* intended clear politicization of the institution in the service of the new regime's National-Catholic precepts. The law required all members of the university community to be affiliated with, and to devote themselves to, the political creed of the Falange and Catholic Church doctrine. Article 1 declared the scholars' devotion to Spain's spiritual and national purpose. The university community became a microcosm of society in general. The law established a system of normalization that regulated the university with a rigorous disciplinary structure to better exercise power and control over its population. The *URL* defined the Spanish university as

> the corporation to which the state entrusts its spiritual enterprise to fulfill the scientific, cultural, and educational activities of the nation, with service as the norm imposed in the current Spanish revolution. To develop this concept, the law restores to the university all its traditional functions, creating, reorganizing, and restoring the proper organs.[13]

The university was given the task of creating a political elite able to fulfill the Francoist spiritual revolution and implicitly to lead that revolution in the broader (male) public realm.

The law consisted of 13 chapters and 101 articles and provisions. The introduction plunged the reader into a bombastic discourse defining the "Hispanic concept of university." Because the primary mission of the new university was to transmit Catholic knowledge concerning morality, spirituality, discipline, and service to the fatherland and state, the Spanish university may be understood as one of those intersections of knowledge and power that Michel Foucault calls *technologies*. According to Foucault, "disciplinary technologies" arise in a large number of different settings, such as workshops, schools, prisons, and hospitals. Their aim is to forge a "docile body that may be subjected, used, transformed, and improved." Of paramount importance for the Francoist regime was the guarantee that those involved in higher learning would remain faithful to the fatherland, just as the soldier in a regular army was expected to do. Throughout the *URL*, one finds an implicit and constant appeal to the university governing bodies to maintain surveillance and discipline over the university departments and population. Chapter 5 (article 36b), for example, described the functions of the School Protection Service in explicit terms: "Exercise surveillance over the life of the students." The same idea of surveillance appeared in articles 41g, 43a, 46a, and 48a. The last chapter was entirely dedicated to "academic discipline" and spelled out the different degrees of violation and the pertinent punishment of faculty, students, and administrative personnel. It advised academic authorities to evaluate the degree to which the individual had escaped or flouted the normalizing network of the university institution. Control of the population remained essential to the automatic functioning of power.[14] Hence, the *URL* established in chapter 5 (articles 31–36) three new departments—the Secretariat of University Religious Instruction, the Spanish Service for Higher Education Faculty of the Falange, and the School Protection Service—and described the norms for their functioning.

The *URL* defined the university individual in the purest male, military sense by his allegiance and devotion to the fatherland and the Catholic hierarchy. Such an individual had to devote himself to Spain's imperial destiny during this time of spiritual revolution that the Francoist regime embodied. The participation of a scholar in the national endeavor involved defending Spain's Catholic homogeneity and exporting those ideas to the world:

> When the time comes for national unity and the supreme moment of Spain arrives, our university . . . appears in its plenitude to serve the ideals of Spain's imperial destiny . . . to produce a knowledge that takes over the world and educates and shapes men who . . . honor Spain and serve the Church.[15]

The SEU, as a division of the Falangist movement, would serve the regime *as the* organizing body to carry out the mission prescribed by the Church and the state. The *URL* required all students, male and female, to register in the SEU upon enrollment. A part of the Women's Section within SEU, the Women's Section/SEU, became the mediator between the state and women university students to preserve true Catholic womanhood along Church lines. The secretary of the Women's Section/SEU was in charge of keeping domestic values alive among women students through mandatory University Social Service. By contrast, men students served the country by completing their military obligations in the University Militia, founded in 1941 to foster within students a militant sense of enthusiasm toward their duties and obligations in the context of World War II.[16] Conscription was mandatory for Spanish young men. By the order of 28 June 1941, a voluntary legion was created to help Hitler in Russia—the Blue Division—whose officers were mainly professionals. The head of the SEU, Agustín Aznar, joined this division. From the university militia the country drew professional officers, and those young men rendered their patriotic services in better conditions than did regular troops.

Although the *URL* did not explicitly exclude women from entering higher education, the legal text created a scholar identity intrinsically the opposite of Spanish femininity. The fulfillment of true Catholic womanhood as prescribed by the regime and learned in primary and secondary schools meant, in the short run, the exclusion of women from higher education, because pursuing a career was foreign to their feminine essence.

Chapter 2 of the law declared the Catholic nature of the Spanish university. It focused on the scholar/subject that such institutions hoped to create. Being a good scholar and a good Catholic were one and the same; the soul of a scholar was that of a soldier; thus, in the introduction to the *URL*, we read, "Such flowering of the university creates a theological army that will fight against heresy."[17]

The main goal of the university was to restore the genuine Spanish identity and Spanish values as prescribed by God and tradition that had been betrayed by the FIL and by laicization:

> We are living through times of crisis and routine in which, if the intellectual education was unsettled, it also succumbed to the hands of academic freedom. Moral and religious education, and even love for the fatherland, was hidden by ominous shame, suffocated by the foreign, secular, cold, krausist, and masonic Free Institution of Learning.[18]

What the Catholic Church and the Francoist regime expected from the woman's soul was quite different. The educational policy of the 1950s with regard to women oriented women's education toward domesticity. According to the *URL* (section 9, article 70f), scholars were to perform university duties "taking into account, when necessary, the *distinction of the sexes*." Although college women who belonged to SEU were the intellectual elite of the Falangist women, their future roles as wives and prolific mothers remained uncontested. Within the institutionalized settings of high school and later college, women learned the "domestic arts" of cooking and infant care through their training in Social Service, in the Domestic Schools, and in the schools of professional training for women. Four months after the URL was published, Spanish women's professional orientation was legally regulated by the law of 17 November 1943, which established the Central Committee for Professional Training of Women. Successive decrees and laws of the Ministry of Education legally limited women's access to knowledge to domestic training. In the words of José Pemartín, director of higher education, "It is necessary to guide women students by preventing them from the feminist pedantry of becoming university women, which should be the exception, leading them to their own magnificent female being. That is developed in the home." To reconcile the self-contradiction between scholar and female identities, the regime demanded of the women of the Women's Section/SEU that they be involved first and foremost in indoctrinating the female population of Spain with the ideological spirit of the Francoist state. Second, they were to enlist the support of male SEU leaders in the most discreet way. Pilar Primo de Rivera underlined subordination, a principal tenet of National-Catholic discourse. "Do not pretend to be equal to men, because you will achieve something very different from what you want: men will detest you tremendously and you will not be able to have any influence on them."[19]

Gender differentiation was also explicit in the URL stipulation (article 34b) that all college women must render Social Service to the state under the direction of the Women's Section/SEU. This women's version of the university militia required female students to complete six months of training in domestic duties. College women completed their service in two phases: instruction, which entailed political indoctrination and home economics; and service, which normally involved working in an office, a nursery, or a shelter. The instruction was delivered in two periods: a winter course during the academic sessions and a "school retreat," which usually took place during the summer or during an academic break. This training made it clear to the women that it was their duty as true women to fulfill their motherly destiny.

Paradoxically, Falangist university women gained some public influence, even as they promoted a submissive female model. They created a space of their own within the public masculine terrain. The regime regarded them as nonthreatening because of their constant rejection of feminism. The Women's Section's domesticated discourse on femininity was not different from that of the state and the Catholic Church, but it granted Falangist educated women the opportunity to be agents in the national enterprise. The best contribution women could make to the construction of the new Spain was excelling in their motherly (private or social) duties, so Falangist women became social mothers, embodying the humane values of the Falange. Ultimately, accepting their *second sex* status helped them to acquire and preserve their own power and space.[20]

VOICING DISCONTENT: THE GENERATION OF 1950

By the 1950s, the Spanish cultural scene was broadening, stimulated by new international and cultural relations, urbanization, and the expansion of the economy. A new generation of students who had not lived through or fought in the Civil War arrived in the classrooms; they were more receptive and open to the changing mentality of the times. For the first time in the history of the regime, university students began to develop dissident ideas. The discontented voices of the 1950s, opposing the official discourse of National-Catholicism, illustrate the power struggle and the transitional nature of 1950s Spanish politics.

The 1950s proved pivotal for intellectual dissidence.[21] Many writers and thinkers became involved in anti-Francoist resistance because they felt a social responsibility rooted in a sense of guilt. After a decade, the regime had not eradicated the postwar material hardships. The new writers who appeared on the cultural scene were known as the Generation of 1950, the Midcentury Generation, or the Children of the Civil War. Their profound contempt for Francoism and their social awareness produced the culmination of the social-realism genre in Spanish literature. They represented the generation gap within the regime's intelligentsia. Many, like Miguel Sánchez Mazas or Rafael Sánchez Ferlosio, were children of well-known Francoist officials or Falangists who rebelled against their parents' stagnant and oppressive world.

The Generation of 1950 gravitated toward two centers, in Barcelona and in Madrid. Those in Barcelona were grouped around the literary journal *Laye,* which gathered names such as Carlos Barral; the brothers Juan, Luis, and José Agustín Goytisolo; Alfonso Costafreda; and Gabriel Ferrater. This group favored a renaissance of Catalan culture with new publications in Catalan and the founding of institutions such as the Institut d'Estudis Catalans. Juan Goytisolo initiated a literary gathering *(tertulia)* in 1951 at the Café Turia in Barcelona, and in 1954 he established a literature seminar at another political and intellectual gathering place, the Bar Club, where the seeds of the neorealist social genre were planted. The Madrid group was more involved in politics and included such writers as Juan García Hortelano, Daniel Sueiro, Gabriel Celaya, Alfonso Sastre, Carmen Martín Gaite, Angel González, and Ignacio Aldecoa. These writers, who met at the *tertulia* of the Café Pelayo, believed in the power of culture to promote change and progress. In 1953, writers such as Ricardo Muñoz Suay and Jorge Semprún, then students, acted as cultural agents for the clandestine Communist Party, encouraging students and intellectuals to join the cause. Most of them were less concerned with Marxism and its political and philosophical meaning, though, than with the excitement of opposing the regime.[22]

There were several psychological elements and historical circumstances that lent cohesion to the groups. The intellectuals of the 1950s experienced a sense of exile within their own country. Their condition as children of the

Civil War made it difficult for them to forget the tragedy of the "two Spains." Their works show an obsession with the recent past and reverberate with fatalism and escapism. Spanish writers and intellectuals were greatly influenced by the Italian neorealism that arrived in Spain in the first half of the 1950s. The caustic criticism of the postwar Italian establishment that was expressed in black and white movies inspired Spanish filmmakers such as Juan Antonio Bardem and Luis García Berlanga, who were both affiliated with the Communist Party. They collaborated in the production of the movie *Esa pareja feliz* (That happy couple), which was made in 1951 but not shown in Spanish cinemas until 1953. This film is a good depiction of gender relations under consumerism, denouncing the ills of consumption and the yearning for conformity that the new society prompted.[23]

Social realism matured in the 1950s with such authors as Carmen Laforet, Miguel Delibes, Camilo José Cela, Alfonso Sastre, and Manuel Buero Vallejo. Cela's novel *La colmena* (The hive), censored in Spain and published in Argentina in 1951, inaugurated a genre that used behaviorism to tell a story. By using this technique, the narrator avoided any psychological analysis of the characters, presenting them through their actions and looking at their everyday lives in postwar Spain. In spite of official censorship, social-realist novels prospered in the second half of the 1950s. In 1959, Cela organized an international colloquium of writers in Formentor, Majorca. This encounter gave cohesion to the group of intellectuals of "the midcentury." Writers from several European countries attended. Michel Butor and Robbe-Grillet represented the French *nouveau Roman,* and Italo Calvino and Elio Vittorini represented Italian realism. Among the Spanish writers in attendance were Luis and Juan Goytisolo, Juan García Hortelano, Carlos Barral, and Carmen Martín Gaite.

Women remained marginal within the Generation of 1950. Many of the women followed their husbands' intellectual endeavors and inclinations. Josefina Rodríguez, for example, who was married to Ignacio Aldecoa, and Carmen Martín Gaite, who married Rafael Sánchez Ferlosio, were among the few female figures in a vastly male group of writers. One of the Madrid group's ventures was the publication of *La Revista Española* (The Spanish journal) in 1953. Both Rodríguez and Martín Gaite participated in this literary experiment, whose purpose was to gather translations of the works of foreign authors such as Truman Capote, Dylan Thomas, and Cesare Zavattini and to gather original manuscripts by young Spanish writers. But the journal had a short life. Published bimonthly, the last issue appeared in the spring of 1954; its demise was due to the lack of subscribers and financial hardship.[24]

Until recently, women authors have been rare in Spanish literature. It was not until the twentieth century, and in particular, after the Civil War, that a feminine tradition flourished in Spanish letters. Only half a dozen female authors entered the canon in Spain before 1936. They were Santa Teresa de Jesús in the sixteenth century; María de Zayas y Sotomayor in the seventeenth century; and Fernán Caballero, Emilia Pardo Bazán, Gertrudis Gómez Avellaneda, and Rosalia de Castro in the nineteenth century. In the 1940s and 1950s, several women writers came to prominence, including Carmen Martín Gaite; Concha Lagos, writer, editor, and hostess of a *tertulia* in Madrid; Elena Quiroga; Ana María Matute; and Carmen Laforet. Martín Gaite's stature now has been confirmed: in 1987 she became the first Spanish woman to be elected an honorary fellow of the Modern Language Association, joining an elite group of approximately seventy contemporary world authors.[25] Her two main works in the 1950s included *El balneario* (The spa, 1954) and *Entre visillos* (Behind the curtains, 1958). In the mainstream of Spanish neorealism of the 1950s, *Behind the Curtains* is a critical scrutiny of traditional mores and social conventions in an oppressive small community. For this work Martín Gaite won the national literary Nadal Prize in 1957.

Recent studies amplify the female voices of Spanish literature, including a work by Carmen Martín Gaite entitled *Desde la ventana*. Although there are those who argue that literature by women is homogeneous, that is, an outgrowth of styles and themes derived from an innate feminine sensibility, when one analyzes the works of Spanish women writers, diversity is the rule. Women's works in the 1950s show deep concern with the recent past, the hardship of the Civil War, and the effects of the conflict on the psychology of the female characters. If any difference exists between men's and women's writings of the Generation of 1950, it has to do with the female characters created by Spanish women writers. Of great interest is Carmen Laforet, who did not belong to the writers/friends group that Martín Gaite frequented. Laforet (b. Barcelona 1921) is considered the prime existential novelist of the 1940s and 1950s. Her literary career was launched in 1944 when she was awarded the Nadal Prize for her first novel, *Nada* (Nothing). In 1946, she married a journalist and publisher, with whom she had five children. Laforet's work remains interesting, above all, for its recurrent discussion of the issue of female vocation in general and of female authorship in particular. Her novels *Nada* and *La isla y los demonios* (The island and the demons, 1952) corroborate the notion that artistic vocation is incompatible with adult female behavior. The only vocation that is successfully pursued by Laforet's female protagonists, other than the traditional one of wife and mother, is a religious one, which is the subject of her third novel, *La mujer nueva* (The new woman, 1955). While riding a train, Paulina, the protagonist, a woman of a licentious life, undergoes a sudden religious conversion that leads her to Catholicism. The "new woman" she becomes rejects her previous life of sin and reconciles her faith with her obligations as wife and mother. The novel ends with Paulina's decision to return to her husband and son. What makes Laforet interesting today is her depiction of the problems that afflicted the female artist in whom the call of art clashes with other more insistent callings of mother and wife.[26]

Although gender was mostly excluded from the rhetoric of the times and the minds of women writers, modernization in the 1950s brought the women's question to the forefront, prompting the official reform of the *Civil Code* in 1958 and the *Law of Political, Professional, and Labor Rights of Women* in 1961. The novels of women writers centered in the inner psychological female world and in issues concerning women's role in a changing society. Most of the female characters struggled with the new feminine identity shaped by the regime while dealing with the psychological impact of the war. The dissident ideals planted in the 1950s by the children of the Civil War led to questions in the next decade on other issues, such as gender relations.

THE MINISTRY OF EDUCATION IN THE 1950S

The spirit of criticism and attempts to reconcile tradition and modernity in intellectual circles permeated the official educational administration and the university community. Joaquín Ruiz Giménez, appointed minister of education in 1951, was a prestigious Catholic layman, a former ambassador to the Vatican, and a member of NACP, as was his predecessor, José Ibañez Martín. Ruiz Giménez headed the education ministry until the university crisis of 1956, when he was replaced by Jesús Rubio García Mina, who held the position until 1962. Stanley Payne considers that "the appointment of Ruiz Giménez placed educational policy in the hands of one of the most idealistic and open-minded of the major Catholic figures."[27] The new minister certainly introduced some changes in the Spanish university system that echoed the progressive and reconciliatory feelings of the intellectual community; his reforms were received with aversion by the Falange and Opus Dei. Nevertheless, his ministry did not alter women's educational curriculum. Rather, it strengthened the emphasis on domesticity and Catholic feminine virtues.

Ruiz Giménez made an effort to open Spanish Catholicism to foreign currents. For example, followers of the French neo-Thomist philosopher Jacques Maritain participated in the international Catholic conferences organized by NACP, such as that at San Sebastián in the early fifties, where a split between conservative and liberal Spanish Catholics—the *excluyentes* and the *comprensivos*—was unavoidable. Part of Ruiz Giménez's initial policy included the appointment of liberal Falangists such as Pedro Laín Entralgo or Antonio Tovar to key positions both in the university system and in the Ministry of Education with the hope of achieving a synthesis between the Falangist vanguard and Catholic progressivism. Laín Entralgo and Tovar occupied the rectorships of Madrid and Salamanca, respectively, and became openly disenchanted with the regime's foundations and goals. They confronted the same discomfort and criticism felt by the writers of the Generation of 1950. Laín Entralgo, for example, published his memoirs in a book entitled *Descargo de conciencia (1930–1960)* (Concience's discharge), where he recounted his political evolution and departure from Francoism.[28]

Under the Ministry of Education, Ruiz Giménez tried, with little success, to take control of the National Research Council from the hands of Opus

Dei. The council was composed of representatives of the universities, the royal academies, and the higher technological institutes, together with technical experts and representatives from private research institutions and industry, whose aim was to attain the fullest coordination in all spheres. Work was (and still is) carried out in a number of institutes, grouped together under eight *patronatos* (foundations). These included the Raimundo Lulio Foundation, for theological, philosophical, and juridical sciences; the Marcelino Menéndez Pelayo Foundation, for history, philosophy, and art; the Alonso Herrera Foundation, for biology and agronomics; the Alfonso el Sabio Foundation, for mathematics, physics, and chemistry; the Juan de la Cierva Foundation, for technical research; and the Diego Saavedra Fajardo Foundation, for geographical, bibliographical, and economic studies. Research staff members were recruited from the universities and institutes.

Ruiz Giménez also initiated reforms at both the university and secondary levels, with better results. The new *Secondary Education Regulatory Law* partially revised the curriculum in 1953, and new university regulations amending the *URL* of 1943 required a more impersonal selection of department chairs with the reorganization of the qualifying boards.[29] Although Ruiz Giménez's ministry proved to be a turning point toward reform and progressivism, gender relations continued to revolve around the same principles set forth in 1939.

In his efforts at reform, the new minister encountered severe opposition within the university establishment. In addition, the Falangist student organization, the SEU, began to crumble during Ruiz Giménez's administration. In 1953, a new group called University Youth contested SEU elections for the first time, and by the second half of the 1950s at least four dissident student groups could be identified at the University of Madrid. On the political left was the clandestine Communist group with Simón Sánchez Montero and Jorge Semprún; two socialist groups, Socialist Youth and the Socialist University Association, gathered around Rafael Sánchez Ferlosio (one of the writers of the Generation of 1950); a small group who followed Dionisio Ridruejo; and finally a dissident section of the SEU itself, which sought to reform the Falangist student union.[30] The emergence of various student organizations on the margins raised the question of whether the SEU was the real power over the student body. Thus the university became a center of dissent against the regime.

The student movement became increasingly violent, leading to the crisis of February 1956 that cost Ruiz Giménez his ministry. Several events accelerated the crisis. The 1954 visit of Elizabeth II of England to Gibraltar sparked the first student protest against the Francoist establishment to end with a violent confrontation with the police. The year 1955 represented a turning point for intellectual dissent and the anti-Francoist student movement. That year former Falangist Dionisio Ridruejo founded a clandestine club called *Tiempo Nuevo* (New times) to discuss the lamentable situation of the university. This gathering assembled anti-Francoist intellectuals of different ideologies. In addition, Ridruejo, along with other liberal intellectuals and some students affiliated with the Communist Party, organized the Conference of Young Writers in Madrid to take place at the end of the year. An unexpected circumstance changed the plans and led to further confrontations between the students and the government: José Ortega y Gasset, the most polemical intellectual before and after the Civil War, died on 8 October 1955. Although he had not been admired by the anti-Francoist left, he became the catalyst of the student movement. Since his return to Spain in 1946 from exile, he had kept a discreet silence toward the regime and had become very popular among people such as Julián Marías, José Luis Aranguren, Pedro Laín Entralgo, and Antonio Tovar. Students distributed pamphlets that read *Ortega Filósofo liberal* (Ortega liberal philosopher), and the funeral turned into a political demonstration against the regime. Under these circumstances, the young writers' conference was suspended by the government.[31]

Official control of the situation lasted only a few months. On 9 February 1956, a Falangist student, Miguel Alvarez Pérez, was shot in the head in a confrontation with a group of *anti-seuistas* in Madrid. This event acquired extreme symbolism in the press, not because it represented the rejection of the SEU by part of the student body, but because twenty-two years earlier another Falangist student, Matías Montero, had been killed in the very same place and because the events of 1956 happened after a memorial. Although Alvarez Pérez was still alive, the daily newspaper *Arriba* published a headline the next day that read: "They've killed Matías Montero again." The Francoist press ascribed the root of the crisis to a Communist conspiracy and in this way justified a repressive official response. Franco immediately proceeded to eliminate major figures from the educational and Falangist administration. He removed Ruiz Giménez and named Jesús Rubio García Mina the new minister of education; Luis Arrese replaced Fernández Cuesta as secretary general of the Falange. The events that occurred in the Spanish university in 1956 favored the emergence of three new currents within the ranks of the Falange: some abandoned the Falange altogether, others created "purist" Falangist groups, and some members of the Youth Front and SEU remained at the margins of the establishment, in order "to play the system."[32]

The events of 1956 certainly demonstrated SEU's unpopularity and lack of support and forced the government to reorganize the Falangist student union by a law of October 1958. The minister from 1956 until 1962, García Mina introduced the reform that established a more democratic representation of the student body by college, based on elections for the new college assemblies. Elections only accentuated the university's political nature, both as the reproducer of the regime's ideals and elite and as the focus of anti-Francoist resistance.

EDUCATIONAL LEGISLATION AND GENDER IN THE 1950S

In the midst of all the turmoil in university and Spanish intellectual life, gender relations remained unchanged. The policy of the Ministry of National Education followed the Catholic Church directives and polarized men's and women's roles even further during the 1950s. Women were channeled to primary and professional training "appropriate" to their gender in Christian terms. The *Law of Elementary Education* of 15 July 1945 had stated in article 11, "Elementary education for girls must prepare them for the home, the arts, and crafts." In contrast with the urgency with which the *URL* was promulgated, occupational training was regulated by the statute of 1928 until 1949. The *Law for Secondary and Professional Education* of 16 July 1949 established the labor high school, in which students had one year of general academic learning and four years of occupational training. The areas of study were agriculture, industry, mining, and "female occupations." This law was complemented by the *Law for Professional Industrial Training* of 1955, which responded to the economic and social changes the country was undergoing and reiterated the separate instruction and qualifications for men and women.[33]

Throughout the 1950s, the Ministry of Education passed a series of laws regulating secondary education that channeled women into certain careers, if they decided to study at all. The *Secondary Education Regulatory Law*, enacted in 1953, declared in its first paragraph the state's service to the Catholic faith: "Since the beginning of the National Movement, the constant preoccupation of the state has been to promulgate juridical norms that guarantee the intellectual and moral development of Spanish youth in the service of the high ideals of the Catholic faith and the fatherland." Analyzing the *Secondary Education Regulatory Law* from a gender perspective is significant for two reasons. First, secondary education was a prerequisite for those who wanted to pursue any higher education; and second, this stage of education was crucial in the life cycle of an individual because it was when female and male identities were forged. Like the *URL* of 1943 for higher education, this law, ten years later, was intended to guarantee the rights of the state, the Catholic Church, and the family in the learning process, as prescribed in *Divini Illius Magistri*. It also declared the need to reform the curriculum so that students could learn and devote themselves to the "essential subjects." Furthermore, it established official inspection of the educators to avoid any deviation from the "proper educational right."[34] Surveillance continued to be essential for the political stability of the Francoist regime, especially in the context of changing times.

The law, signed by Francisco Franco, consists of 11 chapters, 117 articles, and 5 final provisions. Chapter 1 delineated the fundamental principles for the juridical and pedagogical structure for secondary education. Article 1 defined secondary education as follows: "Middle schooling is the level of education whose essential intent is the spiritual and cultural development of the youth and the preparation of those especially capable for access to higher studies." The law declared, in article 15, the need for a separate education for girls and boys at the secondary level, as prescribed by Catholic doctrine: "The principle of separate instruction for the students of each sex will be applied in secondary education."[35]

Christian domesticity was explicitly promoted by the state through the imposition of gender-segregated schools. Segregated classes would make it easier to determine who was the most qualified to enter university, and girls and boys could be directed into different career choices. The main difference was that girls had to pass the home economic classes to obtain their diplomas, whereas boys were exempt from this requirement. There were two types of high schools: official and unofficial. In chapter 2 (articles 23 and 24), the law divided each type of school into masculine, feminine, and mixed schools and specified that in the mixed schools, boys and girls were to receive separate instruction. Patriotic instruction, religion, and physical education were mandatory for all students. Girls had to take home economics in addition. The faculty teaching these subjects were members of the Falangist Youth Front and the Women's Section and were appointed by the Ministry of Education. Boys and girls had to take several courses on "construction of the National Spirit," which delineated the different national duties of each gender. The curriculum for girls focused on domesticity, whereas the boys' curriculum focused more on the political nature of the regime.

Chapter 4 of the law regulated official inspection of the schools' academic progress and observance of the regime's moral and political values, giving the state and the Catholic Church specific powers of inspection (article 58). State powers were related to instruction in the national spirit, physical education, public order, and health and hygiene; the state also determined whether the legal requirements for the recognition and authorization of each center were being followed. Church authority lay in all things connected to the teaching of religion, the orthodoxy of doctrine, and moral customs.[36] The ministry dictated the norms for inspection and supervision, which were carried out by its own agents. Included among these regulations was one that required the keeping of a school record book that identified each student and registered his or her academic performance and disciplinary record.

Chapter 7 covered the curriculum. Secondary education, for students between ten and sixteen years of age, consisted of six years of learning in two phases: the Bachillerato Elemental, or lower certificate, and the Bachillerato Superior, or higher certificate. Equipped with this training, all students would embark upon Preuniversitario, a preparatory course for entering the university that replaced the exam traditionally required to enter higher education. An order of 20 August 1939 had granted exemption from the university entrance exam to those who were persecuted during the "Marxist domination" in the Civil War. Segregated curricula for male and female students were mandated and explicitly defined in articles 67 and 85. The law imposed separate academic norms for girls' schools that included training appropriate to domestic life, particularly instruction in those disciplines that guided them into feminine occupations. "Female high schools will develop their own curriculum, in which teachings suitable for domestic life and those that especially prepare students for feminine professions will be considered obligatory." To strengthen this bipolar design, the Ministry of National Education was in charge of the editing and authorization of textbooks. No other publications were allowed in the classroom.[37]

In 1955, the Ministry of National Education established new curricula that would provide "national spirit and political indoctrination" in the secondary schools. Two separate orders of 9 February 1955 were published in the *Boletín Oficial del Estado* on 28 July that regulated separate male and female instruction. The order regulating the program of studies for male students declared "the constant preoccupation of the state with the development in youth of respect for, love of, and service to the fatherland."[38]

The program designed to develop national patriotism in male students was divided into six courses in the high school years. In the first three courses, they studied the quintessence of Spanish identity on the individual and the national levels. Spanish young men learned about the National Movement and its leaders, José Antonio and Francisco Franco, who embodied the ideal of Spanish masculinity. Fundamental male virtues rested upon the fusion of Catholic spirituality and national devotion. Thus, a true Spanish man aspired to be half monk, half soldier, always ready to serve the fatherland. The idea of masculinity implied at all times a public, aggressive attitude, in great contrast with the female virtues of true Catholic womanhood. From the level of individual behavior, lessons moved to the concept of nationhood and defined the idea of the organic nation in agreement with the traditional Spanish values of religion and order propounded after the Civil War. This new nation incarnated the modern concept of *Hispanidad* and the virtue of the charismatic single leadership of a caudillo. Finally, students learned about the role of Spain in history and the essential role of Christianity as a fundamental factor in the construction of Spanish nationhood. Lectures emphasized the religious and national significance of the Reconquista under the Catholic monarchs. In the fourth, fifth, and sixth courses, students learned about the disintegration of Spanish values under the Republican aegis, the restoration of the national spirit after the Civil War, and the victory of the National Movement.[39]

By contrast, the new curricula to develop national spirit in girls included more lessons and activities related to domestic chores and social etiquette. The lessons required more hours than those for boys. Since the intent of the *Secondary Education Regulatory Law* of 1953 was to restrict the curricula only to essential subjects, it is clear that according to the new curriculum, the study of domestic matters was essential to girls' training in their patriotic duty to the fatherland. Girls' instruction included a synthesis of the political indoctrination prescribed for male students, physical education, and home economics. The program for the first three courses consisted of formation of the patriotic spirit, family and social norms, physical education, sewing, and music. The fourth, fifth, and sixth courses added to these subjects a program of cooking, home economics, and infant care.[40]

The program of family and social instruction was meant to imbue in girls specific habits to build their Spanish femininity. Piety, circumspection, order, and hygiene composed the essence of the Catholic ideal woman. For example, one of the family education lessons in the second course focused on Christian etiquette and emphasized piety as a crucial virtue. Several lessons were devoted to "order" in the first, second, and third courses; they referred to the arrangement and tidiness of both the household (the bathroom, the living room, the kitchen) and the immediate physical environment of the student in the classroom: her desk, her books, her notes. Order was understood as harmony, balance, and softness, within the private sphere. Because the family reflected Francoist society as a whole, order within the family in the physical sense was a metaphor for the political order the regime aspired to impose.[41] Women's visible contribution to the national endeavor resided in their building harmonious homes.

A few lessons dealt with silence as a virtue, discussing when it was appropriate to talk in different social settings (at the dinner table, in the classroom) and posing several such questions for study: "Is laughter good? When may a lady sneeze? What is the importance of overcoming pain? What should a lady never touch? What would people think of a cheeky girl?"[42]

Being good and pious was inherent to the ideal femininity these courses imparted. An entire lesson was dedicated to the ways in which girls should correct their "bad character" and arrogance.[43] With these lessons Spanish women learned the most important feminine virtues: being kind, submissive, tidy, clean, and quiet. The inclusion of all these issues in the government curriculum for girls clearly evidenced the state's desire to perpetuate true Catholic womanhood. All Spanish ladies had to conform to this norm for the good of the fatherland as much as men had to become half monks and half soldiers. Although Ruiz Giménez's ministry proved to be an attempt to open the regime to criticism in the political arena, when analyzed from a gender point of view, it perpetuated traditional Catholic values in women's education.

Girls continued to be trained in the art of cooking. Culinary topics such as "the importance of milk" would be followed by a practical exercise such as making rice pudding. In the sixth course, students took "home economics." The lectures provided a detailed analysis of household cleaning, divided into three lessons: daily cleaning, weekly cleaning, and monthly cleaning. Within these lessons, the laundry process (such as the washing of silk dresses) received special attention, as well as ironing. Girls learned that a good housewife had to be "gentle with the servants and prudent in expenses," designing a detailed household budget.[44] These lessons were obviously aimed at middle-class students, who constituted the majority of the student body and could afford domestic service. Students were also trained in infant care to better fulfill their destiny as mothers.

Those Spanish young women who finished high school, equipped with this knowledge, had to decide whether to go to college and to choose a career. This was a predicament if they wanted to preserve their femininity, especially if they remembered some of the class discussions such as "Is reading appropriate for a woman?" The *Secondary Education Regulatory Law* of 1953 and the orders of 1955 perpetuated female domesticity until the end of the decade. If women went to college, they concentrated on specific careers. For example, women were banned from legal professions until the *Law of Political, Professional, and Labor Rights of Women* was passed in 1961. Those careers that implied some caretaking or artistic qualities were the ones most often chosen by women students, such as nursing, philosophy and letters, and the *carreras de tipo medio,* or middle careers (secretary, librarian, tourist guide, or laboratory assistant). In the end, being a true lady became inimical to any intellectual or scientific endeavor. Although the country's economic and social reality was changing, women's contribution to the national enterprise continued to center on being mothers and wives. If they did not follow a professional career, at least going to college improved their chances of marrying a successful husband. Female high school graduates were influenced by such manuals as *Amor* by the Jesuit Father Remigio Vilariño, in which they read about the kind of education they needed to seek to better themselves as wives and mothers:

> Prepare yourselves to assist men, being similar to them in a certain way. Be housewives, not learned women. Know much about housework, which concerns not only the kitchen and the needle, but rather difficult and important things: for example, the science of cleanliness and hygiene, and everything about the management of the home.[45]

This text captures the spirit of the high school curriculum reforms of 1955. The rationalization of the economy had reached the home as well. Imbuing women with a thorough knowledge of cleanliness as applied to housework remained more important than encouraging them to pursue an intellectual career. True Catholic womanhood prevailed in the 1950s as the country ventured into consumerism. Women who went to college followed those careers that bore the least threat to their femininity.

WOMEN IN HIGHER EDUCATION

Francoist statistics on higher education pose a central paradox when analyzed from a gender perspective. Although the official National-Catholic discourse defined studying as inimical to femininity, the number of women who attended college in the 1950s doubled, from 7,667 in 1950 to 15,338 in

1961.[46] Candidates for admission to a university were required to possess a high school diploma (which in the case of girls included home economics), pass the maturity examination after the preuniversity course, and be over the age of 16. There was no limit on the number of students who could enroll and follow courses in any college, although the first-year course was generally selective and students were required to pass the end-of-year examinations before being allowed to pursue their studies any further.

The university was an urban experience. The two major metropolitan areas, Madrid and Barcelona, experienced the most growth in the 1950s, in part because these two cities attracted most of the country's internal migration. Growth was not so significant in other medium-size university districts such as Granada and Santiago de Compostela, the sites of older institutions located, respectively, in Galicia and Andalusia, two of the most underdeveloped regions in the country.

The University of Madrid had the highest registration, with over 17,000 students in 1950–1951 and almost 25,000 a decade later. The University of Barcelona was next in enrollment with 5,700 students in 1950–1951 and more than 9,000 in 1961–1962, whereas Granada and Santiago each had an average of 3,000 students throughout the decade. Between 1950 and 1962, the student enrollment grew at the University of Madrid by 43 percent; Barcelona had an enrollment growth of 57 percent.[47] University experience constituted a key element in urban life. Sociologist Amando de Miguel points out that, for the period 1955–1969, the three richest regions in the country—Barcelona, Madrid, and the Basque Country—experienced faster economic and demographic growth as a result of the development plans initiated by the regime after the Stabilization Plan of 1959. Madrid and Barcelona were centers that attracted immigrants, whereas both Santiago de Compostela and Granada were located in underdeveloped areas that provided the emigrants who were drawn to the centers of development. Santiago is located in Galicia in northern Spain and Granada is in the southern region of Andalusia, both of them areas where rural structure and Catholic traditions prevailed.[48] Therefore, it is not surprising that the two largest metropolitan areas registered the highest enrollment of students. In addition, the number of women students in the two largest universities of the country doubled. At the University of Granada, women were 15 percent of the total in 1950 and 23.5 percent in 1961; Santiago's female student enrollment went from 26.8 percent in 1950 to 29.7 percent in 1961. Percentages for the major growth areas of Barcelona and Madrid are much the same. Thus, although actual numbers of women attending these universities rose dramatically, the percentage of female students grew more slowly. Women's presence in all of Spanish higher education did not represent more than 22 to 24 percent of the entire university population at the beginning of the 1960s.[49]

The colleges of Spanish universities included philosophy and letters (including education), science, law, medicine, pharmacy, political science, economics, and veterinary medicine. For teaching purposes, the colleges were divided into sections, subsections, and special branches. The universities offered courses of study leading to the first degree of *licenciado* (equivalent to a master's degree) in all colleges, ranging in length from five years in philosophy and letters, science, law, political science, and economics to six years in the colleges of pharmacy and medicine. All universities awarded the doctoral degree.

The teaching body was composed of tenured professors (established posts), acting professors, associate professors, lecturers, and junior lecturers. Tenured professors held the doctoral degree; they were responsible for all activities connected with their chair and lectured on their main subject. Acting professors filling vacant chairs had to have the same qualifications and carried out the same duties. Associate professors held a doctoral degree and might occupy a vacant chair, but they were normally only responsible for seminars. Lecturers usually held a doctorate, but most of them were just *licenciados;* they assisted professors in practical, laboratory, clinical, and seminar work, usually working in close contact with the students. In accordance with the *URL* of 1943, professors were appointed to established posts by order of the Ministry of Education. In Madrid and Barcelona, vacant chairs were filled either by competitive selection *(concurso)* from among professors already holding a university chair or by open competitive examination *(oposición)*. In the rest of Spain, appointments were normally made by *concurso*, and an open examination was held only if the vacancy was not filled. The *concurso* was open to titled professors from other universities whose area of study was the same as that of the vacant professorship. The appointment was strictly based on merit and was decided upon by a specially appointed board; preference was always given to the candidate who had served well as the acting professor in the vacant position. The open competitive examinations were always held in Madrid, before a board specially constituted for each case, and the candidate's scientific publications, teaching qualifications, and experience, as well as his or her concept and method of approach to the subject, were taken into account. Only holders of doctoral degrees who had completed two years of teaching or research in a state institution were admissible as candidates. Associate professors were appointed in the same way, except that they were recruited for a term of four years, renewable for another four years. Acting professors and lecturers were appointed by the Ministry of Education on the proposal of the rector after consultation with the appropriate faculty. The appointment was a three-year term for acting professors and a one-year term for lecturers. Junior lecturers were appointed every year on the proposal of the dean of the college after consultation with the professor of the subject concerned.

In 1950, the total number of professors in the Spanish universities was 3,439, of which only 248 were women. The highest number of faculty women for any given academic year were in the disciplines of science and of philosophy and letters. Women professors were scarce in the rest of the disciplines. There were only 15 women professors in pharmacy, 9 in law, 4 in medicine, 3 in political science and business, and 2 in veterinary medicine. Of the 651 full professors in the Spanish universities in 1953, only one was a woman. María Angeles Galino, a member of the Teresian Institute, was the first woman to hold a chair at a Spanish university; she became full professor of history of education at the University of Madrid. In 1961, three more women gained chairs: Asunción Linares in paleontology at the University of Granada, Carmen Virgili Redón in historical geology at the University of Oviedo, and Gloria Vegué Cantón in political economy at the University of Salamanca.[50] Junior lecturers became an essential segment of the teaching staff. Although they were supposed to teach only practical and laboratory classes, in reality they lectured and carried out full instruction, but for a lower salary. Junior lecturers represented 80 percent of the total of faculty professors for the academic year 1959–1960. The Ministry of Education statistical reports show some irregularity regarding the total number of professors for the years 1960–1961 and 1961–1962. There is a discontinuity in the figures that can only be explained by the assumption that the auxiliary faculty was not included in the total number for these years.[51] In addition, the distinction by gender disappears from the statistics starting in 1960. Women were underrepresented in all the faculty segments throughout the 1950s. There was a slight increase in the number of female faculty throughout the decade, from about 7 percent to about 9 percent. The disciplines that had more women faculty were pharmacy, philosophy and letters, and the sciences—all disciplines that had no political prospects, as opposed to law or political science.

The concentration of women students in certain career paths followed the same pattern. Although the number of women students grew significantly during the 1950s, by the end of the decade women were still underrepresented in Spanish universities. They remained primarily in three disciplines: philosophy and letters, pharmacy, and the sciences. In the sciences, 20.2 percent of the students were women in 1950–1951, and ten years later it was 23.2 percent. Women were even more numerous in philosophy and letters and in pharmacy. At the beginning of the decade, women represented almost 70 percent of the student body in philosophy and letters, but that percentage decreased gradually to 62.6 percent in 1961–1962. Many of the women students majored in history, geography, philosophy, literature, and art, and some of them moved into teaching positions, although they were less likely to teach at the university level than in primary and secondary schools. Pharmacy attracted a significant number of women: throughout the 1950s, they constituted around 50 percent of all students in the field. Professional opportunities in pharmacy included opening a dispensary, which traditionally was a family business. A pharmacist was regarded as a caretaker, whereas a doctor and a veterinarian were not, and therefore these careers attracted fewer women; they were more likely to enter nursing and infant-care careers.[52]

The state was the determining factor in the wide divergence between men's and women's courses of study and eventual careers. Gender difference inspired the Ministry of National Education policies during the 1950s that shaped female and male identities. True Catholic womanhood acquired national and political significance. The official discourse praised submissiveness, frailty, and self-sacrifice as the ultimate feminine virtues and promoted an education in accordance to these principles. Women were limited in many ways in their pursuit of intellectual and professional activities. The reform of the *Civil Code* in 1958 and the *Law of Political, Professional, and Labor Rights of Women* tried to accommodate the economic and social changes the country experienced during the decade without abandoning the essential virtues of Spanish femininity. The university was a locus of state power from which it drew its political elite. Not only was the image of a scholar that of a soldier at the service of the fatherland, but men also dominated the professions that were indispensable to the state and public power. By contrast, the definition of a true woman was the opposite of that of a scholar; women were encouraged to choose careers that were better reconciled with their feminine soul. Although women gained access to the universities in greater numbers, they concentrated in those areas of study most suitable to traditional family and social roles of women.

The women who entered the classrooms of higher education in the 1950s were under the supervision of the Women's Section of the Falange/SEU, who policed and ensured their domestic training. But some women joined other Catholic organizations, which allowed them to develop alternative Catholic femininities that would not contradict a love for knowledge and learning.

CHAPTER FIVE

THE WOMEN'S SECTION
OF THE FALANGE

"To guide the Women's Section's educational task, we are going to
follow, as always, the teachings of José Antonio. He said: "We must
bring men down to earth." And for women that realm is their family.
That is why, besides offering our members the mystique that elevates
them, we have to attach them, with our teachings, to the daily routine,
the child, the home, the garden. Our goal is that women find there all
their purpose in life and find in men all their comfort."

—Pilar Primo De Rivera, *Teresa*, October 1959

T he Women's Section of the Falange (WS) survived until
1977 as a division of the FET de las JONS. It endured the ups and downs of
the National Movement and provided Francoism with a maternal mask. The
WS's leitmotiv was to serve the fatherland with abnegation. Their faith in
God and in the Falangist enterprise guided them to do no wrong, and their
resilience in sacrifice made them strong. Such moral superiority was considered genuinely feminine and indispensable to the survival of the regime's
Falangist principles in the 1950s when Franco removed the members of the
Falange from his government.

When examining the discourse on femininity articulated by the WS in the 1950s, it is particularly useful to discern how it contributed to women's access to the public realm (power) in general and to the university (knowledge) in particular. Modernization created a tension between the imposed Falangist doctrine that WS officials struggled to preserve and initiatives favoring women's agency and contestation. As a result, by the end of the 1950s, WS officials acknowledged the decline in membership and lack of genuine enthusiasm among the women who joined the Falangist family. Modernization produced a multiplicity of identities that WS tried to counteract by forging a Falangist elite among college women through the mandatory University Social Service (USS). But what of the Falangist women of WS who preached the doctrine of ideal Catholic womanhood? Did they conform to that model themselves?

THE WORK OF THE WOMEN'S SECTION

The WS and the SEU were born simultaneously. José Antonio envisioned a violent dimension to his organization and was reluctant at the beginning to allow women to join the party. Nonetheless, the WS was born in 1934 within SEU. A year earlier Justina Rodríguez de Viguri, a student in the college of philosophy and letters, had joined the SEU (masculinizing her name to "Justino"), although Ramiro Ledesma Ramos had opposed the entrance of women in the student union. Ledesma Ramos was the leader of the JONS, an organization that merged with the Falange Española after the meeting in the theater La Comedia in 1933. The SEU was attached to the JONS movement. Ledesma Ramos, along with the other male Falangist leaders, came to the realization that women could distribute propaganda with less risk than men, and he admitted them into the movement. By 1935 seven women constituted the new WS. Four of them had official responsibilities: Pilar Primo de Rivera, national head of the organization; Dora Maqueda, secretary; Luisa María de Arambúru, head of the WS in the province of Madrid; Inés Primo de Rivera, county secretary. Three members did not hold office: Dolores Primo de Rivera; María Luisa Bonifaz, who later entered a convent; and the British national Marjory Munden. The WS was declared a separate entity within the party by formal decree of 28 December 1939.[1] Women were not admitted to men's politics but were given the opportunity to take care of their own business.

The indoctrination of Spanish women remained the primary mission of the WS in the 1950s, a decade of economic and political transition. The autarchy's productive/reproductive model of women shifted to include the consumer-housewife and the professional woman by the beginning of the 1960s. The WS's task was to smooth this transition, helping to redefine femininity in accordance with the new circumstances, without losing its power.

To perform its duty in the most effective manner, the WS maintained a hierarchical structure, with Pilar Primo de Rivera as national head and a web of provincial delegates throughout the country. The National Schools of the WS imparted basic instruction on the principles of the Falange, preparing women for their domestic duties.[2] The WS orchestrated its program of indoctrination from several departments, each with its own function. The religious secretary took care of the spirituality of Falangist women under the counsel of Fray Justo Pérez de Urbel, a Benedictine monk from the monastery of Silos. The political secretary was in charge of the dissemination of Joseantonian ideals, and all the legal matters were administered by the legal secretary. The National Council every two years brought together national and local delegates; the Consultative Junta met on special occasions; and Delegates' Assemblies met monthly on a local level.

The services offered by the WS were divided into three categories: general, educational, and social. General service departments served the other divisions, recruiting new members, selecting leaders, administering the finances, and projecting the WS's image to the public. The educational services were performed within several offices. The technical secretary was in charge of organizing WS's activities and regulating the relations between the organization and the state. This secretary edited a pedagogical magazine for Falangist teachers under the title *Consigna*. The secretary of culture organized Home Economics Schools, which were located in the high schools all over the country and whose instructors were affiliated with the WS. There were other schools with a missionary aim. They were created to eradicate illiteracy and were equipped with small libraries (whose books had to be authorized by the leaders of WS) to perform their instructional tasks. The cultural secretary also organized choral and dance groups of men and women who traveled around the world performing traditional regional Spanish songs and dances. As cultural ambassadors of the regime, these groups offered to the world a quaint image of the new Spain.

The secretary of the WS/SEU was responsible for guiding Spanish university women on the road to domesticity. This office organized the USS as well as summer retreats that enrolled around three thousand college women yearly.[3] Young women were also encouraged to devote themselves to the practice of sports and the "domestic sciences." The WS/SEU encouraged social involvement among university women and organized cultural activities— such as seminars, lectures, and plays—in its residential halls. This secretary cooperated with the appropriate agencies to provide financial aid for students. The secretary of youth and the secretary of physical education had special importance. The former was in charge of the indoctrination of girls between the ages of six and seventeen in elementary and secondary schools; this office also organized summer camps where girls' physical education was promoted, within the parameters of Catholic morality, in order to produce healthy mothers. The WS also had a director of health and social assistance, a director of labor, and a director of social service. Through this bureaucratic machinery, the WS instilled Catholic and patriotic femininity in Spanish women.

During the 1950s, as the advent of consumerism complicated the traditional definition of Catholic womanhood, the WS directed women, for the good of Spain, to obey and accept with abnegation what the circumstances dictated. The modernization of the country must not eradicate traditional Spanish Catholic femininity, and to its preservation the WS devoted its efforts. Although Spanish women were permitted to work, they were expected to quit their jobs when it came time to devote themselves to their families and children. Motherhood remained the highest patriotic offering to the fatherland. The WS's challenge was to reconcile the essence of the autarchy model of femininity with the new consumer-housewife, who was ready to abandon the hearth and enter the workplace. The organization conducted several surveys at the beginning of the 1960s to study the educational alternatives for women entering the labor force.

A good example of the rationalization of women's work (public and private) that characterized modernization may be found in the WS papers:

> A fundamental knowledge and the development of a feminine pedagogy appropriate to women's mentality remain to be created. It is important to inculcate both social and individual behavior appropriate to women's work, uprooting any collective ideas that, right now, only represent an obstacle for a woman's service to modernization. [Technical] orientation and management are also necessary to correct her frequent psychological evasions, her disregard for the value of time, her need to chat, and her rivalry with fellow women workers outside the workplace.

The regime confronted the dilemma of assuming modernity without betraying the traditional principles that gave birth to the Francoist state. To a certain extent, the 1950s provided the opportunity to reconcile the struggle between continuity and change, between tradition and modernization. The economic, social, and cultural changes of the 1950s favored a new approach to traditional Spanish femininity and gender relations. The WS developed a discourse of its own on Catholic womanhood in tune with the regime's dictum. The economic demands required a change of mentality, a certain acceptance of women's independence, but within well-established limits. A WS report on work opportunities for women asserted the motherly nature of the Spanish female character even outside the home. "[O]utside the home, in society, a woman continued to be a mother, an educator, and a guardian of her children. Her tenderness, sensibility, and maternal instinct were the most valuable things society needed from her; for these there were no age or time limits."[4] The political circumstances had also changed, as the crisis of 1956 showed. In order to adjust to the changing times, the WS redefined its goals and action in successive National Councils that occurred in the 1950s. In addition, several circular letters from the national head of WS, Pilar Primo de Rivera, noted the need for a revision of organizational principles, according to the new political and economic circumstances. Circular 54 of December 1955, for example, announced the preparations for the Eighteenth National Council of the WS to be held in Málaga a month later. "Because of significant national and international political changes occurring in the last twenty years since the war, this National Delegation proposes to the Council a total restatement of issues, to be studied and resolved there." It was important, though, to preserve the Falangist essence and political direction in the context of the Cold War: "A new orientation in the political instruction is appropriate, *not in essence but in form,* in accordance with the evolution experienced by the world since the last world war and the new conception of global structure that groups nations in a common destiny."[5]

The new international scene made Spain a partner of the United States in the crusade against Communism. The Falange's fascist overtones were domesticated in the context of the Cold War. The university disturbances in 1956 led Franco to remodel the government, excluding Falangists from key ministries. By contrast, the WS enjoyed greater official support in the 1950s. The *Secondary Education Regulatory Law,* for example, had been enacted in 1953, establishing mandatory home economics classes in all secondary schools and assigning WS instructors to teach those classes, along with political indoctrination in Falangist principles. In her circular of 8 March 1957, Pilar Primo de Rivera addressed the removal of Falangist elements from the government.

> Considering it calmly, the change may be positive for us in the long run, although at first sight it seems to be moving toward a removal of Falange from official life. . . . On the other hand, if a Falangist government had been formed now it would have been worse. Given Falange's public discredit, because of us and others, there would have been tremendous reactions that would have made us all unpopular. Besides, the presence of technocrats in the government gives an aura of utilitarian security that Spain needs.[6]

The new members of Franco's cabinet who were affiliated with Opus Dei incorporated an ethic of success and rationalization of the economy that led to the modernization of the country with the Stabilization Plan of 1959 and the development programs in the next decade. By contrast, the WS assumed the humane (Falangist) values of the regime at this juncture, and its programs for domestic learning were well received by the new cabinet. With a discourse that celebrated domestic Christian femininity, the WS secured both the survival of Falangist principles and a power space of their own until 1977. (Claudia Koonz's study of Nazi women provides a superb analysis of the participation in politics of totalitarian women's organizations, which has relevance to an evaluation of WS access to and participation in power.) The WS offered a maternal face, more benign than that of the Falange, and provided essential social services at a very low cost for the regime. The WS followed the Joseantonian ideals, which saw the state's political bases as the family, the municipality, and the syndicate. The family became more than an emotional domain in the hands of the WS: it represented a political tool and a site of female power.

> Thus, following as usual the words of Jose Antonio, who affirmed on repeated occasions: "A true State, like that which Falange Española wants, will be based neither on the inconsistency of political parties, nor on the Parliament they generate. It will be based on the authentic vital realities: the family, the municipality, the guild, or the syndicate. Hence, the new State will recognize the integrity of the family as a social unit; the autonomy of the municipality as a territorial unit, and the syndicate, guild, or corporation as the real basis of the total organization of the State. Nobody feels ambiguity, dispersion, or contradiction between who he really is and what he represents in public life. The individual thus becomes involved in the State as somebody who fulfills a function, and not through political parties, not as a representative of a false sovereignty, but because he has a job, a family, because he belongs to a municipality. This way he is both an industrious laborer and *repository of power*."[7]

Rather than competing for power in the men's world, Falangist women defined themselves as mothers and wives, as "industrious laborers and repositories of power" within the home. Women as Falangist individuals in the new national project became involved in the state as much as their male counterparts by performing functions "appropriate" to their gender. In the case of women bearing and raising children, by staying at home they expanded and protected their own sphere of power from male intervention. Women's major contribution to the construction of a new Spain consisted of excelling in their motherly (social or private) duties. Pilar Primo de Rivera clearly defined the political purpose of the WS:

> It is necessary to clarify certain points in order to refocus our unique purpose.
> 1. Our only goal, in Spain's quest, is to serve a political position.
> 2. This political position is the Falangist one, born of the ideas of Jose Antonio and incorporated in the State apparatus as the only one able to make suggestive, just, and transcendental, in the universal sense, the historical reality of our fatherland, Spain.[8]

The WS turned into the guardian of the Falange's political values. In a metaphorical motherly fashion, Falangist women assumed in the 1950s the task of protecting the Falange's survival against change. Nonetheless, the transitional nature of the times made it necessary to adjust to the new political and economic conditions. As Pilar Primo de Rivera's words attest, "It is essential to mold ourselves to the circumstances of each moment; thus, although inspired by the same immutable principles, the Women's Section evolves to encompass, for the better, as many areas of influence as possible."

It was imperative that WS officials not forget the characteristics of their Falangist responsibilities. "Abnegation, self-denial, authenticity, strength, austerity, justice, joyous self-discipline, comradeship, exemplary behavior" remained the foundation of the WS personality.[9] The WS leadership had to symbolize the ultimate femininity. There was no doubt that women constituted a key element in the national endeavor:

> Nobody compelled anybody; all of us [women] joined this enterprise separately, because all of us felt in our own heart the need of the fatherland. And only the political thought of Jose Antonio made us surrender comfort, praise, and possessions to build all together a better Spain.

To achieve a better Spain, political indoctrination certainly was a must, and the WS assumed such responsibility. In a circular letter, Pilar Primo de Rivera made it clear that it would be inadmissible to question the teaching of "political form." "Because our presence, as part of the state's task, is justified by our goal to promote a political consciousness among Spanish people," she remarked, "we must direct them toward what we firmly believe as the only possible solution to achieve a better and more just Spain." Political propaganda, especially directed toward the younger generation, was a means used by all nations: "This fervor to shape a political consciousness belongs to all nations, even the most liberal and democratic, because they see it as the better means to attract particularly the youth to what they consider true."[10]

The WS became the protector of the Falangist spirit when the regime weeded out male Falangist elements in the mid-1950s. Falangist women would not suffer their male counterparts' political ostracism, because they had never been part of the male political sphere. On the contrary, they created their own site of power and fueled their enthusiasm with a women's interpretation of Joseantonian principles. Their interpretation, which celebrated domesticity and Catholicism, appeared nonthreatening to the regime. Falangist women created a state within the state by offering basic social services to the regime at a low cost and by serving as propaganda agents of the official National-Catholic femininity.[11]

The 1950s were pivotal in the evolution of the WS and its definition of femininity. The WS preserved traditional Catholic womanhood yet motivated Spanish women to enter the workplace. It redefined Spanish femininity to accommodate traditional gender roles to the demands of modernity. The technocratic rationalization of the economy introduced by Opus Dei permeated the private sphere. The WS's task was to become the guardians of spiritual values, as the Falangists had been.

The WS's zeal to preserve a domestic femininity within a changing economic reality led to the development of a guide to feminine occupations. There were two types: intellectual or university occupations and those occupations that required some kind of technical training. The most highly recommended of the latter were nursing; social work; jobs within the movie industry, such as script writing or film editing; journalism; tourist guide work; and teaching, either in elementary or high school. In addition, there were occupations created by the WS and regulated by law throughout the 1950s. The following job titles were included: general instructor of youth, teacher of home economics, music and dance instructor, rural instructor, social health educator, and physical education instructor. As decreed on 7 July 1950, only WS instructors could teach home economics, and the degree of "Home Economics Teacher" was recognized by the Ministry of Education by a decree of 10 November 1960. Rural instructors, who were in charge of the domestic training of peasant women, received official recognition by both the decree of November 1953 and by the Ministry of Agriculture order of July 1954. All of these occupations required a Christian and Falangist spirit, total discipline, and devotion. Even though a woman entered the public realm, she was expected to maintain her duties as a mother and an educator within her home. "In conformity with the great importance a woman has as an educator of her children and for her influence in the home, [WS] will pay special attention to her cultural and family training. To fulfill this goal, it creates the Home Schools." These home schools were a WS venture sanctioned by the state.[12]

To a certain extent, the personal lives of the WS officials and affiliates contradicted the model of the true woman that they prescribed. In contrast with Franco's fatherly image as a grandfather in the 1950s and early 1960s, Pilar Primo de Rivera never married; she devoted her entire life to the construction of the ideal new woman for the new regime. Falangist women developed a public persona very different from the private motherly Christian figure their discourse promoted. The National Councils, held every other year, were the WS's most obvious public function with political connotations. These events represented an opportunity to unify positions and adjust to the political and economic changes. The WS affiliates had to travel and assemble for several days to discuss politics and propose solutions to confront the changing times. The Eighteenth National Council, held in Málaga in January 1956, opened the debate about the need for reform. At this meeting, carefully arranged since September 1955, the delegates discussed political matters such as the Falangist concept of empire inspired in the Catholic monarchs' reconquest of Spain in the Middle Ages rather than domestic female issues. The imperialistic approach was now revised and replaced by that of "supranational community," which fit better in the Cold War international context. At the same time, the council decided on an administrative reorganization of the WS, delegating more authority to the provinces, and reaffirmed its training activities.[13]

Particularly important was the Nineteenth National Council, which convened in the Castle of la Mota in Medina del Campo in 1958, a year after Franco remodeled his government. This meeting undertook a serious discussion of the future of the WS and the survival of Falangist principles in a time of crisis. In her inaugural speech, Pilar Primo de Rivera acknowledged, "Undoubtedly a new political era is dawning. And at this juncture, the important thing for us is that neither the essence nor the efficacy of the Women's Section is lost for Spain."[14] The council vowed to maintain cooperation with the state to secure specific legislation to better the educational development of Spanish women in accordance with Falangist precepts. It was necessary also to coordinate the action of SEU, the state's Social Service, and the Labor Organization. Finally, to enhance their social services, the council proposed the creation of a new profession: social worker. This decision implied that not all Spanish women were homebound. The WS women developed a space of their own to provide essential (and low-cost) health and educational services for the regime. Women Falangist officials construed a feminine mystique based on nurturing female qualities. The entrance of women into the public sphere was conceived and perceived as an extension of domestic duties, thought of almost as a missionary vocation of religious charity in the tradition of working for the poor. The discourse articulated by the WS was class-based and condescending, its main purpose being to indoctrinate the lower classes in the middle-class spirit of the Falange. By the end of the 1950s, the WS began preparing women for the labor-force demands of the new economy, particularly by endorsing the *Law of Political, Professional, and Labor Rights of Women*, which was approved by the Cortes in the summer of 1961. The modernizing drive included an improvement in women's educational opportunities. Spanish young women aspiring to enter college would enjoy certain advantages under the new legislation, since some additional careers were opened to them.

THE SPANISH UNIVERSITY STUDENT UNION

Pilar Primo de Rivera in her memoirs, *Recuerdos de una vida,* expressed the close relationship between the WS and the Spanish University Student Union (SEU). The WS was born within the SEU, and they shared the same goals and actions. The first university women members of the SEU were Clotilde Salazar, Justina Rodríguez de Viguri, Mercedes Formica, Pilar Anadón, Parusa Nieto, Cheli Valcarce, Vicky Lago, and Pilar Lago. Pilar Primo de Rivera recounts the relationship of the SEU and the WS as follows:

> In the early Falange, the Women's Section and the SEU were the same thing; we all appeared in the same files as students and, as such, members of the union; we shared risks and hopes with the groups of medicine, law, philosophy. We made the SEU's flags our own and embroidered the emblems of the SEU; only when the organization started to grow were we separated. But in many of us, that first union and intellectual vocation has remained forever like underground links that unite us at all junctures.[15]

Each organization had an ideological raison d'etre. The student union was born, much as the WS, to serve the Falangist political agenda. According to Raimundo Fernández Cuesta, general secretary of the Falange movement at the time, the purpose of WS could be expressed in three words: education, propaganda, proselytism.[16] These goals accurately described the rationale of the SEU as well.

By order of Fernández Cuesta in 1951, the national plan for the political instruction of the SEU was established.

> The prime mission of the Spanish University Student Union, approved by the *University Regulatory Law*, is to bring to the student masses the doctrine and purpose of Falange. As a political alliance, this mission pertains to the SEU with the maximum urgency and it must accept it with the greatest enthusiasm, hoping to find and secure the best university individuals to incorporate them in the service of Spain. All the syndicate's activities must pursue a triple end of winning, selecting, and training university students.[17]

The purpose of this ministerial order was to enhance political indoctrination of the university student body through the SEU. To do so, it created three means of control: the Center of Political Studies, the front line of the SEU, and courses specially designed to train leaders. The theorists of the Center of Political Studies provided curriculum material for both frontline and leader courses. The task of political proselytism belonged to the activists in the front line of the SEU, and to accomplish this responsibility, they were divided into groups of political and social action. The frontline SEU mission was to incorporate, upon arriving at the university, those young men and women already affiliated with Franco's youth phalanxes and the WS. Articles 14 and 15 of the order called for students' total devotion to the service of Falangist principles, a combination of militaristic and Catholic discipline. "Art. 15.—Manners will be exemplary. Military discipline, intellectual rigor, religious authenticity, and enthusiasm are essential elements of the style that a Falangist university student must possess."[18]

The national SEU leadership conference held in Madrid in September 1952 addressed the university union's duties as it ventured into a new decade. The National Department of Political Instruction encompassed frontline SEU members, the Center of Political Studies, leadership instruction, the press and propaganda, and cultural and artistic activities (theater, music, and creative writing). The SEU's goals were not only cultural but social and political as well. To achieve a fraternal link between university students, workers, and peasants constituted an important political end. Social harmony would be thus fulfilled by spreading the Falangist concepts and style of life. The eradication of illiteracy, as well as a new approach to the rural world that involved increasing the understanding of its problems and reality with "programs of rural and labor hygiene," became a priority. In addition, to complete its cultural enterprise, SEU—with the aid of WS work teams—registered folklore traditions, village festivals, songs, romantic stories, and legends.[19] Women of WS/SEU contributed significantly in the student union cultural extension task. They performed these duties diligently through the USS, the chorus and dance office, the mobile libraries and educational teams, and the rural programs of hygiene, which were administered by the national delegation of WS until the end of the 1970s.

A high point for the SEU came with the decree of 11 August 1953, which enacted the *Student Statute,* identifying the SEU as the only legal university organization through which students could participate in academic life. But three years after this high point, the SEU began to crumble. The crisis of 1956 destroyed the ministry of Ruiz Giménez, and Luis Arrese replaced Fernández Cuesta as general secretary of the movement. The Government Presidency Order of 18 October 1958 further reorganized SEU as a part of a general reform of the movement's Services and General Secretariat. The legal document acknowledged SEU's loyalty to the national endeavor in masculine terms. SEU members were conceived of as soldiers more than anything else, through their past participation in the Civil War. "From [SEU] were drawn many magnificent combatants for our Liberation War; it also later provided the basis of the university militia that created higher premilitary instruction."[20]

The SEU provided an important infrastructure for Spanish students. Its services included health insurance, dining facilities and residence halls, grants and financial aid for graduates, a university job-opportunity office, a travel agency, and an international students' exchange. Nonetheless, the crisis of 1956 confirmed the students' rejection of SEU and caused a much needed revision of its structure and meaning. The State Order of 1958 therefore reaffirmed the corporative and professional character of the SEU and added a representative bent, but within the boundaries of the National Movement. The SEU was now defined as follows: "The Spanish University Student Union, part of the National Delegation of Associations of the Movement, is the students' corporation in the institutions of higher education, through which they are represented in the organs of the state, whose decisions affect them."[21] Seuistas (student members of the SEU) were part of the corporate structure of Spanish society at large. The order's emphasis on the representative character of the SEU was an innovative official attempt to alleviate its unpopularity among students, particularly after 1956. The representational reform affected the SEU's structure on all levels, from the officials in charge of college syndicates, colleges and institutions, and local and provincial syndicates to the head of the university district and the national head.

According to the SEU statutes of 1937, class delegates had been selected by the syndicate's local head, but with the reform of 1958, class delegates were replaced by Class Councils, the most elemental cell of SEU structure. During the first month of the academic year, all students in a class elected ten students to be part of the Class Council. A delegate and a subdelegate, selected from the ten members, led the council. Their functions, though, were strictly limited to academic issues.

Above the Class Council was a Branch or Section Council, which replaced in 1958 the College or School Junta headed by the College Delegate, who now was elected every two years from the class representatives rather than appointed by SEU local authorities. The Syndicate Council of the Center included all the Class Councils, the heads of syndicate services, and the WS secretary. This organ held private meetings to discuss academic matters.

Local and provincial heads of the SEU and the head of the university district were chosen by being first proposed by academic authorities and the national secretary of the movement and then appointed by the national head of the SEU. The head of the university district participated in the administrative meetings of the college and counted upon the assistance of a Syndicate District Council, which assembled all the center's delegates, the heads of syndicate departments, the district head of the WS/SEU, and the district secretary of the SEU. The national head of the SEU was composed of several central departments, arranged by the 1958 reform as follows: auxiliary organs to the national head, the central secretary of the WS/SEU, and departments of the SEU National Services.[22]

The reform of 1958 was completed by a decree of 18 September 1961. But the government's attempts to democratize the SEU from within proved ineffective. Student mistrust originated in the contradictions present in the SEU's postulates and practices. Although the SEU officials proclaimed their interest in students' social and political involvement, in reality the student organization's actions were limited to academic matters. Finally, on 5 April 1965, the SEU was officially disolved, and the government replaced it with the Student Professional Associations, which were equally unpopular. The student social and political movement grew significantly from this point until the end of the regime.[23] By contrast, the WS survived until 1977, even after Franco's death. At the university level, the WS secretary of students and graduates continued carrying out the SEU's work and aspired to maintain a women's Falangist elite.

THE WS/SEU SECRETARIAT

Until the demise of the SEU in 1965, it had been mandated that college women join that organization, and those already affiliated with the WS were expected to carry out a proselytizing duty. The national secretary, Syra Manteola, pointed out in a circular letter of 6 March 1950 that

> It is of great importance that among the college women mandatorily enrolled in SEU, there be Falangist comrades affiliated with the WS and graduated from the "Juventudes" [Youth Front]. They must be completely united through the

syndicate activities, because this is the means to realize a true proselytizing campaign within the university and because this elite, even more than the UD [University District] officials, can instill a political interest and show to the growing amorphous mass our style and philosophy.

WS university graduates comprised the women's Falangist elite who discussed political matters at the organization's National Councils. Falangist university women considered themselves creators of a women's political consciousness. This activity, according to a report issued by the graduates' office, was "performed in the service of the majority" and would "open the path to political action dedicated to the minorities." A new professional woman would be the means by which the WS would regain its strength over the "educated woman," saving her from the bourgeois way of life that her preparation favored. The WS aspired to promote "currents of opinion in Spanish society about burning and important national issues" and to "boost, profit, and empower the action of Falangist elites in the professional and political domains."[24]

The WS had representatives in each of the SEU administrative agencies. Every six months, WS delegates in the University District Councils had to report on the development and problems of the WS activities in the three levels of education (elementary, secondary, and higher education) of their university districts. They were to report on each university district meeting for the national secretary of the WS/SEU and inform that office in case the meetings were not held.[25]

The WS/SEU was organized as a pyramid headed by Pilar Primo de Rivera. Its authorities were divided into several levels: national, university district, provincial, local, college or educational center, and university residence hall. The secretary of students and graduates answered to both the SEU and the national head of the WS. The main task of the WS/SEU was to organize a USS and to help affiliates to find jobs once they graduated. By the end of the 1950s, the organization tried to recruit its leadership from college students and graduates. They had been drawn from the cultural activities organized within student residence halls in Valencia, Salamanca, Valladolid, and Santiago and from the summer literacy courses arranged by Cheli Valcarce, head of the WS/SEU in the 1950s.[26]

The dual administrative and ruling roles of the central secretary of the WS/SEU were established in a joint circular order of October 1944 by the national heads of the WS and the SEU. The delegate of the WS/SEU described this arrangement in a report a few years later:

This, actually, has caused an interlacing of responsibilities, which on many occasions puts WS/SEU in an unstable and false position that is strongly reflected in its activities. Hence, considering the last few years' experience . . . we believe that it is necessary to determine and regulate the position of the WS/SEU with regard to the dual authority, clearly explaining in detail the duties of each, the Women's Section of the Movement and the head office of SEU, as well as the relation between the two, at the same time evaluating the activities already developed, to see what has to be rectified, what maintained, and what gaps are to be filled in the present work.[27]

The WS and SEU relations were based on the subordinate position of the WS. In this report, the WS national secretary proposed a revision, noting that the WS within the university community had a mission of its own. Such a mission was a dual one: on the one hand, to guide university syndication in accordance with the SEU, and on the other, to train women students in feminine matters. The responsibilities of the secretary of the WS/SEU were organized under the dual authority of the WS and SEU officials. The WS/SEU also had an auxiliary central command, a national inspector, and five departments: Personnel, Press and Propaganda, Social Service, Retreats and Residence Halls, and Physical Education. In addition, each university district had its own WS/SEU delegate, who was required to attend the National Councils.

The secretary of the WS/SEU promoted certain professional options for women graduates, especially within the teaching profession. Because of the WS's interest in covering those positions in colleges of education, the national delegation offered classes to graduate affiliates to prepare them for the government exams for teachers. Explicit ideological motives were behind this interest. To benefit from the preparation classes, graduates had to be affiliated with the WS and commit themselves to teach Falangist principles. Each WS university district secretary was to meet with all graduate affiliates and insist on this loyalty.

> You will emphasize the importance for the Falange, and for Spain, of an entire renovation of the Colleges of Education by introducing Falangist elements within the faculty. This should be done with the greatest discretion to make it available only to our members, for it is not beneficial for it to go beyond our community.[28]

Colleges of education prepared elementary school teachers, and by instilling a Falangist spirit in them, the WS secured its influence on Spain's younger generation. The selection of those teachers who would benefit from classes to prepare for the government exams was very strict and subject to the personal decision of the WS university district officials, who chose women affiliates who met the following conditions:

> 1. Professional commitment; be sure they study their career with vocation and interest even if they do not get the best grades.
> 2. Make sure they are trustworthy and interested in the exams, so that they do not leave us halfway through the preparation process, causing great inconvenience for everybody, as has happened frequently.

3. Be sure they are really incorporated into the Women's Section and we can be certain that once they pass they will carry out Falangist work and keep in touch with us. Our effort and economic investment are too big for us not to receive some compensation later on.[29]

Nonetheless, professional promotion of the WS affiliates did not constitute the most prominent duty of the WS/SEU secretariat. In accordance with article 34b of the *URL* of 1943, the administration of the University Social Service was more important. The USS depended exclusively on the national delegation of the WS. The unpopularity of this program among college women at the beginning of the 1950s brought about a revision of the USS and the implementation of a new USS plan. This decision was made at the meeting of women SEU officials in 1952 held to unify criteria about Social Service for college women.

> It is true that USS is unpopular within the university, just as all mandatory activities are unpopular. But this unpopularity is not so important that we need to modify the USS completely or to allow university women to perform the ordinary Social Service.
> We believe that all university women must provide Social Service according to the same plan.[30]

The new plan required the completion of a six-month USS for college women in two phases: instruction and practical training. The instruction was delivered in two periods: a winter course and a school retreat, which together would be worth two months of Social Service. Enrollment in the USS coincided with the university registration period at the beginning of the academic year. The winter course was mandatory for all first-year women students; it consisted of fifteen classes during the academic year on different topics related to the university community and the activities of the SEU. When the course concluded, the district secretary of the WS/SEU sent a detailed report to the central secretary.

The school retreat cost two hundred pesetas (about two dollars in today's currency) and lasted one month in a residence at the seaside or in the mountains. Attendance was mandatory for first-year students, who at the end of the retreat had to pass a series of oral and written exams on national syndicalism, religion, home economics, and physical education. The final exams on these subjects were graded by the Committee on Studies, composed of the local delegate of the WS, a religion instructor, the local secretary of instruction, the university district secretary of the WS/SEU, and the retreat director. The young women attending the retreat received a character and behavior evaluation (detailing their qualities and defects), which appeared in the Social Service record book along with the exam grades. Only those who passed obtained their Social Service record book; those who failed had to take additional exams. Women had to keep their Social Service record book as proof that they had done their service to the state, not only to receive their diploma at the end of their studies but also to get a driver's license or a passport.

A second phase, practical training, completed the USS. Young college women received a two-month credit toward the fulfillment of their Social Service for the home economics classes they had taken in high school. After the instruction phase was completed, they worked only two months more at the sewing workshops or offices of the WS.

The WS retreats were an important part of the organization's instruction process. Each year for a month, first-year college women lived together in a "pure" Falangist environment. The retreats were designed to provide a perfect women's Falangist universe and were administered by the Retreats and Residence Halls Department within the Secretariat of WS/SEU. Some retreats had different purposes; for example, some were designed for women performing USS or for elementary school teachers, whereas others were either dedicated to leaders' training or simply offered affiliates a summer vacation.

Special attention was given to university students who attended the summer retreats. They were required to wear a uniform (white shirt and blue skirt)[31] and apply themselves to understanding their familial and political duties. Domestic knowledge imparted by WS officials in WS schools and retreats offered Falangist women some professional promotion in itself. Once they graduated, they could work as instructors of home economics, physical education, or music. Home economics classes covered such topics as organization and management of the household, family relationships, and domestic education of the children. Far from being secluded at home performing their domestic duties, WS officials and members could develop active careers within the boundaries of the organization, though in the name of self-sacrifice, not emancipation.

The internal correspondence of the WS indicates a strict hierarchical management of the retreats. Pilar Primo de Rivera, in an official Circular Letter of 3 April 1957, noted the general norms for the instruction in the WS retreats and schools. The purpose was to inculcate in women feminine virtues covering a variety of facets: religious, political, and domestic instruction. Special attention to religious training included voluntary daily mass and mandatory attendance on Sundays and Catholic holidays. Detailed reading of the Gospel and congregational prayers constituted part of the religious program. To guide the liturgical life in the WS schools and retreats, officials used the *Liturgical Directory*, which was edited by the national delegation.

Political tutelage was also given great importance in the WS intern schools and retreats, where political instruction was imparted in an orderly fashion to attract female leadership. The entire group of women was subjected to WS influence, with the level of education of each group of women taken into account, so that very different material was given to future university leaders than to those women enrolled in ordinary Social Service. The doctrine of

command and spirit of leadership that inspired the political program was imparted by Falangist officials to train future WS leaders to lead the organization's activities. Self-awareness of their duty, which would become their life
and career, determined their conduct, Pilar Primo de Rivera emphasized:
"With their bearing and their behavior they will be more than instructors of a
course, but rather Falangists who perceive themselves as servants of a great
destiny, helping those they serve to shape the soul of the women students
subject to their discipline."[32]

The women officials in charge of WS intern programs were trained to consider themselves trustees of a national responsibility. They were to become
not mere supervisors who imposed the norms, but real matriarchs, exercising
a maternal social role that would compensate for the lack of a family of their
own and allow them to become exemplary social educators and "mothers."
The fact that they were performing a public function was socially accepted
because of the very nature of their work, which was carried out and perceived
as an extension of their domestic duties. One of their main responsibilities
was to facilitate the rationalization and good management of the household.
An official circular of Pilar Primo de Rivera concluded with a quotation from
the Holy Scriptures about the strong woman that the WS aspired to mold:

> She searches for wool and linen and does the work with her own hands. She is
> like the merchant ship, which brings its bread from afar. Before dawn she rises
> and prepares food for her family and the duties for her servants. She sees a field
> and buys it, and with her own hands she plants a vineyard. Her arms are
> strengthened and given force. She is content that her business goes well, and
> even at night her lamp does not go out. She takes the distaff in her hands, and
> makes the spindle dance. She extends her hand to the miserable and helps the
> needy. Her family does not fear the cold of the snow because all of them have
> double clothing. Covered with strength and grace, she smiles at the future. Wis-
> dom opens her mouth and on her tongue is the law of goodness. She watches
> for all her family and does not eat anything she does not earn herself.[33]

A life of self-denial and service (public and private) to others became the
leitmotiv of the Falangist women. Much in the same vein, María Dolores
Bermúdez Cañete, WS/SEU central secretary, prepared a lengthy report
(Circular Letter 8) in 1962 about the retreats' spiritual and instructional values. The retreats possessed a dual formative role: a general one directed to all
university women and another that was particularly aimed at molding a com-
manding elite. Women who showed promise in the general retreats were tar-
geted for more training in a series of other courses for college leaders.

> We invite those university women who are outstanding in their activities during
> the general instruction and who are eager to lead and guide, as a minority, the
> instruction of their university counterparts to attend a course for province

college leaders, a course for national college leaders, a course for province retreat leaders, a course for national retreat leaders, and a course for graduates at
La Mota Castle.

The appropriate training of leaders, thus, was crucial for molding university
women's minds and trying to make them accept the dictates of the regime.
WS officials realized that the indoctrination of university women required an
extra effort on their part.

> We must not forget that the university woman tends to rationalize everything . . .
> and our mission will be to teach her not to condemn the imponderable, what
> reason can not wholly accept: the world of sentiment, affection, generosity, and
> renunciation. But this will be achieved only by conviction, never by imposition.[34]

Exemplary conduct was necessary for a leader to succeed at her task of
"conviction." The posture and attitude of WS leaders was to be enthusiastic
and joyful. Those retreats dedicated to leadership had an elitist character, as
witnessed by this statement by National Secretary María Dolores Bermúdez
Cañete:

> [F]rom the retreat devoted to training leaders, each summer there emerges a
> new generation of intelligent, capable, model university women, conscious that
> they are elite, and responsible before God and Spain, university women who
> know their leading mission in the destiny of the fatherland. And if they perceive
> the long-term calling, there is no doubt about their immediate performance as
> an elite of the university body, which is a small part of the Spanish community.

Retreats took on multiple dimensions: religious, political, cultural, athletic, and
especially feminine. The religious dimension was characterized by a profound
liturgical meaning. The retreat chaplain served as a spiritual counselor for each
individual and taught religion classes, which were intended to instill a moral
and social consciousness that would make the women better leaders. The political instruction inculcated in university women a sense of belonging to an elite
with a social purpose. "The university elite must serve a political ideal. They as-
sume the responsibility of being the leadership of the community."[35]

College women's professional development was secondary to their motherly destiny through marriage, which was their main political and national
duty. If college women did not get married, they could have an impact in the
community through the WS. But college women's political involvement was
conceived to serve society with their professional skills, based primarily on
their sense of devotion and service rather than on competitiveness. Retreat
life motivated college women to get involved in their community. Political instruction was intended to link their vocation to the fatherland's permanent
Falangist reconstruction. The cultural, athletic, and feminine dimensions of

the retreats completed the moral and spiritual training of the residents. The feminine dimension included home economics, arts and crafts, infant care, cooking, and practical questions of social etiquette.

The WS/SEU's task in the 1950s entailed the preservation of traditional Spanish femininity. Though college women who belonged to SEU were the intellectual elite of Falangist women, their future roles as wives and prolific mothers were considered of first importance. Women of WS/SEU developed their own discourse on Catholic womanhood in an attempt to reconcile the contradiction between their identity as scholars and the feminine ideal the regime demanded.

COLLEGE WOMEN'S SELF-PERCEPTIONS

By the beginning of the 1960s, WS officials began to acknowledge a membership crisis and to worry about the general apathy of young women toward the organization. María Dolores Bermúdez Cañete's report to the Twenty-Third National Council of the WS, held in Gerona in January 1966, addressed these issues and attributed them to political and technical causes. According to Bermúdez Cañete, by the mid-1960s the WS lacked appeal for young women because they were becoming reluctant to enter a devalued political organization. Furthermore, the Falangist women's organization offered very limited professional opportunities to educated women. Nonetheless, the WS filled the vacuum left in the university domain by the breakup of the SEU in 1965. A year later, the secretary of students and graduates of the WS undertook an extensive study of the university student community and produced a document on women college students entitled *Female University Youth in Spain*.[36] Two sociologists, María Angeles Durán Heras and Juan Antonio Pereda Linacero, both from the University of Madrid, directed the project.

The target population studied was 1,334 first- and second-year young women who were attending their USS retreats during the academic year 1961–1962. They answered a survey that generally avoided any questions regarding the WS, the nature of the retreat, or the Falange in general. Some thirty-five university women who were performing the USS practical phase processed the data. The questionnaires were divided into six parts: the first dealt with general information regarding the university district to which the student belonged; the second asked about professional aspects, students' dedication, and later expectations; the third referred to family life, particularly the young woman's attitudes toward her own family, her friends, love, and marriage; and the fourth focused on religious issues. Parts five and six centered on students' interest and participation in social life and politics. Of the target women, 94 percent were between eighteen and nineteen years old; 75 percent had studied in private Catholic schools, and 16 percent had attended public high schools; and 68 percent lived at home while going to college. (It is important to point out here that Spanish women could not abandon the family household until they were twenty-five years old unless they married or entered a convent, as stipulated by the *Civil Code* of 1958.) Those who were over twenty-five and had gone to study in another city or had moved in from the countryside lived with their relatives in some instances or in university residence halls run either by religious orders or by the WS. According to the report, women who were only children met more opposition to leaving their homes. All the women belonged to middle- or upper-middle-class families. College expenses were being paid by parents in the case of 89 percent of the women; 7 percent combined their parents' support with a grant; only 2 percent worked to pay for their studies. College women whose parents belonged to the middle class made up 75 percent of the group; of those, 39 percent were in the so-called liberal professions that included lawyers, doctors, engineers, and professors. The report noted the elitist nature of college education at the time: "In short, nowadays the university is limited to women from upper, upper-middle and middle-middle classes, and its access is almost impossible for girls from working-class families from agriculture or industry."[37]

With regard to religious attitudes, the report showed an interesting profile: 93 percent considered themselves believers, practicing Catholics, and 41 percent received communion daily. Only 3 percent did so less than once a year, and 6 percent preferred not to answer this question. The figures differ for different university districts. Barcelona, Zaragoza, and Madrid showed higher percentages of women who were not practicing Catholics, but there are no data for other districts. Although only 6 percent were familiar with the Second Vatican Council, the whole group was equally divided when confronted with the question of marrying a non-Catholic. All acknowledged the problems such a situation would entail, but 50 percent would do so anyway.[38]

Answers to the question on college women's political preferences revealed a lack of firm and developed opinions. When asked what political form they desired for Spain, 37 percent responded that they had never thought about it, and 24 percent preferred not to answer. Nonetheless, of the former, 40 percent proposed democratic systems and 17 percent mentioned the republican form of government as their preference. Those in favor of prolonging the current political situation constituted 81 percent of the total.[39]

The section that dealt with students' career orientation and professional expectations discussed the concentration of women in certain careers rather than others. Half of the girls studied the sciences, and the other half, the humanities. Many chose a career because their family resided close to a particular college or university, but in most cases they took into account what was appropriate for a woman to study. Pharmacy and philosophy and letters remained the most popular and were considered the most feminine, although all of the women believed that no differentiation between feminine and nonfeminine professions should exist. Respondents were realistic, though, in noting the problems encountered by women who combined marriage and a professional career and the difficulties related to the nature of each career that created major obstacles (some were too time-consuming and arduous to allow women to devote themselves to their domestic duties). Most of the students interviewed thought that, for a woman who abandoned her studies for marriage, a career in the humanities would always give her some "general education." They also recognized moral and aesthetic factors that limited women's access to careers too rough or dangerous for them, such as medicine or law.[40]

A culture of romance affected these young women's attitudes about the pursuit of a career and later professional life. Love was central to their lives; professional options took second place in their priorities. For example, 77 percent (1,023) would abandon their career to marry; 14 percent (189) would not; and 9 percent (122) did not respond. They considered it ideal to get married between twenty-one and twenty-five years of age. With regard to family size (the national average number of children was 5.8), the ideal for these young women was between 4 and 6 children. This strong inclination toward large families was a result of family background (89 percent belonged to upper-class or upper-middle-class families), very religious feelings (93 percent considered themselves practicing Catholics), and youth (96 percent were younger than twenty years old).[41]

. . .

In June of 1989, I interviewed two former affiliates of the WS from the University of Granada. Neither woman married, and today both are high school teachers in one of the oldest and most popular male high schools in the city, now a coeducational institution. We met at the school, and the interview occurred in the faculty lounge. Remembering their past was "quite difficult, quite exciting." Suddenly, they began to remember things they had always considered unimportant, since they had never thought their lives would become a historical matter. Above all, they let me feel their nostalgia and tried to explain their past decisions in the light of their present situation.

Clara González was born in Granada and María Leiva in Córdoba. Both of their families had lived in the city for generations. Clara's father, with his brother, owned a grocery store, a good business: two families lived off its proceeds. Her uncle had seven children and Clara had three sisters. "Only sisters, four girls," she said.

> Well, I have been from Granada all my life, from Granada for three or four generations. My father was a merchant, and my mother a housewife, which was what was in those days, wasn't it? And at home the first one to study a university career . . . well and the only one that has studied a university career has been me. Because later my sister finished nursing. And I had another [sister] who became a lab technician.[42]

Clara studied chemistry between 1960 and 1965 and has worked as a teacher since graduation. María Leiva studied history during the same years. She and Clara "are like sisters" because they have known each other since high school and went to USS retreat together. Maria went on to explain:

> Well, me too, my family [has been] from Granada always. I was born in Córdoba and have lived some years in Madrid, but from my father's and mother's side, and my grandparents and everybody [have been] from Granada for a very, very long time. I do have brothers and sisters, and for example, my brothers could study in another city because my parents would pay. But we [the sisters] had to resign ourselves to study here. Because I mentioned the possibility of going to Madrid to study languages, and they told me I could go if I wanted but they would not give me any money. If I wanted to study here, it was fine because here it was not as costly. Besides, my father was a teacher in high school and a military pharmacist. He would have liked me to study pharmacy. But he did not have a pharmacy store because he did not have any money. And then I thought, what do I want pharmacy for if I don't have any money? And then, I don't know, sciences were too difficult for me. So in the end I did letters.

When I asked María about her mother, she said: "My mother was a housewife. My mother had a so-called 'general education.' A little of piano, a little bit of nothing."[43]

Although both Clara and María belonged to large families of Granada's petty bourgeoisie, they never married. They acknowledged the deep religiosity of their families. María referred to it in a jolly tone of voice: "Well yes . . . everybody [was] very religious. Everybody went to church, [they were] conservative, religious." Clara was more solemn about this issue. A sister who died some years ago belonged to the women of Catholic Action, and she herself was part of Catholic Action Student Youth during her college years. She explained:

> Going to Mass is still a tradition, because my father has been always a very honest person, and he has inspired this in us. We have seen it not as an imposition but rather as something natural, lived by him. He taught us how to forgive others, how to be generous with others. We have accepted it as something positive, not as something imposed. So, I think that is the reason why my sisters and I have been so. [silence][44]

María remembered her father's religiosity as different from that of her mother:

> Well, my father is very methodical, with a very strict religiosity, more papist than the Pope, as my uncle Pedro the priest says. And my mother is much more open. I mean, she accepts others' ways, doesn't she? Even modern things, and

she reads a lot and so on. So she is open to other ideas and other things. But not my father. My father is much more rigid, in the sense of very strict in conscience. Too much.[45]

When asked about the Civil War and whether their families talked about it, they immediately responded in a serious tone that they hardly discussed it, "just a few episodes." For Clara's family, the war was very difficult.

It was a very painful topic for my father, for example, who had a hard time. Because they even had workers who were, let's just say, leftists, and of course they [her parents] had to hide them. They knew there had been some persecution. So they tried to stay away from those topics at home. You know, in the families there was less dialogue in those days between parents and children. I know my father hid some people. He hid his employees because he knew they would be shot.[46]

María's family lived in the Albaicín, the oldest part of town, a beautiful neighborhood of white houses on the hill facing the Alhambra. Granada was taken and remained Nationalist all through the war, but the Republicans resisted for a few days in this district of the city.

[My parents] had a terrible time in the Albaicín. Because the Albaicín was taken by the Reds and they set up barricades, they [her parents] who lived in a *Carmen* [Grenadine house following the Arab architectural style] had to jump the garden's walls and escape, and they had a hard time. But it was not talked about. Some things were told. My mother used to recount how bombs were thrown and fell in the archiepiscopal palace, and that they hid. But those were little tiny bombs, because they were not very effective. It's true, she said that a bomb laid in a trunk. They went into a basement or something. They [her parents] were helping the family downstairs; he was a law professor and everything was taken from them and they had nothing to eat, so all the war they [her parents] were helping them. And she [her mother] says that it was the most unjust thing. And they [her parents] here in Granada did not notice anything very much. They heard the singing of the *Giovenezza* by Italians who came . . . but no, no they did not have a bad time, because here in Granada they didn't feel it. My grandfather used to say, "We are orderly people."[47]

Clara finished by saying:

In short, they tell you very few things. My parents have not been very political. My father disregarded politics; he never liked to be affiliated with anything, or anything like that. He kept his blue shirt [Falangist shirt] to wear when he was on duty, because he had to live on this side [she refers to the Nationalist side; silence], and maybe if he had been living on the other side he would have cooperated [silence].[48]

Moving to their personal experiences in college, they both remembered not being able to get any fellowships. Their parents paid for their studies, and to a certain extent this determined their career choices. Clara reported that, after talking to her father, she resolved to study chemistry instead of mathematics.

> I knew they [her parents] couldn't pay for me to study in another city. I liked mathematics more than chemistry. But my father posed the dilemma to me. Chemistry I could study in Granada, but for mathematics I had to move at least to Sevilla. We couldn't afford to do that. And I couldn't even get a fellowship. Once I tried in my second year to apply for a tuition waiver, and at the college they said, "How being the daughter of Antonio González do you dare to apply for a tuition waiver?" [heated tone][49]

Neither Clara nor María remembered any mention or discussion of the 1961 *Law of Political, Professional, and Labor Rights of Women.* Clara joined the SEU by pure coincidence. She had been buying her supplies at the syndicate's cooperative, and after a local USS retreat, some members of the SEU asked her to stop by and visit the office.

> Then, when I came, as I told you we used to go and buy all the material at the SEU's cooperative. So they told me at the retreat, "Look, when you go around there at the SEU, come and visit us." And then I went and they told me, "Look, why don't you take charge of the basketball team? See if you get funding, because you have the right to get some money; otherwise the boys take everything and so forth." I remember going to those meetings where the dean, representatives of professors, and students attended. And they told me, "You go to those meetings and say that since you are in charge of the basketball team, you request money for some uniforms and so on, because there is a quota of participation." I found out then, there was a quota of participation out of the money we paid to the SEU that went to pay for extra-academic activities in the university. They said "No, if you don't request that, everything goes to the boys, and they have everything . . . they get balls . . . and so forth, you go complain because you have the right." And I went and made the request. And we got the money for our uniforms. We got them made and were playing all year around.[50]

Clara's memories focus on the playful aspect of her affiliation; not once did she mention any political consciousness or involvement. Clara and María agreed that the most significant part of the WS presence in the lives of university students was their summer retreats. Clara told me cheerfully about her experiences and how she perceived life at a retreat.

> They made you get up in the morning and first thing go to pray, then [there was] a very busy schedule. You had physical education, then some free time.

Normally, you had some time for recreation if there was a pool. For example, at the Viznar retreat we had a pool, so we had some time to swim. At the Gredos retreat we went to bathe in the river and were not very lucky. We went down to the river, and when we came back there always was a thunderstorm. We used to say "Oh well, we had our shower." And then we got to the retreat and there was no water. We got a shower all dressed. We came back from the river in our swimsuits and the rain showered us.[51]

María was a leader in WS/SEU for a year right after graduation, when she was only twenty-two years old. She remembered that the way she got involved was very casual, since she was not interested in the politics of the organization but rather was searching for a job.

But then in 1965 when I finished, the former "regidora," that was the title, she was secretary of the SEU, [who] belonged to the WS within the SEU, either got married or was going to, and she asked me, "Do you want to work in the office?" and I didn't have a job that year, so I said, "All right." I didn't know it was related to anything [silence] . . . nothing more than office work. I had an office in Santa Paula [street in Granada], and then I had to go down to Paseo de la Bomba [street where the WS's central offices were located]. So that year I was in charge of supervising a little bit how the practical training phase of USS was progressing. I don't even remember what they did; I guess the girls would do clerical work or something like that. And then I prepared for the retreat. And that summer I had to organize and direct the retreat all by myself. Besides that summer, since there were fewer and fewer retreats because they were very expensive, I had all of the Sevilla and Granada university districts, around 80 [participants], I remember. And later I was told that I was receiving the district of Valencia as well, and 80 more arrived. Can you imagine?[52]

María remembered all the women who helped her carry out her duties. She was in command of fifteen women who taught home economics and physical education. She was in charge of the political indoctrination class.

I had to teach politics, and of course, since I had no previous experience at all, I didn't teach anything. There were some little programs to follow [silence] that the class passed by. Then we had to teach sewing in the afternoon, physical education in the morning, and later at night we had campfires with play representations, songs, and so on. Walks in the afternoon, free time. . . . Anyway the retreat was a huge stupidity.[53]

María does not remember indoctrination as an important part of the retreat she directed in the summer of 1966. She not only does not remember the political implications of her job that summer but even devalues them by calling the whole experience a "huge stupidity." With hindsight, she thinks of

her participation as something totally circumstantial: "Well, I just got enrolled." When I asked María for an evaluation of those years, she said:

> An experience. A very hard and laborious experience, but in the end, just that, an
> experience. I mean, it is not that I regret it, but I did immediately disenroll myself.
> Because . . . all that didn't make any sense anymore in that time. Because the stu-
> dents used to complain. They got along very well. So the retreat went very well,
> but it was something without meaning. And I wondered, "How did it happen
> that I got into this?" Later, you tell yourself, "All right, it was an experience."[54]

Both Clara and María remember their participation in the WS as a mere circumstance, stripped of any political consciousness. Going to the WS retreats
represented an opportunity to socialize with other young women and enjoy a
summer vacation. The participation of women in the Falangist enterprise has
been analyzed from polarized positions that accentuate only a guilt and
blame cycle. In Clara's and Maria's words we can read between the lines a
sort of justification a posteriori. They try somehow to make sense of a now-
embarrassing past, particularly in the case of María, who was a leader in one
of those retreats.

The evaluation of women's experiences under Francoism brings out issues
of "guilt" or "responsibility." Spanish feminist scholars emphasized the subordinate position of WS women within the Falange, whereas Falangist
women leaders remembered those days as full of solidarity, dedication, and
empowerment. For Clara and María, for example, they were years of personal
self-discovery and growth. They remembered their experiences within the WS
devoid of any political consciousness; instead, they believe they joined the
Falangist organization by accident. As Kathleen M. Blee points out, American
women members of the Ku Klux Klan had similar experiences:

> The women's klan of the 1920s was not only a way to promote racist, intoler-
> ant, and xenophobic policies but also a social setting in which to enjoy their
> own racial and religious privileges. These women recall their membership in one
> of U.S. history's most vicious campaigns of prejudice and hatred primarily as a
> time of friendship and solidarity among like-minded women.[55]

The WS retreats offered both Clara and María the opportunity to enjoy a certain independence from parental control; and since they never married, in the
long run they never assumed any type of domestic duty as prescribed by the
Francoist official ideology.

The same dynamics of guilt/victimization and responsibility emerged in
the analysis of the role of women under National Socialism. According to
Claudia Koonz, "Nazi women shared many assumptions of other women activists in Weimar politics. Accepting conventional stereotypes about women's
special nature, they worked to improve women's public status."

Women in other political movements took their concerns into the male-dominated political sphere. But Nazi women, like members of nonpartisan Catholic and Protestant organizations, worked outside the political framework altogether. Rather than competing in the men's world, they expanded their own sphere beyond men's direct intervention, relying on men for protection against external enemies. Nazi women calculated realistically that women had not achieved sufficient force to make much of an impact on men. Their experience bred the cynical prediction that men would never change. Whereas feminists worked for an egalitarian future, conservatives spun out a vision of a past that never had been, in which strong men dominated public space and tender women guarded humane values. Nazi women accepted the promise of second-sex membership in Hitler's movement in exchange for the hope of preserving their own womanly realm against male interference.

Koonz's book opened a heated debate among German feminist scholars who discussed issues of women's victimization or responsibility under National Socialism. In 1989, Gisela Bock, one of the most prominent women's historians in Germany, lashed out at Koonz's thesis. In Bock's view, National Socialism was particularly pernicious for women because it invaded their maternal sphere, which the author romanticized as being women's own. Whereas Bock considered that the Nazis' crime consisted of denying women motherhood and attacking motherly values, for Koonz the crime consisted of instrumentalizing motherhood as a mobilizing tool.[56]

As the Nazi women did, the WS created a women's state within the regime that survived the regime itself. The transitional nature of the 1950s offered the WS the opportunity to fill the vacuum left by the Falange in the political scene and by the SEU at the university level. The regime confronted the challenge of modernization. At this juncture, Franco opted for the Opus Dei formula of economic rationalization and got rid of the Falangist elements in his new cabinets. The 1950s, however, proved to be pivotal in the evolution of the WS. It became the guardian of Falangist values and created a power space of its own with a women's interpretation of Joseantonian principles. The women of the WS redefined Spanish femininity, preserving true Catholic womanhood as the country ventured into modernity. Family, municipality, and syndicate constituted the three pillars of the new state and the only sites for political participation. By making the family and domestic duties their main concern, Falangist women placed themselves in the center of the political arena. They relied on men only for the enactment of their own domestic agenda, which was presented, however, in a nonthreatening fashion, never with a feminist flavor.

At the university level, the WS confronted the dilemma of reconciling domesticity with intellectual aspirations. In its zeal to preserve true Catholic womanhood, the WS developed a list of so-called feminine professions that included nursing and teaching. Aside from those, the careers most populated by women were philosophy and letters and pharmacy; very few chose law or medicine.

At the Cold War political juncture, Falangist women proclaimed themselves to be the guardians of the humane values of the Falange and the regime. The WS became the Francoist state's vehicle in the nationalization of Spanish women. The WS's tame discourse on femininity was not different from those of the state and the Catholic Church, yet it granted them the opportunity to be agents in the national enterprise. Nonetheless, with the advent of modernization, the influence of the WS agenda on Spanish women began to wane.

IN THEIR OWN WORDS
Women in Higher Education

"In Spain, the Women's Section was given the task of formatting women. The Women's Section prepared perfect women, but only perfect housewives, perfect child-bearers. Or that single woman, a little mannish in her ways, whose role consisted in devoting herself to prepare others. But that was all. So when you stepped out of that mold, you were completely out of place."

—Purificación Prieto, Madrid, 20 October 1994

In addition to the WS, other organizations existed in which Spanish university women developed a public persona. Among these, three were most important: the Teresian Institute, Catholic Student Youth within Catholic Action, and the Association of Spanish University Women. They presented alternatives to the WS and shaped a discourse of their own on Catholicism in contrast to the official one on true Catholic womanhood. These organizations were also different from the WS in that they lacked a political agenda. Although they challenged univocal Catholic womanhood, their Catholicism safeguarded them from official control and allowed them space to pursue knowledge in spite of the official discouragement of the woman scholar. The personal experiences of the leaders and members of these organizations link past and present as a unique reality, for memory is subject to present political and social conventions. Present realities affect one's memory of past experiences.[1]

Oral sources refer to and emanate from a sphere that historian Luisa Passerini calls *subjectivity*. Memory is the production of meanings. The use of oral sources enlarges the scope of historical analysis and includes the subjective hopes, dreams, and interpretations of its subjects.[2] Oral sources also show a multifaceted relationship between the informants and institutional power in the past and in the present. The way informants remember their experiences is a result of present political and social constraints and conventions. Analyzing the life stories of these women reveals not only how they related to power institutions (such as the university) but also how their discourses shaped such relationships. The power dynamics here are the result of the link between the past and the present. The very fact that they created their own definition of the female self empowers them and illuminates issues of women's agency within the Francoist regime. The analysis of this issue of the agency of women within a dictatorship brings up the question of the ideological nature of the regime when explored from a gender perspective. The contested discourses of Catholic womanhood highlight the limits of state control, especially when confronted with a modern consumer economy.

THE TERESIAN INSTITUTE

The origins of the Teresian Institute date to the turn of the century. Its founder, father Pedro Poveda Castroverde, created this pious union to foster the pursuit of knowledge among women.

> In our program we place knowledge after faith, or rather we place them together at the same level. You are daughters of God and Knowledge, daughters of whom the Holy Scripture says "Deus Scientiarum, Dominus est." The author of faith and knowledge is only one, God, and the subject of that faith and knowledge is the human creature. I asked you the other day to be women of much faith; living faith, felt faith, and never say no more faith. I also tell you today: long for knowledge, seek knowledge, acquire knowledge, work to obtain it and never desist, or ever say no more knowledge. Much knowledge leads us to God, little knowledge alienates us from Him.[3]

The history of the Teresian Institute (TI) is inseparable from the life of its founder. Father Pedro Poveda Castroverde was born in Linares (Jaén) in 1874 and was executed by the Republican militia in Madrid in the summer of 1936, at the beginning of the Civil War. Ordained in 1897, he graduated three years later in theology at the University of Sevilla. From the beginning of his ministry, he showed a passion for education. In 1902 he moved to Guadix, a village near Granada, and opened first a shelter and later a school for the poor people who lived in the outskirts of the city in caves, poverty stricken and ignorant. Teresa Barrenechea (born in San Sebastián in 1914), general vice director of the TI in the 1950s, recounts Poveda's first pedagogical experiences as she explains the origins of the institute:

> [Father Poveda], a young zealous priest, started going out there and he realized that those poor people had no words to defend themselves . . . because they could not read or write, and they hungered, they simply didn't know how to express themselves. So he thought that the first thing to do was to seek the means to better their living, so at least the children could eat, open some dining rooms and then educate them, teach them to read and write. [Poveda] considered that if they learned to read and write they could defend themselves, but if they didn't . . . well, they would never have a voice to defend themselves. And he founded some schools. And he sought help in many places. He went to see the king, he sought other support and went out to the surrounding villages to beg, etc. . . . and he was very successful.[4]

In tune with social-Catholic reformers such as Andrés Manjón and Ramón Ruiz Amado at the turn of the century, Father Poveda perceived education as both the path to salvation and the key to social betterment. He considered the articulation of a Christian educational program crucial for Spain to achieve modernization. However, Poveda's work at the caves in Guadix became the target of deep anticlericalism at the time, and this situation prompted him to move to Covadonga (Asturias) in the north, where he accepted a canonry in 1905. During the next six or seven years Poveda produced several pedagogical writings refining his Christian concept of education, which was in contrast with the secularization of government education. The Free Institution of Learning, active at the same time, responded to the lay spirit of the period. The Ministry of Public Instruction initiated in 1902 a policy in this direction with a series of decrees that imposed state primary education, voluntary study of religion as one subject in school, and the requirement that teachers of private schools pursue a state teaching license. Along the same line with regard to higher education, the Junta for Postdoctoral Studies and Scientific Research was established in 1907. According to Barrenechea, Poveda believed that "one who can read and write and is a good Christian possesses three wings [sic] to be able to struggle in life." He envisioned an education that took into account man as a whole, born to be part of society and civilization, who would never deny his essence as a creature of God.[5]

Poveda also understood the potential and valuable contribution of women to the learning process. By a royal decree of 8 March 1910, women were allowed to teach from primary school to university level, and the same year the government created the Professional and Home School for Women. This development attracted Poveda's attention to the Normal Schools. His *Pedagogical Essay* (1911) contains the core of his educational message and his proposal for a national plan for a Catholic educational program under the supervision of the Church hierarchy. The essay's educational guidelines would be developed within academies, conceived as centers for the training of professors and teachers in the spirit of the Holy Scripture. As Barrenechea points out, Poveda did not want to create schools in the traditional sense but rather as a space where teachers and students cooperated in the learning venture.[6]

The very same year that *Pedagogical Essay* came out, Poveda opened two academies, one for men in Gijón and another for women in Oviedo. The latter, called the Academy of Saint Teresa, was inspired by the figure of Saint Teresa de Avila. He named it for Saint Teresa, says Barrenechea, "because he found her to have her feet on the ground; she was human, completely human, but at the same time profoundly transfixed by a life of God—a woman who prayed, who had a relationship with God, an extraordinary woman." He celebrated Saint Teresa in his *Spiritual Warnings of Saint Teresa de Jesús* as the prototype of the educated Spanish woman. Saint Teresa's spirit should permeate the academy's life. "Nobody else but this phenomenal woman, doctor of the universal Church, Spanish, and saint, could guide the path for those women devoted to teaching, who are proud of being Spanish, who aspire to sanctity, and consecrate themselves to this task."[7] In 1912 and 1913, two other Teresian academies for women were founded in Linares and Jaén, respectively. But the TI did not receive official Church sanction until 1924. Pius XI's pontifical brief *Inter Frugiferas* approved and recognized the TI as a "Pious Union."

At this point, the TI interested young women with a passion for learning, ready to devote their lives to the task. When asked why it appealed more to women than men, Teresa Barrenechea responded:

> Well, I don't know what to tell you. I can just say that that was the historical reality. The historical reality is that women understood him [Poveda] more or their needs were greater, or who knows. . . . And to be a teacher in Spain was the very last thing a man could do. But for a woman it represented a promotion, since she did not find employment in other areas, because she couldn't work in a bank, or a post office, or those kinds of places, because she still wasn't allowed, that path remained closed. [Teaching] became a respectful way into society and having a job and being capable. . . . And then also, since teaching is tied to motherhood, women had more qualities to take care of children, etc.[8]

Barrenechea emphasizes women's nurturing qualities to explain their devotion to Poveda's project. They saw it as a respectable way out of their predetermined domestic destiny as mothers and wives. The assumed motherly instinct of every woman would be fulfilled in the TI as she offered her life to teaching others.

Two women particularly embodied ideal Teresian womanhood: Antonia López Arista and Josefa Segovia, both of whom became teachers in their early twenties. They were described in the institute's histories as "studious, reflective, generous with others, happy, deeply spiritual human beings." According to Barrenechea, Poveda met Josefa Segovia through a priest he knew in Jaén. Before World War I, Segovia entered the College of Education in Madrid when she was only sixteen. There she studied sciences at a time when the school offered only three diplomas: sciences, humanities, and home economics. Upon her return to Jaén in 1914, Segovia met Poveda and became so excited about his project that she went against her parents' will and offered to direct the academy of Jaén. God's calling was the only acceptable justification for a young woman's parental disobedience. Antonia López Arista, a cousin of Poveda, was appointed director of the academy in Linares. Well aware of their qualities, Poveda selected the two women to govern not only the academies but the Teresian venture. But Arista died in 1918 as a result of the Spanish influenza, and Segovia was appointed the first general director of the TI, serving from 1919 until her death in 1957. She became the ideal of the Teresian woman that Poveda aspired to forge, what Barrenechea defines as the "intellectual woman":

> And certainly, she became later the incarnation of Pedro Poveda's idea, the idea of "intellectual women." Educated women, prepared. Women who had gone to college and had studied, etc. . . . But then, women ready to influence at all levels, from the legislative level of education to the schools, the university . . . to exercise their influence at all levels. I mean, not just as a mere teacher who arrives at a village simply because she is making a living, but with vocation, with the desire to realize a whole task, to educate parents and youth, to cooperate with the priest . . . to be an active element in the village.[9]

Those "intellectual women" became the quintessence of the Teresian Institute. They embodied the combination of knowledge and femininity that was only possible through the power of their Catholic faith and their renunciation of worldly temptations. Poveda wanted to contest the idea that Catholicism and backwardness went together, or that Spain's decadence derived from its Christian tradition. He disagreed with the view that laicization represented the only solution for achieving modernization and social improvement. During the Second Republic (1931–1939), the process of laicization accelerated. Article 26 of the Constitution of 1931 proposed the dissolution of religious orders that had an obedience vow to an authority different from the state. In 1932 the Society of Jesus was dissolved, and by a law of 1933 clergy were forbidden from teaching. But in spite of the Republican efforts to secularize the educational system, the TI continued to found several university residence halls for women in the 1930s. The first was in Madrid, and other establishments followed in the districts of Valladolid, Salamanca, Santiago, Zaragoza, Granada, and Valencia.

Father Poveda dedicated some writings to university women: *Faith,*

Virtue, Science, You Are the Chosen Elite, and *About Learning* were written in 1920 and *To University Women: Our Program* in 1930. All of them were published for the first time at the beginning of the 1960s by Angeles Galino, a member of the institute. The publication of Poveda's writings represented an attempt of the TI to evaluate the economic and political changes that the country underwent in the 1950s. The new consumer culture required an up-to-date reading of the founder's teachings. These writings described the pedagogical and spiritual essence of the Teresian woman. Poveda's approach to women's education derived from his conviction that women were the heart of society and that their moral superiority freed them from corruption. Such moral superiority had to be preserved while educating them in a strictly male curriculum. Poveda's objective entailed educating women to be "[e]ducated, virtuous, healthy of body and soul, but as women not as men; with the characteristics proper to their sex elevated to perfection, but never confusing the perfection of their sex by judging, as mistakenly happens, that the most perfect woman is one who imitates men."[10]

Being well educated opened possibilities in the public realm. Therefore, the aim of women's education in modern society was to make women better mothers, Christian educators, and professionals. Poveda's message served well during the transitional nature of the decade. His writings attempted to redefine women's influence in society as coactors with men. Preserving women's Catholicism and rejecting the assumed atheism of feminist discourses were the goals.

> Strict justice demands that women be active participants with men in the configuration of a more humane world.
> Who ever would have thought that the cultivation of thinking does not square with women?[11]

Poveda refuted those who believed that, for women to be pious, they should remain uneducated. Teresian women embodied the Catholic woman intellectual, whose virtue rested on knowledge. The character traits emphasized most in Teresian training were strong will, self-discipline, and prudence. A Teresian woman would possess a solid faith in Jesus Christ and the Catholic Church and would evaluate modern world problems from a Christian perspective that sought truth and justice.[12] Their faith and religious vows differentiated them from other women's organizations such as the WS or Catholic Action.

Jesus was the driving force, the foundation, the model; He was everything. "For us the word of God," says Barrenechea, "the Gospel, of the New and Old Testaments, is our guidance to act by imitating Jesus, who was a man among men and never rejected anybody . . . for us, first of all, this is a vocation, a calling, because it will demand renunciation." The main vow that Teresian women made was that of celibacy, which allowed them, according to

Barrenechea, "to devote [themselves] completely" to Poveda's project. The founder expected from them an absolute dedication and total devotion.[13] Mysticism and castimony (the union of the religious with Jesus Christ) was the alternative to marriage and the path taken by women in Catholic tradition. Certainly, celibacy constituted an important vow for Teresian women. Although both men and women were members of the TI at its beginning, women incarnated the Teresian ideal that Poveda sought. Because women entering the institute renounced their biological destiny as mothers and instead espoused chastity, their religious commitment and sexual purity made them socially respectable and redeemed them from any accusation that they had a deviant interest in knowledge per se. Their virginity was an intentional rather than an accidental state, resting, as scholar Jo Ann Kay McNamara points out, "on a concept of the soul and even the body as malleable to the perfect will."[14]

Chaste celibacy allowed Teresian women to escape a domestic destiny and to engage in intellectual endeavors reserved historically to men. It was precisely their celibacy and the renunciation of biological sex that somehow erased gender differences. This gender-blind philosophy was based on the assumption of the triumph of the soul over the body that would encourage cooperation rather than antagonism between the sexes in worldly matters. In the eyes of God, the souls of men and women were equal. With the challenge of modernity, women were supposed to participate in the public sphere, but within the Christian parameters promoted by the Catholic Church in general and Poveda's project in particular. Teresian women's celibacy fostered their independence and the development of an intellectual and professional life that continued a tradition developed throughout history by nuns, who had created, in McNamara's words, "the image and reality of the autonomous woman. They formed the professions through which that autonomy was activated."[15]

To become a member of the TI, one was (and still is) required to be a practicing Catholic, to be twenty-one years or older, to accept the institute's spirit, and to possess a Christian and cultural education (normally a technical or college degree). Members were divided according to their specific vocation and commitments into a Primary Association and Collaborating Associations. The Primary Association, made up exclusively of a core of women devoted to the institute's task, was the driving force of the TI. The Collaborating Associations of the Teresian Institute could be local, regional, national, or international, and each had its own statutes. The Primary Association has always directed the institute. A general assembly, a general director, and a government council exist within the Primary Association. Each Collaborating Association has an assembly, a president (either a man or a woman), and a directing junta.[16] During the 1950s, Pius XII declared the TI a secular institute under *Provida Mater,* but the institute fought and finally regained in 1990 its original canonical status. The internal structure remained untouched during all those years, and the core of TI women extended the Teresian spirit through-out the world.

The TI was already established in Portugal, Italy, and Chile during the life of Pedro Poveda, and with Josefa Segovia, the institute began to enter non-Latin countries as well. Teresa Barrenechea became part of the Primary Association's governing council in 1950 and was in charge of the international re-lations of the institute until the death of the general director, Segovia, in 1957. In the early 1950s, Barrenechea and a few other members of the insti-tute were offered the opportunity to teach in the Catholic University of Peking. To prepare themselves for this mission, they went to London to study English and Chinese. The Korean War prevented them from going to China, but Barrenechea moved to Ireland and later to the United States. During the 1950s, she became the bearer of Pedro Poveda's idea, and the TI expanded throughout Europe and Latin America.[17]

Teresian women believed that only through knowledge could they perfect their spiritual essence. In 1953, María Angeles Galino, a member of the insti-tute, was the first woman to occupy the History of Education chair at the Uni-versidad Complutense de Madrid. A year later the TI published *Eidos*, a jour-nal of scholarly works and creative writing, founded especially for the members of the institute. Segovia wrote the introduction to the first issue and described the journal's ultimate goal as "to contribute to the spread of Catholic truth in the scientific world." Issued twice a year, *Eidos* voiced the position of the insti-tute with regard to women's matters in the 1950s and 1960s.[18]

In an article entitled "Hacia qué mujer vamos" (What kind of woman are we heading toward), Rafaela Rodríguez depicted the ideal woman of the modern-day TI. The author reviewed and criticized Simone de Beauvoir's *The Second Sex*, proposing that to study the question of women in modern society implied a dual approach. First, the study must address the human di-mension, which is equal for men and women. A providential outlook of the relationship of the sexes led Rodríguez to equate men's and women's souls. "With regard to their personal dignity as children of God, men and women are absolutely equal, as well as in their ultimate goal in human life, which is the eternal union with God in Heaven."[19]

Social and biological differences do not alter one's spiritual dignity in the eyes of God. The key question resided in accepting those differences as com-plementary aspects of the sexes. According to Rafaela Rodríguez, *The Second Sex* devalued religious beliefs and placed them in the category of myths. The existential philosophy guiding Simone de Beauvoir perplexed Rodríguez, whose transcendental view of the world excluded the idea of female inferiority.

> Summing up the thought of the French author, we find that love is a purely erotic sentiment; the family, an egotistic association; motherhood, a burden to bear. The stations of wife and mother are for her other risks directly derived from the existential female structure, and women must guard themselves against

them, because they are the obstacles that, in fact, cause the personality of most women to fail. Husband, home, and children are the three circles that tomorrow's woman must dismantle around her, so that she can realize herself satisfactorily.[20]

By contrast, Rodríguez maintained that women embody human nature in a different and unique way. She proposed a Christian model of femininity as the right and honorable path for modern women of the 1950s and 1960s. For her, inculcating the redeeming nature of Christian doctrine in women was imperative.

To establish and make explicit the redeeming message that Christianity renders to women today, and to extract from it the possibilities of action that it offers us, seems the most urgent task of those who have understood that the new order we await demands the cooperation of all, men and women.[21]

This dignifying of Christian woman's ethos permeated the writings of members of the TI when addressing the new problems Spanish women confronted in the changing society of the 1950s. Rather than being a drawback, Christian spirituality elevated a woman's worth and provided a singular imprint to her participation in public matters.

Family, dutiful service, and motherhood continued to be highly praised as inherent Catholic virtues in several articles of *La Revista,* the official organ of the institute, at the beginning of the 1960s. In an article entitled "A las universitarias" (To college women), María Angeles Galino defended women's access to higher learning, arguing that this vocation was secondary to, but not less important than, marriage for Catholic college women.

On the one hand, if Spain needs experts in all orders, why not take advantage of those already prepared, even if they are women? And on the other hand, it is our firm conviction that mere professional success will never fill completely the feminine heart. Is this a justified cause to avoid other aspirations, certainly less important than marriage, but also legitimate and often urgent?

Motherhood as the primary destiny of all women was particularly emphasized in *La Revista.* Nevertheless, motherhood should not prevent them from undertaking professional work. In an article entitled "La mujer cara al tiempo" (Modern-times women), Ana María Macias remarked:

At the same time we must not forget that women's activities must be subordinated, in everything, to their motherly function—as Pope Pius XII pointed out in his radio speech to the Italian C.F. [*sic,* probably the Italian Women's Center] in October 1956—and when designing the work for women, "*a wise discrimination* in both its quality and quantity, must be taken into account."

> Evidently, women retain an immutable function prescribed by nature, which is motherhood, but this should not prevent them from taking care of their family and home and, at the same time, developing their abilities in all social spheres.[22]

According to the Teresian outlook, to gain men's respect in the labor market and the professional world, women had to improve their education. Education would transform them into freer individuals who knew their place in modern society, while at the same time preserving their feminine essence. Three dimensions of a woman's life were taken into account: education for the home; education for a professional life; and the woman's social life. M. A. Pascual advocated the complementarity of the sexes as an enriching source of social advancement. In line with the maxim "equal dignity, complementary mission," coined by John XXIII in 1960, Pascual argued:

> To the woman who finds herself with capacity and vocation, no force should prevent her from reaching the highest knowledge in Science and Letters or devoting her life to a profession that she feels inclined to by duty; because truth, freedom, and justice are rights of the human person.
>
> In the way she performs her work, in this certainly, a woman should be true to her own nature to cooperate with God's will, because not in vain has He created a society of man-woman.

A woman's nature led her to motherhood whether she was a virgin, a wife, or a mother. Society would benefit from the maternal essence.

> Maternal instinct is the prime instinct in a woman's soul and the most spontaneous, too, and that is why all women possess it, whether they are *virgo, sponsa,* or *mater.* And it can even happen that a *virgo* is more maternal than a *mater.* Men need maternal care when they are children, when they are old, when they are sick. They need it as well to legislate and administer justice.[23]

This outlook emphasized motherhood as the principal mission and drive in every woman's life, an inherent part of female fulfillment whether or not it was biologically realized. All women by nature were either private or social mothers. Thus, Teresian women, although celibate, would perform a motherly function in society.

According to María Angeles Galino, the Bible prescribed women's obligation to be society's "heart" and the guardians of humane values. Men lacked such moral superiority, and women's contribution was necessary to maintain a social equilibrium. To cooperate in a constructive way with men, women had to educate themselves. For Galino, it was a major mistake to conceive of the relationship of the sexes from an antagonistic standpoint, as a war. By contrast, Catholicism offered them the opportunity to approach their differences with love and cooperation.[24]

The *Law of Political, Professional, and Labor Rights of Women* in 1961 was well received in TI circles. It stated implicitly that marriage did not represent the only life option for women and that, furthermore, their access to the labor market and liberal professions (lawyers, professors, physicians) promoted a healthy economic autonomy among women. Galino considered it a mistake to recognize the right to work only for those women whose families needed an extra income, because "the right to work belongs to *all* human beings."[25]

According to scholar and TI member Ana María López Díaz-Otazu, although the *Law of Political, Professional, and Labor Rights of Women* provoked intense discussion in the national press about women's professional opportunities, little attention was devoted to working-class women's options. The Christian concept of human value included work as a facet of personal realization, from which women could not be excluded. Díaz-Otazu believed it was necessary to develop "a common opinion that responds to the complete acceptance of the Christian concept of women's personal dignity and to value work as a means to develop one's own personality, as a means of participation in the creating labor of God and the redeeming mission of our Lord Jesus Christ."[26]

Participating in the public arena as women, rather than as mimics of men, was the challenge confronting Spanish women. Teresian discourse on Catholic womanhood envisioned a truce in the "war of the sexes." For these women, their Catholic faith, far from limiting them, invigorated their self-esteem. In Barrenechea's opinion, Catholicism did not engender discrimination against women; rather, this was a problem of society in general.

> But that [women's discrimination] does not belong to Catholicism. It is a social problem that has perhaps permeated Catholic cadres, originally created by society in general. It doesn't pertain to the Church. Look, the Catholic Church has always encouraged women and recognized their dignity. Although there are certain things, for example . . . [the Church] doesn't admit women to become priests. But this is not about disdain or less appreciation of women but rather because Jesus wanted it that way. . . . You know one thing is the theory and another the practice. Look, women have entered the Vatican very slowly. There is no law prohibiting them access, but it is a male hierarchy. And besides, often women cannot voice their concerns, but rather men speak on women's behalf. And yes . . . as it happened that certain minorities have been silenced, the same has happened to women. But this never discouraged us: to be a women's institution to the core, governed by women.

Barrenechea occupied the office of vice president from 1957 until 1967. From 1967 to 1980, she directed the institute's center for vocations in Rome. Only women have, in fact, governed the TI. For these tasks, women entering the institute retreat and meditate about their commitment for one year. The future members confront the demands of a life of study and celibacy. They are women who have a career. The purpose of the year-long retreat is to decide whether the candidates are "psychologically calm and have a truly Christian faith to struggle as it is required." Teresian life involves renunciation of family life and, to a certain extent, embraces a life of solitude. Barrenechea recalls that she used to have larger groups than nowadays.

> I was director of the center, which is located outside of Rome, for thirteen years. When I was there, the groups were numerous, because there were also more people. Now those groups are smaller, but we always have between 25 and 30 persons in them. I once had up to 60 girls, or rather 60 women. They spend the whole academic year. They take a sabbatical from work, etc. . . . And this is a year to confront seriously that resolution, that vocation of making of their life an offering to the Church in the academic realm.[27]

Barrenechea is now in her eighties. Always active and eager to learn, she founded a historical archive of the Teresian Institute in 1977. In 1993, she resigned from the vice presidency of the institute.

The version of Catholic womanhood promoted by the TI celebrated learning as a path to salvation and glorification of God. Teresian women proclaimed their differences from men and aspired to contribute to the construction of a better society as partners with the opposite sex. Rather than preventing women from entering the public realm, Teresian spirituality created a femininity that celebrated the pursuit of knowledge and the performance of a profession. Although the members praised motherhood in their writings, they remained celibate and free of the obligations of a family so that they could offer themselves to God's will, thus acquiring a public persona of their own.

The TI was (and still is) part of a long tradition of learned religious women. It was their religious affirmation, their marriage to the family of the Church, that protected them from social criticism as educated women. Their faith and religious vows also differentiated them from the WS's political agenda, particularly when Spanish society became increasingly secular.

CATHOLIC STUDENT YOUTH

Historically, Catholic Action owes its origins to papal initiative and the support of the bishops of different countries. It developed gradually as an international Church lay organization with national peculiarities. The popes repeatedly declared that Catholic Action, as the apostolate of faithful and Church collaborators, was as old as the Catholic Church itself. As a secular apostolate organization under the authority and coordination of the bishops and the Pope, though, it constituted a modern religious entity, a product of Pius XI's Pontificate (1922–1939).[28]

Pius XI defined the nature and aims of Catholic Action as the active participation of the lay faithful in modern society to restore Christian values in all public realms.

> True Catholic Action [he said], in the sense we have conceived it and defined many times, [is] lay participation in the Church hierarchy's apostolate, for the defense of religious and moral principles, the development of healthy social action, under the direction of the ecclesiastical hierarchy, outside and above any political parties, within the family and society.[29]

This social commitment expanded a traditional practice in ecclesiastical matters starting at the parish level. Lay participation in the Church's mission derived from a variety of historical circumstances. First, it was a result of the shortage of priests and their inability to penetrate certain social, political, and economic milieus; and second, it was pressured by the increasing laicization and paganism of modern industrialized societies.

To maintain its inner unity, Catholic Action remained above political parties. Nonetheless, its members, as independent citizens, might participate in political activities; and in joining a political organization or party, they would always accept the practice of Church doctrine in worldly matters. In Pius XI's words:

> Catholic Action must be careful not to interfere in political parties, given that its very nature makes it foreign to political dissensions. . . . But if any political question deals with issues of Catholic religion and its moral doctrine, Catholic Action can and must interpose its activity, postponing any particular interest and with its members devoting themselves to the glory of the Church and their souls.[30]

The Pope's assertion of the nonpolitical nature of Catholic Action made it a good forum for women's public participation, since they were considered to be not political beings but rather guarantors of morality and Christian values. Consequently, Catholic Action's mission projected itself beyond the ecclesiastical community by reaching specific groups such as workers, peasants, students, women, and youth. After Catholic Action was founded by Pius XI in 1923, the three decades that followed saw it undergo an internal transformation. Originally conceived as the deaconry of the clergy, it became a socially involved secular organization of the faithful.[31] The Pope's definition of the secular organization constituted the doctrinal basis for the foundation of Spanish Catholic Action (SCA).

SCA began with the establishment of Women's Catholic Action, and Catholic Youth was established in 1924. In 1931, the Conference of Metropolitans, as the highest SCA authority, set Spanish Catholic Action's foundations. In 1939, the Conference of Reverend Metropolitans approved SCA's reorganization that prevailed for twenty years. Between 1939 and 1945, the organization grew rapidly under the presidency of Cardinal Isidro Gomá. It was divided into four branches: the Men's Branch of Spanish Catholic Action, the Women's Branch of Spanish Catholic Action, the Young Men of Spanish Catholic Action, and the Young Women of Spanish Catholic Action. Between 1945 and 1950, the labor sections, such as the Labor Fraternities of Catholic Action and the Labor Youth of Catholic Action, emerged. These sections expanded during the second half of the 1950s, whereas the significance of parish-based communities decreased.

The final phase in the historical evolution of Spanish Catholic Action began in 1956 and lasted until the end of the Second Vatican Council. A more diversified movement flourished during these years, particularly among young people. SCA's youth branches divided into several new movements: Catholic Workers Youth (Juventudes Obreras Católicas, JOC) for working-class youth; Rural Catholic Action Youth (Juventud Agrana Católica, JAC) for rural communities; Catholic Student Youth (Juventud de Estudiantes Católicos, JEC) for student involvement in the intellectual community and society in general; and Independent Catholic Youth (JIC) for clerks. Each of these movements had girls' sections. The youth organizations offered Spanish young people a means of participating in the solving of social problems from their own environment. They were also able to cross class barriers through cooperation among the varied organizations under SCA. In order to maintain a certain level of unity within the organization, the Supreme Junta of Reverend Metropolitans passed the Statute of Spanish Catholic Action in 1959.

The objective of JEC was to bring the Church doctrine and life to university youth, and it was organized on three levels: national, diocesan, and by college. At the national and diocesan levels, men's and women's committees existed, each with a spiritual counselor (consiliario). The consiliario, always a priest, represented the Church presence and guidance in the lay organization. Each college had a Catholic Action center and organized class teams; but in general, at this third level, the organization was not as rigid, and its existence depended on the number of affiliates in each university district. The movement operated by the "active method," with campaigns and "revision of life" questionnaires. Retreats and spiritual exercises were held for members and other university students. There were three national meetings, an annual assembly, a prayer workshop, and a summer course for members.[32]

Under the aegis of Pius XII, SCA grew and developed. Key to his pontificate was his redefinition of the role of Catholic lay men and women in modern society. The Pontiff exhorted them to rechristianize the world, in order to combat a world dehumanized by machines in the name of progress. In a Christmas radio message in 1952, the Pope argued against modern industrialized society and urged laymen to get involved in social matters with a Christian approach.

We know where we must look for technological progress in society: in the giant enterprises of modern industry. It is not our intention to utter a judgement about the need, utility, and obstacles posed by such forms of production. No doubt they are wonderful realizations of human creative and inventive power; rightfully they attract the world's admiration. In turn, we must deny their ability to serve as a general model to conform and arrange modern social life.

Such industrialized society impoverished the human spirit and threw the human race into a state of anguish and antihumanism. In Pius XII's words,

> [W]e can understand the origin and point of departure that pull the modern man to an anguished condition: his "depersonalization." He has been deprived of a face and a name; in many of the most important life activities he has been reduced to a mere social object, because such society has transformed itself into an impersonal system, a cold arrangement of forces.[33]

Hence, the rechristianization of society was key. Only a solid faith could relieve such a state of despair and provide an escape path from the distractions of the modern world.

The Church considered women, as mothers of the human race, morally and spiritually superior souls; they were therefore central to the rechristianization of modern society because of their role of preserving family and hearth. Modern order demanded that women take a more active role in society and in the labor force. However, they were expected to infuse humane values into the public realm. A "new Christian woman" with a new duty to society was the core of the Church's doctrine for modern times.

Spanish women were organized within Catholic Action in two branches: the Catholic Action Women's Association, for those thirty years and older, and the Catholic Action Young Women's Association, for those between seventeen and thirty years of age. The High Board of Catholic Action Women served as the central committee at the national level; its services included information and guidance of the affiliates in their religious, moral, social, and cultural apostolate; publication of instructional journals; coordination of internal diocesan activities; and training of central and diocesan leaders. Most of the affiliates of the senior Women's Association were housewives (single or married) who cooperated with the parish. The younger women, however, were involved in different activities and accordingly were incorporated into different organizations for workers (JOC), students (JEC), and peasants (JAC) that flourished in the second half of the 1950s.[34]

The nature, mission, and goals of the Catholic organizations for older and younger women were similar. They grouped women who placed their calling under the patronage of Saint Teresa de Jesús and Christ, the King of Nations, to help the Church hierarchy in their apostolic mission. Some activities involved campaigns against "unhealthy tendencies among modern women, such as withdrawal from the home, pagan feminism, disrespectful fashion, frivolous and dangerous social gatherings, and ostentation of wealth."[35] Senior members organized a mother's week to educate women about their domestic mission and duties.

All activities followed the teachings of Pius XII. In 1953, the High Board of Catholic Action Women published a series of papal documents about the Christian female personality, and *Senda,* the national organ of women's Catholic Action in Spain, echoed the Pontiff's concerns and teachings for Catholic women in modern society. "The Pope is very worried about the family. Modern winds are hostile and threaten to destroy it," reads an article by Father Emilio Enciso, national consiliario, recounting a papal speech to Italian women of Catholic Action in July 1949.[36] The main causes leading to the destruction of the family were war and modern materialism. The Pontiff pointed at materialism as the essential problem:

> It is superfluous to remind you how the radio and the cinema have been used and abused to spread materialism. And how radio, cinema, bad books, licentiously illustrated magazines, shameful shows and performances, immoral dance, and immodesty on the beaches have contributed to increase the superficiality, worldliness, and sensuality of the youth.[37]

To put an end to family disaster, an appropriate social policy, built on a strong parental faith to guide the children, could instill morals in the young people. Women's motherly functions were of primary importance to achieve such a goal.

The senior women of Catholic Action in Spain enthusiastically embarked upon the task of strengthening the family and the home. Throughout the 1950s, *Senda* helped to quicken the domestic spirit of Spanish women confronted with consumerism and modern society. Nicolás González Ruiz published a monthly column entitled "Familias numerosas" (Large families) in 1951. In the first article of the series, he compared the family, in its organization and management, with the state. Freedom should exist within certain limits: reciprocal respect, order, authority, distributive justice, hierarchy, and unity. The father was granted the supreme authority by God, the mother acted as minister of interior and finances, and the law of public order prescribed a moderate freedom of speech, punishing any excess. To guarantee a happy home, *Senda* provided its female readers with the "Decalog of happiness in the Christian home":

1. In the family you will always be happy.
2. With your smile you will make all of your loved ones happy.
3. You will only speak, in public, about those things you are allowed to.
4. You will show a great deal of interest in the small things of your loved ones.
5. You will heroically banish from your home any excess of asceticism.
6. You will be eager to serve and reward everybody equally.

7. You will forget about yourself and worry about your loved ones showing happiness.

8. You will not initiate any discussion and will always talk prudently.

9. You will be patient, always responding kindly.

10. You will gain the affection of their souls and hearts with good will.

Creating a Christian home was the mother's task. According to an editorial, "La mujer española" (The Spanish woman), that appeared in *Senda* in January 1953, "the stupendous growth of vocations in our fatherland proves that Spanish Catholicism, despite its many flaws . . . is very efficient." It continued: "Vocation, in general, is the result of a Christian family of a generous and sacrificing spirit. There it is born, grows, and flourishes. The cultivation of this plant is the work of the Christian mother who, even without knowing it, thanks to God, is the key, the base, and the soul of most Spanish homes."[38]

Motherhood was intensely admired in the pages of *Senda*. To avoid having children was "almost . . . mocking God mischievously." Within the family, the mother's mission was regarded as sacred. She could either be a "saint or nothing." According to Catholic Action's national consiliario, Father Enciso, "Other people may aspire to be mediocre, but not the mother. . . . She has been chosen by God to cooperate with Him in the creation of new human beings and the sanctification of their souls." Pius XII celebrated motherhood as the quintessence of Catholic womanhood, particularly in a time of pagan materialism in which the family was threatened. *Senda* echoed the Pope's teachings and proclaimed Catholic Action's pride and joy in motherhood for Spanish women. "Because of you," read an editorial, "we have a high esteem of our body and our spirit, both temples of divinity molded by God for a mission so great and beautiful as that of being a mother." In Pius XII's words, a woman was a "mother even in the most spiritual sense. To that end Our Creator ordered all female essence; her human organism, and even more, her spirit, and more than anything her sensitivity." Mothers had an important role to play in modern society. "The public world needs you, as women, as mothers," said the Pope. "Female cooperation in spreading and defending God's kingdom has never been more necessary and appropriate than in these present times."[39] Safeguarding the Christian home, as well as bringing motherly values into the public realm, constituted the Catholic woman's path in society.

No doubt participation in worldly matters was the challenge women confronted in the modern industrialized world. To guide them and unify the Church efforts to rechristianize society in different countries, international Catholic women's forums were held, such as the World Union of Catholic Women's Organizations (WUCWO), to which Spanish women of Catholic Action belonged. Pilar Bellosillo, president of the High Board of Catholic Action Women, became a member of the WUCWO executive committee in

1952. She reported on the conference the WUCWO held in Rome in April that year on the topic "Peace in the World and the Contribution of Catholic Women." In different interviews granted to *Senda*, Bellosillo discussed the important role of Catholic women in social matters. She became the ambassadress of Spanish Catholic Action women. In 1956, she visited Paris, London, and Dublin, as well as several Latin American countries (including Mexico, Costa Ríca, Panama, Colombia, Peru, Chile, and Argentina), to contact their women's organizations. In Mexico, she attended the Conference for the Protection of Young Women and in Bogota, a seminar sponsored by the WUCWO in cooperation with UNESCO. "Catholic women have a lot to do in present times," she declared in an interview given to *Senda* while she was in Mexico, and "that is why they bravely raise their voices at meetings and conferences in the five continents, so they can tell the Holy Father, in the next conference to be held in Rome, 'Your Holiness, we have finally discovered the perfect profile of the modern Catholic woman; we have once more reevaluated female personality following the guidelines of the program Your Holiness designed.'"[40]

The moral duty of Catholic women in the public arena was to make capitalist society more humane. For this purpose, Catholic Action women took on the task of awakening social consciousness among Spanish wives, mothers, and daughters, making them aware of their Christian social obligations. *Senda* promoted certain careers: for example, a woman could be a social worker, an air hostess, a tourist guide, a specialist in infant care, a hygiene inspector, or a hotel or restaurant manager and use and enhance her feminine qualities in the course of her work. Social workers received their training at the School of Social Work, whose director, María Sabater, declared, "Spanish women have a social awareness and are conscious of their responsibility in the modern times in which they live; they want to prepare themselves the best they can, to be useful to others and to the fatherland." Over a span of three years, young women attended classes that taught them religious, philosophical, and social principles, along with some medicine, hygiene, and labor legislation. Once they received their degrees, they would work as social consultants for different firms and companies, Sabater continued, arguing that this was the most feminine career because it implied "delicacy and a spirit of sacrifice."[41]

María Pilar Vila Domínguez, a twenty-five-year-old AVIACO air hostess, pointed out that patience, courage, and understanding were virtues she had developed in her profession. Described as tall and attractive, with "a charming smile that gave the impression she possessed 'the joy of living,'" Vila Domínguez affirmed that women were more understanding than men when it came to listening to the needs of the passengers. "Besides," she said, "we also have a very important role with regard to children. When children travel alone, you feel like they belong to you."[42] Maternal feelings were of utmost significance in this young woman's analysis of her professional qualifications.

An important common element in all these careers was a constant zeal to incorporate some sort of eternal female virtues in their professions. Hygiene inspectors, for example, "had taken to the streets to bring to others the essence of femininity, through the habit of cleanliness." Their mission, since the first one was hired in 1941, was to carry out fumigation campaigns in city slums. This occupation, exclusively for women, said a hygiene inspector, was based on the mother's responsibility for family neatness. "If she is convinced of the need for cleanliness, the entire home transforms itself."[43] Rather than valuing intellect in the workplace, an emphasis was placed on women as caretakers or nurturers in these feminine occupational options that *Senda* described for its readers.

In an interview with six college women between eighteen and twenty-three years of age, the magazine tried to decipher the spirit of a university woman. As one of the interviewees put it, "nobody understands a woman's vocation to study. Her parents, especially the mother, worry more about their daughter getting married than finishing a career. In general, when she has already entered college, they would like her to conclude her studies, but they would rather have her abandon them to get married than to see her graduating without a boyfriend." Their male classmates ignored them for the most part, and these young women found it hard to attract a boyfriend in the college environment. Men did not even invite them to talk about their studies, based on the reason that "college men, in general, did not look favorably upon the fact that a woman followed a career, much less if she took it seriously." They believed their male counterparts were "afraid of their competence as colleagues and the possibility of not having a docile wife." According to these young women, men were convinced that women possessed "inferior intelligence." In spite of everything, all of the women interviewed aspired to marriage. Nonetheless, they also assumed that "fewer university women get married, because they become more selective in a partner. . . . They prefer mature men." One of them affirmed, "[F]or a seventeen-year-old girl, the ideal husband must be over thirty. They want their husbands to be more knowledgeable than themselves and well established."[44]

Purificación Prieto was a member of the Catholic University Women Youth (a part of JEC) in Madrid during her studies in the late 1950s; she became national president of the JEC in 1961. Prieto, born in 1936, was the daughter of two teachers, the youngest of seven siblings and the only daughter. When I interviewed her in 1994, she began by saying that the Christian values she gained at home explained her decision to join Catholic Action when she was older:

> My family was a Christian Catholic family, but from the north, from León. That means that it was a traditional Catholic family but very serious. Christianity was not an adornment, it was something we lived sincerely, with formality. For

example, I always say that I have certain values that I did not receive from the school, society, Catholic Action, or anybody. My family gave them to me. So I have, for example, the sense of justice, of equality, of equity, something very deeply felt at home. I mean, at home injustice was never tolerated.[45]

Purificación studied with the Sisters of Charity until 1953, when she went to college in Madrid. Although her real desire was to study mathematics, her family "convinced" her to go into something "less arid for a woman." After two years in chemistry, she started philosophy in 1957 and soon after joined Catholic Action at the university to satisfy her "nonconformist" spirit.

I think that I have always been very nonconformist. . . . there were many things I was not convinced of, I didn't like them, [things] about society, people's religiosity, about how to go about things. And by chance, I made contact with Catholic Action. And in a very curious way. Catholic Action in Madrid had a choir, and I started to sing in the choir. From that point on, I joined Catholic Action . . . university Catholic Action of Madrid. And within two years I was president in Madrid. . . . Very soon, I became diocesan president, from the diocese of Madrid. And then when I was in my last year in college, I entered the national committee as national president of JEC.[46]

Her participation and activism within JEC gave Prieto a self-awareness of historical agency. Catholic Action's specialized movements offered her, on the eve of the 1960s, the opportunity to be more involved in social and—in hindsight, although not declared at the time—political issues. The young people who encountered each other in JEC shared a sound religious faith. Women protected the prerogative to rule themselves and to maintain a separate association where men could not intervene. Prieto explained:

I think Catholic Action was managed by the people interested in it. . . . they were the first movements where young people ruled themselves. The men by the men, the women by the women. I mean, young university women were led by themselves. That was very important. There were consiliarios, but the consiliario had only an advisory role; he never conducted, never. And furthermore, we did not tolerate him to do so [a little laughter]. That was very important. We were the protagonists of our own history. For example, many times it was discussed whether to unify the movements and transform them into mixed movements, and finally that happened, but it took a long time. Because we were very worried that a JEC, for example, or a JOC in which the men and women were together would turn into a male JEC or a male JOC that admitted girls. In Spain at the time, the issue of the presence of women in the public arena was still very difficult. And if the movements united, what could happen was that it would be a male movement with women who participated but who were managed by men.[47]

Although separate, the women's and men's movements coordinated their efforts in organizing campaigns and retreats for the university community. In these gatherings, participants confronted problems of all sorts: political, economic, or simply academic. At the time, JEC members were committed to reforming Spanish social reality with an infusion of Christian values. As Prieto said:

> There was an obligation to your surrounding world. In other words, the specialized movements were not just pious movements, which doesn't mean they didn't have a religious aspect, but their religious aspect implied that the person, the Christian, had to be immersed in his/her social reality, trying to provide solutions for the problems around him/her. This was nothing new, except that they participated with others in the solution of problems. So if there was a strike, they were the first to participate, for example. Of course, strikes were more serious within certain groups than others. But to show you an example, in the famous strike of Asturias [1964], Catholic Action made some proclamations and the national president of JOC and the national consiliario were imprisoned.[48]

The pontificate of John XXIII, and particularly the Second Vatican Council, provided an important stimulus for the progressive sector of the Spanish hierarchy, thus breaking the ideological unity of the Spanish Catholic Church. Nonetheless, the move toward social involvement made by the specialized groups within Catholic Action, particularly after the wave of strikes in 1962, suffered from the backlash of the conservative Catholic hierarchy: the movements were dismantled by the mid-1960s. This process, the "Catholic Action crisis," came when Church fathers and Franco began to fear the disobedience to official Catholic doctrine of the youth of Catholic Action.

Paradoxically, their Catholic creed and social awareness transformed the specialized movements into enemies of the Francoist National-Catholic regime. The movements were perceived as a threat, not only by the Francoist establishment, but also by the orthodox Church hierarchy, which regarded them as subversive. The young interpreted Pius XII's mandate to get involved in society by infusing their actions with ideals of justice, honesty, and compassion. By 1966, Casimiro Morcillo, archbishop of Madrid, was appointed president of the Commission for Secular Apostolate, and with the cooperation of bishop José Guerra Campos, he disbanded Catholic Action's specialized movements. Franco, for his part, was not going to tolerate any dissidence, not even from Catholic circles. The state repression of any opposition was handled by Camilo Alonso Vega, an old friend of the dictator, former head of the Guardia Civil, and a wealthy investor in Banco Popular, who became minister of the interior in the 1957 government realignment. Franco regarded Alonso Vega as a hard-line military man, one who would confront with draconian measures any opposition to the regime.

Purificación Prieto embodies young people's rebellion and shaping of a new social Catholicism that challenged Church hierarchy mandates, a Catholicism followed in turn by the senior women of Catholic Action and voiced by *Senda*. Prieto spoke passionately about her experience within JEC and how JEC members stood against Church hierarchy and Francoism.

> Catholic Action was smashed. There was an absolute conspiracy to smash it between the government, meaning Camilo Alonso Vega, and some bishop, specifically Guerra Campos, bishop of Cuenca today. He was appointed bishop consiliario of Catholic Action. I lived this day by day with him, because I had many meetings with him, since I was the secretary for the youth conference. Guerra Campos spent two years gaining the trust of Catholic Action, very quietly, and when he had all the threads in his hands he demolished it completely, he destroyed it, he smashed it. . . . For the government it [was] the biggest threat. And for good reason, because [Catholic Action] was a well-organized movement, and no one else in Spain could do this; it was legal and protected by the Church and the Concordat. So, for example, a leader of Catholic Action could not be arrested without an order, or it was a very serious matter. And on the other hand, it was a Church movement, and Franco became ill every time anybody mentioned it to him, because he believed he embodied Spanish Catholic essence, and could not bear to be questioned from the Catholic Church.[49]

The crisis within Catholic Action proved that discontent existed among Catholics about Church doctrine. All Catholics did not necessarily follow the official line. Prieto's words highlight the multiplicity of discourses shaping true Catholicism under the Francoist dictatorship. With regard to gender relations and the position of women in the modern world, there was a sharp contrast between the domestic ideal popularized by *Senda* and the activism of the young university women of JEC in the late 1950s and early 1960s. Although they shared faith in God's word of salvation for men and women, the outcome and goals of this faith differed. For Purificación Prieto, the message of hope was of the utmost importance because it also allowed a Catholic woman to be "liberated," to be herself.

> Well, I feel completely liberated. Above my conscience there is nothing else, absolutely nothing, absolutely nothing. And I tell you more, I think that being a believer . . . being a Catholic woman, I am not sure what it is, I know what being Christian is, but a Catholic nowadays, I am not so sure. I think that being a Christian woman means to believe in very few things, very, very few. I think there is only one dogma of faith. All the other dogmas we may interpret in a more dynamic way. But there is one, and that is that God sent His Son to the world to deliver us *all*, and there is only one thing that is worthy: to trust that message. Nothing else.[50]

In Prieto's words there is a clear belief in the triumph of the spirit over the body, which implies a transcendental and gender-blind vision of the world. In this light there are no differences between men's and women's souls.

Prieto devoted three years to JEC, traveling in Spain, running campaigns in the provinces, and organizing lectures and cultural activities. The meetings were held in private homes or in the Catholic Action center of each province. Usually the groups were no larger than ten or twelve people. Recruitment of members took place through mutual friends' inviting each other to activities open to the public and sponsored by JEC. Prieto belonged to the organizing committee of the Youth Conference held in Madrid in 1964; after that, she moved to Paris, where she studied theology at the National Institute of Liturgy because "I wanted to study on my own," she said, "and have my own opinions." Upon her return to Spain, she became a professor at the Pastoral Institute of the Universidad Pontificia de Salamanca in Madrid. For two years, she taught "Liturgy Foundations" and the "Sacrament of Penance," mostly to priests and nuns. She found resistance to her being a woman professor and left the position to teach in high school for a year. After these dissatisfying experiences in teaching, she decided to open a bookstore, which she currently manages. "And apart from the bookstore," she pointed out, "I haven't done too many things, because I have spent seventeen years looking after old people." Prieto justifies herself by saying: "I have done all this because I wanted to, being aware that it wasn't my responsibility. I did it not because I happened to be the girl, the youngest, and the only woman, who was also single, so it was my duty, wasn't it?"

Prieto accepted her role as caretaker of the family and regards it as a personal choice, according to the times in which she was living. As she explained it with hindsight: "In life one is born in a time, and things are the way they are. And maybe if we want to run away, it only makes us feel bad."

Regardless of the circumstances, Purificación considers herself an independent-minded woman. She does not regret what she did for her family, but she always questioned the constraining boundaries of Francoist femininity.

> I think that certainly, within Francoism women had a role to play, but only after they went through certain channels. I'll explain myself. In Spain, the Women's Section was given the task of formatting women. The Women's Section prepared perfect women, but only perfect housewives, perfect child-bearers. Or that single woman, a little mannish in her ways, whose role consisted in devoting herself to prepare others. But that was all. So when you stepped out of that mold, you were completely out of place. . . . Beforehand, being a woman constituted an absolute hindrance. Hence, the only place where you could escape such measurement was within the specialized movements of Catholic Action. And notice I do not say within the Church.[51]

Joining Catholic Action allowed Prieto to step out of the Francoist feminine mold in her own way. When she moved to Paris to study theology, she sought to escape from a deep dissatisfaction with the conventions about Catholic womanhood. For her, the specialized movements of Catholic Action offered an opportunity to realize the word of God. Far from being constraining, her faith constituted the root of her personal liberation. Although she became a caretaker for seventeen years, she does not regard that period of her life as an imposition but rather as a choice and, with today's hindsight, a product of the times and the circumstances. Highly educated and unable to find a professional activity that matched her qualifications, she ventured into the business world when she opened her bookstore in the 1970s. She is still taking care of herself and others.

As it was in the TI, the religious element was most important for the young people who joined JEC. The specialized movements of Catholic Action offered them the opportunity to get involved in social and political matters and even to protest the state of things in the changing economy of the 1950s. In an increasingly industrialized society, the members of the branch of Catholic Action for older women viewed it as their duty to bring feminine moral superiority to the modern world dehumanized by machines, a world in need of rechristianization.

THE ASSOCIATION OF SPANISH UNIVERSITY WOMEN

The Association of Spanish University Women (ASUW, Asociación de Universitarias Españolas) was established in Madrid at the beginning of the 1950s by Carmen Gayarre Galbete (1900–1996), a former professor at the Universidad Complutense de Madrid, and a group of graduate and professional women.[52] This association emerged as a Catholic counterpart to other university women's organizations, such as the Spanish Association of University Women (Asociación Española de Mujeres Universitarias).

The Spanish Association of University Women, originally called Young University Women, was founded in 1920 and belonged to the International Federation of University Women. Dismantled after the Civil War, it reappeared when a group of American university women (Edith Hellman, Isabel Pope Conant, and Mary Sweeney) associated with the International Institute for Girls in Spain and a few Spanish women in exile (Carmen Zulueta, Isabel Palencia, and Justina Ruiz de Conde) got together in Boston. Their idea was to establish a liberal-minded university women's association that followed the principles of the Free Institution of Learning.[53]

By contrast, Asunción Ibarra, cofounder of the ASUW, defines this association as a "foundation thought of and matured for years by Carmen Gayarre, to unite a group of university women who sought perfection as professionals in tune with the Catholic Church doctrine."[54] Ibarra emphasized that the association was to be exclusively for women and independent from political or religious organizations: "a *female and independent* association that occupied a place along with other female organizations exclusively Catholic—such as Catholic Action or Congregaciones Marianas—others of political or social character—such as the Women's Section of Falange—or cultural associations—such as the university women of the Institute of Boston."[55]

The founder of ASUW, Carmen Gayarre Galbete, was born in Pamplona on 14 August 1900 and died in January 1996. Her father, a merchant, died when she was young; her mother, a well-educated, pious housewife, reared her and a brother. After she finished her studies in the Normal School of Pamplona, Carmen arrived in Madrid in 1929, where she continued at the University of Madrid, studying philosophy.

> I was told to study law. The reason why, I do not know, maybe because of the activities I had already initiated. I had organized, first of all, a women's alumni association at the Normal School; that was my first step. . . . I found myself lacking the memory that law required, on the one hand. And on the other hand, I could not conceive of defending an unjust cause. . . . And a professor friend, precisely, professor Zubiri, recommended that I study philosophy. And I said, "What am I going to do with philosophy?" and he said, "Well, you will structure your mind." And indeed I said, "All right, I'll do my best to follow that path."[56]

Like Teresian member Teresa Barrenechea, Carmen Gayarre followed the advice of a male authority to choose her career. The former accepted Father Poveda's suggestion to study classics, and the latter accepted the advice of professor Zubiri.

Carmen Gayarre's religious zeal and piety encouraged her to get involved in education during the Second Republic. She was concerned about the children of Catholic families who attended the classes of the FIL at the Instituto Escuela, so she talked to Angeles Gasset—a personal friend and one of the teachers at the institute—and offered to teach religion to those children and to prepare them for their first communion.

> And when the Republic eliminated religion . . . the teaching of religion in all schools and all religious symbols, I told Angeles: "Look, there are many families who brought their children here for a modern education, because they think that your institution is better than any religious school." . . . So I told her, "Look, you know Jimena [Jimena Menéndez Pidal, another teacher at the FIL] much better; see if she will allow you to ask the families of the children who you know are practicing Catholics, if outside of the Institute we could teach the children religion and prepare them for their first communion, which is required at an early age." So Angeles did that, and we were indeed able to organize, on Serrano Street number 50 I believe, religion classes, and the children from the Instituto Escuela attended twice a week . . . I think one day during the week and on Saturdays.[57]

Carmen Gayarre married Dr. Carlos Gil y Gil, a gynecologist and radiologist, in 1931, after finishing her doctoral courses. She remembers that her husband commented to a friend, "My wife has caused me only one sorrow, not completing her Ph.D. She never defended her dissertation." Carmen shared forty-four years of marriage in spite of, she said, her husband's "grave authoritarianism" and reared six children.[58] Although she never finished her dissertation, she competed in 1932 for one of two teaching positions at the University of Madrid in the newly created section of pedagogy. María de Maeztu (1882–1948), director of elementary education at the Instituto Escuela and of the Ladies Residence Hall of the FIL, competed for the other. Maeztu got the position of assistant to Professor Luis de Zulueta (1878-1964), who became minister of foreign affairs for the Republic, and Carmen gained the position of assistant to Professor Domingo Barnés (1879–1943), who became general director and later minister of education. The Civil War interrupted her academic career. She remembers how difficult those years were: she and her husband had to leave Madrid and reside in Pamplona until the end of the conflict.

> It was 1936. A policeman, whose mother he [her husband] had treated, called him. Apparently he hadn't charged them; he was so good to everybody. So that man told him, "Don Carlos leave Madrid because Calvo Sotelo has been murdered, and nobody knows where to find him yet. But this is a very serious matter and they will look for you. Leave." And indeed, he [her husband] told me, "Look, we have to pack." Already in 1936 we had three children, one of them very small. Well, one year old. Carlitos had been born in July 1935, and it was July [1936], so the child was one year old. And the other two were two and three years old. So we left. That summer he had thought of taking me to Germany. He was looking forward to it because he had become a Germanophile. He had specialized there where he had learned radiology treatments. He thought of taking me to Freiburg, his alma mater. We stayed in Hendaye waiting to see what was going to happen. And then, when he was able to, we moved to Pamplona. And in Pamplona, he fixed an old machine and treated those who came from the front and those going.

Carmen does not comment on her husband's Germanophile sentiments at a time when National Socialism was in power in Germany. For her, being a wife and a mother came first in her life. She remembers the birth of baby Carmen during the war in Pamplona:

> And I spent the war there, and had my baby girl, the fourth of our children; it was a girl. Baby Carmen. He [her husband] was so happy with her birth. . . . And we were in the country near Pamplona in the year 1937 when she was born. And he was really happy, poor thing. And in 1938 she died. It took me twenty years to recover from that trauma, and to accept it.

The death of her child is what she felt as the most traumatic experience; she does not mention any of the horrors of living in the midst of a civil war. Once the war was over, she went back to her position at the University of Madrid; but she decided to give up her profession three years later to fulfil her motherly duties and take care of her sixth child, born in 1942 with Down's syndrome.

> [It was God's will] that our sixth child was a son with Down's syndrome. Besides, he was so miserable a creature that when he came into the world and was in my bed, the pediatrician who saw him called him a "human wretch." At the time, I was assistant professor of Paidología [early childhood development] at the university, what today is the Complutense, the University of Madrid. Then I thought, "If I continue here, this poor baby is going to die; I have to leave this and do whatever I can for him." And that's it.[59]

In the 1940s, right after the Civil War, Spain lacked any infrastructure to educate retarded children, and Carmen became the pioneer in the field. She devoted herself to save her son and took good care of him. "He turned fifty-two this year," she points out proudly. In 1958, she opened a school for mentally deficient children, and in 1964, this school became a foundation that still exists today.[60]

In spite of her personal setbacks, Carmen continued to be interested in intellectual matters. Although removed from the university environment, in the early 1950s she decided to create what she refers to as a "totally independent" association for university Catholic women, ASUW. "Certainly," she says, "the 1950s were the most important years, because we started then." ASUW's main goal was to strengthen the ethical and religious training of its members, who were professional university graduates between thirty-five and forty years old, described by Carmen as "independent, right-wing women."

> How would I say . . . essentially in the classical term [we were] right-wing women, essentially, but not involved in politics. We belonged neither to the Women's Section, nor to the monarchist movements, not even to Catholic Action. Without being political, it had a more institutional imprint. [We were] totally independent, always, from the beginning.
>
> [We were] not only Catholic in theory but absolutely practicing Catholics and right-wing . . . I mean with the idea that all the Church ideology had to be preserved intact and carried into education and lived in practice. This is as far as the Church is concerned. And with regard to politics, well, there could be no socialist theory. Let's speak bluntly so I can express myself more easily and generally.[61]

Carmen's emphasis on the ASUW's nonpolitical affiliation as "Catholic right-wing women" under the Franco regime highlights the conscious alternative discourse on Catholic womanhood and is a statement of women's individuality and agency within the dictatorship.

The members of the first board of directors in 1954 were all educated professionals with college degrees: Josefina Pérez Mateos, president; Asunción Ibarra, secretary; Matilde Revuelta Tubino, treasurer; and Pilar Fernández Vega de Ferrandis, committee member. Two years later, three more committee members joined the board: Manolita Fernández Arroyo, Consolación Morales Oliver, and Carmen Gayarre Galbete. According to the association's statutes, approved in 1957, the board of directors had to be elected every five years by the general assembly. The association counted on the guidance of a spiritual counselor, or consiliario, Father Jesús Solano, S.J., a member of the Jesuit order and a professor of theology at the University of Oña. The Catholic nature of the organization was well defined in article 2 of the statutes, which stated: "Those activities devoted to the members' personal growth as well as their professional enrichment and public actions are subject to the norms of the ecclesiastical hierarchy, as is the Association itself." The activities organized by the association were both religious and intellectual. "We lived the Church doctrine day by day," declares Asunción Ibarra, the first secretary of ASUW. "The Church way of life gave us strength to be good professionals, being always alert to what happened in the cultural and scientific world."[62]

Asunción Ibarra, born in Albacete, was the oldest of four sisters. Her parents encouraged the girls to gain an education, for they considered that the key to a better life. She graduated in 1946 in Romance languages, receiving the Ministry of Education's National Award. In 1954, she passed the government examinations for archivists and librarians and joined the National Library professional staff. She began as the head of the National Library Official Publications, and by the time she retired was in charge of the Section of Rare Manuscripts. Simultaneously, she was a professor of technical training for archivists and librarians at the defunct General Board of Archives and Libraries and Researchers School.

Asunción Ibarra never married; she devoted her life to seeking knowledge. For her, a university woman "is a person who does not have her mind closed to any kind of knowledge, and that thirst for knowledge does not conflict with femininity."

> Why wouldn't it be feminine? I remember once, when I was in high school, a professor of philosophy or something, said, "Write on a piece of paper why you study." And I must have written something very unusual because I said "To learn, to seek knowledge." And when he read that, he said, "Here we have a very interesting answer; it says to learn." And I thought, "What do we study for, then?" So given what is said about women, I don't know if this professor found it a little odd. I don't know what the other girls said about why they studied.[63]

When considering the domestic role attributed to women in the 1950s, Asunción does not see a sharp difference between a housewife and a university woman, because

> there are housewives who went through university and are perfect in both realms. The university woman puts before any activity her zeal to seek knowledge, which does not end in the classroom. She searches for alternative means to continue expanding her knowledge without neglecting any scientific area, following the evolution of the thought of the times she is living in.[64]

Nonetheless, she never married.

The ASUW was affiliated with the Pax Romana International Movement of Catholic intellectuals. For ASUW's members, their Catholicism constituted an essential part of their intellectual endeavor, as agents of rechristianization of modern society. Carmen passionately explains their commitment to the Catholic Church doctrine about women in the modern times.

> We thought a path to that [rechristianization] would be the intellectual life, the professional life with a sound formation. Because what happened then, and now also, is that the intellectual who follows a career and a professional and social path forgets his or her religious training, and only retains what they learned from their mother and then at school. But further than that, nothing. And we understood it was necessary to break out of that pattern and move on without searching for great theological answers, but getting to the bottom of the revealed doctrine that we practiced and had learned when we were young and didn't sufficiently understand. So the goal was . . . to show it by osmosis more than preaching, through our own life penetrating the environment we were in, either family, profession, work, society.[65]

To strengthen their Catholic devotion, ASUW members attended spiritual exercises organized by the association and directed by Father Solano. These gatherings consisted of a retreat of five days to pray, meditate, and discuss themes such as "The Meaning of Our Existence," "Jesus Christ Our Savior," "In the Kingdom of Christ," and "Children of Mary."[66] Initially, there was a series of lectures on theological issues prepared and delivered by Father Solano, but the members thought that holding the lectures in a private retreat would give them a better opportunity to enhance their pious zeal. Hence, since its origins, the association has organized retreats for the members every year.

The ASUW organized other activities as well to help members improve themselves as professionals, such as tutoring in foreign languages (French, English, German); assistance with publications and notes for the government professional examinations; a series of lectures on intellectual and professional matters; cultural trips; and leisure activities such as cooking, interior decoration, and photography. The organization also had a library and offered financial support for research projects, publications, and travel in Spain or abroad. Every month the ASUW distributed a schedule of activities to members and friends. The foreign language tutoring service included conversation, reading comprehension, writing, and translation. The tutors, all native speakers, taught a group of six to ten students twice a week for one hundred pesetas (about one dollar in today's currency) per month.[67]

In 1958, the ASUW sponsored a series of lectures about university career orientation for women that were held in the lecture halls of the National Research Council. University of Madrid professors from different disciplines spoke on topics such as "Women's Dilemma in Choosing a University Career: Psychological Orientations," "Perspectives of the Sciences for College Women," "Is It Suitable for Women to Study and Practice Medicine?" and "What Does the School of Law Offer to the University Woman?" Father Solano's lecture "Life's Horizons" was the last one in the series.[68] It is important to note that all of the speakers were male professors. In both intellectual and spiritual matters the association sought the guidance of male experts.

The ASUW opened a women's university residence called "La casa de la universitaria" (the university woman's home) with private funding, but it lasted only five years. The bishop of Madrid-Alcalá granted ASUW the privilege to hold the Blessed Sacrament at this residence, located at 35 Espronceda Street in Madrid. The house was blessed by Father Solano, who celebrated an inaugurating mass before the board of directors. Manolita Fernández Arroyo, a graduate in philosophy and letters, was made director of "la casa," and Felicidad Beltrán, a graduate in law, became the administrator. The ASUW members wanted to create a "Christian home" for university women and a space where they could satisfy their thirst for knowledge. Residents had a library, a journal archive, and a billboard for cultural events and entertainment. In spite of ASUW's good intentions, however, "La casa de la universitaria" did not survive, "due to financial, and staff problems," comments Asunción Ibarra. "[B]ut the girls were very happy, because they enjoyed a lot of freedom, and participated in the activities of the residence."[69]

The founders of the ASUW emphasized the cultural and intellectual character of their organization. They never intended to promote social activities, but members could participate by personal choice in other organizations. The ASUW was not conceived of as a charity association; their focus was limited to seeking knowledge and following the doctrine of the Catholic Church. The founders insisted that the organization be independent from any religious or political organization, believing that a social consciousness would emerge on its own in each member. In Asunción Ibarra's words:

> The intention is to form . . . the university woman so that she can later carry
> out those social activities in other realms. But we did not create or facilitate the

means for social action. We wouldn't say, "You are going to do such social activity." However, if there is a person interested in going to the slums and helping the poor, she may do it. She may have gained that consciousness in our association, but she does it as a personal question, a personal choice. [The ASUW] does not impose any activity of that kind, no activity that is charitable.[70]

The ASUW never spread farther than the Madrid area. Although its statutes considered the possibility of expanding to other parts of the country, it never happened. Carmen Gayarre thought the reason was "that the members are all professionals who work in Madrid." They were (and still are) a minority of educated and pious women interested in their professional and spiritual growth, not in politics. When asked about Francoism, Carmen commented:

> Frankly, I thought very little about Francoism. I just took advantage of the situations that it offered. So, how would I tell you, I have been eminently practical. I saw who could help us, and looked for them. And I have been criticized in this sense. "You go wherever you need to go, you call whenever it is convenient for you, you look for what you need." So, more than the general situation, it was the opportunities that the situation opened for us.[71]

The members of the ASUW were educated women who sought intellectual and spiritual growth. Their Catholic faith was in tune with the official discourse on domestic femininity, yet they aspired to be professionals in the public arena. Francoism opened for them the possibility to develop a public persona that would contribute to the national endeavor but within the parameters of the official discourse on Catholic womanhood. They were conscious of their independent definition of Catholic womanhood and, in a utilitarian way, took advantage of the opportunities their religious zeal afforded them under the dictatorship. By emphasizing their search for pious knowledge and their lack of a political agenda, these women created a public persona of their own.

• • •

The organizations studied in this chapter developed their own discourses on Catholic womanhood in tune with the Francoist feminine project (enforced by the WS), yet different from it. They represent three different responses from right-wing women's organizations to the demands that modern consumer society placed on women. Being better educated was certainly necessary in order to improve the social conditions. For all these organizations, women's participation in social affairs was crucial to achieve the rechristianization of industrialized society. Each organization elaborated *its* own public persona, within Catholic parameters. All of them encouraged women's involvement in the public arena. They all considered themselves independent (meaning nonpolitical) but socially conscious right-wing women. That social consciousness arose from a belief in women's moral (meaning Christian) superiority. Their religious zeal made the dyad knowledge/femininity not an oxymoron. It is for all these reasons that these organizations illustrate issues of the agency of women under the Francoist dictatorship and point to the tension between official and marginal discourses of identity building.

The fundamental component in the Teresian Institute was the vow of celibacy and devotion to knowledge. For the senior women in Catholic Action, family duties were crucial to their self-perception as true Christian women, whereas for the young students of JEC, such as Purificación Prieto, the main issue was social activism. And for members of ASUW, their commitment to intellectual growth was central. All of the organizations shared several elements. First, they all glorified motherhood, both social and biological. Women's social mission in the 1950s was to bring motherly virtues to industrialized society, thus making it more humane. Second, none of these organizations had a declared political agenda, as the WS did, but rather considered themselves pious associations. Only in the JEC did political involvement become evident, when they cooperated in the labor strikes and the anti-Francoist student movement and when they assumed a dissident position against both the Catholic Church hierarchy and the regime.

Finally, all three organizations believed in the transcendental equality of the sexes. Christ's message was one of salvation for the human soul, both male and female. For these women, gender consciousness became a signifying element within social relations. Gender consciousness was sacred. Women had a role of their own to play in society, not as male mimics but rather as their complementary companions. Hence, for them the Christian message was a liberating one. By articulating a discourse on Catholic womanhood of their own, yet without contradicting the official National-Catholicism of the 1950s, these women created a public space of their own and placed themselves beyond politics. Their very spirituality protected them from official control and eliminated the threat of broad social censure.

CONCLUSION

Authoritarian Politics and Modernity from a Gender Perspective

To preserve tradition in the face of unavoidable modernization was the challenge the Francoist regime confronted in the 1950s, and the "woman question" constituted a crucial part of this clash. This decade saw Spain's transition from postwar isolation to Cold War Western ally. Additionally, it spawned the advent of a modern capitalist/consumer economy that wrought changes in gender relations and in women's access to education. These changes prompted two cabinet reorganizations and the regime's implementation of a National-Catholic agenda to create and sustain a popular consensus and to maintain Franco's stability in power. Some of the measures undertaken by the regime under the aegis of Opus Dei included the revision of the *Civil Code* in 1958 and the enactment of the *Law of Political, Professional, and Labor Rights for Women* in 1961. These legal texts demonstrate that National-Catholicism embodied a strict definition and observance of men's and women's roles and relations. Women were to be mothers, men were to be providers, and both were to continue being pious Spaniards even with the advent of consumerism.

A discourse of "true Catholic womanhood" was integral to National-Catholicism as instituted by the Francoist state. Sixteenth-century treatises such as *La perfecta casada* by Fray Luis de León and *La educación de la mujer cristiana* by Juan Luis Vives provided the foundation for this discourse, as did papal encyclicals (particularly *Casti Connubii* and *Divini Illius Magistri*), as well as the ideological indoctrination of the Women's Section of Falange. This discourse is most clearly seen in the Francoist educational system, which served to create and perpetuate the regime's political elite. Decoding the Francoist nationalization of women and the power dynamics that such nationalization involves reveals the essential roles education played, both in enforcing unity and uniformity and as the site where the individual related to the concept of the nation. The Francoist educational system instilled a sense of individual duty to the National-Catholic agenda based on gender. According to the regime and the Church, these differences in duty provided stability and social order to the nation and clarity of purpose to the individual.

In Francoist Spain, as in other authoritarian or totalitarian regimes (such as Nazi Germany, Fascist Italy, or Stalin's Soviet Union), the drive to nationalize the female populations implied the politicization of the private sphere. The Spanish case raises again questions concerning women's agency and responsibility under such regimes as well as women's consciousness building and resistance in the transition to a market economy. As Victoria de Grazia and Claudia Koonz have demonstrated for Germany and Italy,[1] for Spain, motherhood and the politics of the body (or "bio-power" in Foucauldian terms) were inherent to authoritarian body politics. Nazi Germany was a particularly clear example of this since nation building was based on race and sex; a racially pure state needed racially pure mothers[2] devoted to educating children in Nazi values. Similarly, Stalin imposed a "traditional" family model. For example, a law of 8 July 1944 abolished common-law marriage, increased family allowances, and created the title of Heroic Mother for those women who had more than ten children. In addition, unmarried mothers were no longer allowed to file paternity suits. The Soviet family was to be preserved and the state would guarantee it.[3] As under Stalin's regime, the main duty of mothers under fascist or Francoist rule was to be the first agents of indoctrination for the regime, rendering the family a site of particular concern for authoritarian politics. In the Francoist model, the family became the means to achieve total loyalty to the state. Women were the "heart" of the family in National-Catholic Spain, as much as they were in Nazi Germany, Fascist Italy, or Stalinist Soviet Union. The glorification of the maternal role of women under totalitarianism is essential for understanding how gender was and is central to authoritarian politics. Motherhood represented the essence of national strength and orchestrated an orderly relation between the sexes.

The sense of order between sexes that inspired the policies of authoritarian regimes was not confined to European countries. Glen Jeansonne's book *Women of the Far Right: The Mothers' Movement and World War II* explores these issues in the American context. Shortly after the German invasion of Poland in 1939 the Mothers' Movement emerged in the United States. The movement expanded from California to the rest of the United States and reached a membership of between five and six million women. Most were white, middle-class, and Christian. Elizabeth Dilling (1894–1966), the leader of this movement, was the most important woman to emerge from the far right in the United States during the 1930s. "She was so notorious," Jean-sonne points out, "that Sinclair Lewis based a character on her in *It Can't Happen Here*, his novel about fascism coming to America."[4] Dilling was especially enamored with Franco's fascism because of his adherence to Catholicism. Although an Episcopalian, she had attended Catholic school.[5] Christianity played a very important role in shaping the Mothers' Movement in the United States because these women were convinced that Christianity defined Americanism in the same way that National-Catholicism defined Spanishness during the Franco regime.

The Mothers' Movement considered Hitler, like they did Franco, a good Christian and fervent protector against Communism. When Dilling visited Germany in 1938 she was so impressed with Nazi rule that she would later write: "there is no question about it. The German people under Hitler are contented and happy. . . . [D]on't believe the stories you hear that this man has not done a great good for this country."[6] Dilling's travels also took her to Spain, where she witnessed Franco's crusade against Communism, later writing that Spain was "a paradise of order and decency compared to dirty Red Russia which wants Franco overthrown."[7] Dilling's Mothers' Movement supported the isolationist cause during World War II. The anticommunist and anti-Semitic campaigns that her movement launched in the 1930s were kept alive by the pro-fascist propaganda in the United States. In the 1950s Dilling supported Sen. Joseph McCarthy in his quest to root out Communism. Like the women's organizations in European authoritarian regimes, the Mothers' Movement was openly antifeminist. The movement and the European organizations did not challenge the privileged status of males in society, but rather they sought to create a separate sphere of power using a discourse that emphasized the eternal feminine roles of mother and wife in society. For them gender difference and Western Christian values ordered the chaotic male world.

Exploring authoritarian regimes from a gender perspective requires addressing right-wing women's definitions of self, specifically within the boundaries of Catholicism for the Spanish case. Francoism created the possibility for women to contribute to the national endeavor within the parameters established by the official discourse on Catholic womanhood. Women's social contribution was realized within their participation in the Women's Section of the Falange and in different Catholic organizations such as Catholic Action or the Teresian Institute. The official National-Catholic discourse emphasized fixed, binary political, and social definitions, including the meaning of gender. The ultimate guarantee of the truth was God, and the individuals gained a sense of self by identifying with the word of God as read by the Catholic Church and the Francoist state.

Former Falangist women leaders remembered the Francoist past as days full of solidarity, dedication, and self-discovery. Rather than entering men's worlds, they expanded their own sphere beyond direct male intervention. The three pillars of the new state—family, municipality, and syndicate—were the only sites for political participation. By making the family and domestic duties their main concern, Falangist women placed themselves at the center of the political arena. They relied on male politics only for the enactment of the Women's Section's domestic agenda presented in a nonthreatening, highly antifeminist fashion. At the Cold War political juncture, Franco purged male Falangist elements from his government to gain international acquiescence. However, the Falangist Women's Section survived until 1977, beyond the death of the dictator. Female Falangist officials proclaimed themselves to be the guardians of the humane values of Falange and the regime. While the Women's Section's tame discourse on femininity was not different from that of the state and the Catholic Church, it did grant them the opportunity to be agents in the national enterprise.

Besides the Women's Section, other women's organizations elaborated their own definitions of the Catholic female self—in tune with the Francoist feminine project, yet different from it. While the official discourse encouraged women to remain at home, it assigned to the Women's Section a legitimate, but maternal, public purpose: the participation of women in the national endeavor of fulfilling their biological destiny as mothers at home. This perspective broadened somewhat in the 1950s to recognize women's participation in social affairs, necessary to the creation of a modern, industrial, but still Christian society. Operating in this context, each of the organizations discussed (TI, JEC, and ASUW) elaborated their own definition of Catholic womanhood. The discourse on true Catholic womanhood, hence, proved to be not monolithic but multifaceted. Gender difference remained the key to Teresian, Catholic Action, and ASUW women's definition of selfhood. At the same time, they believed in the transcendental equality of the sexes and the salvation of the human soul, both male and female. For them, gender consciousness became a signifying element that was sacred within social relations. Women had a role of their own to play in society, not as male mimics but rather as their partners. The Catholic organizations studied here represented the competing discourses on true Catholic womanhood, the alternative ways of giving meaning to the female self, and the various Catholic paths to female empowerment.

The language and nature of true Catholic womanhood was not fixed. The Francoist version of femininity stressed an obedient and submissive woman whose national duty remained attached to the family realm. Teresian, Catholic Action Women, and ASUW members developed public personae of their own that diverged from, but did not openly challenge, national gender ideology. Their spirituality and declared antifeminism protected them from official control and allowed them to develop outside the home. Yet each of these women's organizations presented distinct and contesting discourses of true Catholic womanhood. The dynamic interaction, relation, and tension among the different discourses on Catholic female subjectivity are evident in the reading of a variety of texts. One set of meanings appears in the written documents produced by the regime, the Catholic Church, and women's organizations: legislation, statistics, encyclicals, newspapers, and correspondence. A different viewpoint emerges as one listens to the oral testimonies of university women who belonged to Catholic organizations and the Women's Section.[8] These women's memories link past and present to create a unique reality. Unlike the more static documentary record, their memories are the product of present realities and prove how consciousness is always in the making.

The gendered discourse of Franco's Spain has much to say to scholars who study gender ideology and authoritarian politics in Latin American and Eastern European countries. In the case of Argentina, Sandra McGee Deutsch has explored the ties between right-wing women's organizations and social Catholicism from 1900 to 1932.[9] The triumph of Franco in Spain, as well as Hitler in Germany and Mussolini in Italy, inspired the right to proclaim these regimes as models for the future of Argentina. Especially important was the influence of the Falange on like-minded activists interested in a "purifying Argentine renewal."[10]

The recent transition to the market economy and democratization of Eastern European countries has also led some scholars to the Spanish model of transition to democracy after Franco's death. As Kenneth Maxwell notes, "Spain and Eastern Europe are different in many basic ways; nevertheless, Eastern Europeans have learned from Spain's democratization."[11] Although the process of democratization in Spain has received scholarly attention, the interaction of the new regime with other geopolitical areas has been little studied. According to Geoffrey Pridham, "the purpose of a comparative framework is to accommodate complexities and to encourage a dynamic rather than static approach to transition."[12] Pridham distinguishes three separate but interconnected levels of the transition process: state, intergroup relations, and society. Surrounding these levels is the environment that may include the international framework or the state of the economy. Spain offers a fairly convincing historical case of socioeconomic transformation. The Spanish "economic miracle" initiated by the Stabilization Plan of 1959 created such large-scale changes that political ramifications were inevitable. Particularly interesting is the impact of the transition at the society level, especially on gender relations, ethnic divisions, and national identity. Hence it is important to analyze the Francoist redefinition of national identity in general and gender identities in particular during the transition from autarchy to a market economy, as well as to analyze the ways modernization undermined the regime and aided the transition to democracy. Barbara Einhorn has explored such issues in the East European context in *Cinderella Goes to Market: Citizenship, Gender, and Women's Movements in East Central Europe*.[13] Central to my study are the adjustments Franco's regime made to the changes brought about by the modernization of the country and the impact of modernity on the construction of Spanish national identity articulated along gender lines.

It is in the realm of consciousness building that the Francoist regime underwent profound changes and eventually collapsed, opening the way to a democratic transition. Throughout this study, I have dealt with the tension between, on the one hand, the official discourse on National-Catholicism and its elaboration of Catholic womanhood and, on the other hand, marginal discourses of dissidence as well as those discourses within the right-wing spectrum. This tension was accentuated in the transitional decade of the 1950s with the advent of the market economy, which illustrates how the "politics of the everyday" rather than party-led collective movements can lead to the transformation of a political system from a dictatorship to a democracy. The personal changes in subjectivity and self-representation prompted by consumption, tourism, and emigration had a real effect in the perpetuation of the regime beyond Franco's life. Modernization signaled the beginning of the end of Francoism. The regime struggled to accommodate its foundations to the multiplicity of contested discourses at play. In part because of the deep resonance of the discourse of true Catholic womanhood within Spain, however, the nation did not achieve qualitative political change until Franco died.

Gender provides a unique window through which to look at the process of modernization and political change from an authoritarian regime toward democracy. As we have seen in this study, many discourses on Catholic womanhood coexisted along with the official female model, which raises questions about the effectiveness of official propaganda in a dictatorship. It also points out the significance of identity politics as a strategy of resistance and agency in modern consumer societies, what Victoria de Grazia calls "post-political citizenship."[14] Although there was some indoctrination of the female population, the official message was generally filtered, reinterpreted, and accommodated to the particular needs of each group within the right-wing women's organizations studied here. The presence of women in the public sphere in 1950s Spain was defined not so much by the transformation of the political system as by new notions of female self and collective gender roles. The synthesis of all of these discourses engendered and eventually gave birth to a new woman for a new Spain—not Francoist but democratic.

NOTES

INTRODUCTION

1. Victoria Enders, "Nationalism and Feminism: The Sección Femenina of the Falange," *History of European Ideas* 15 (1992): 673–80; Rosario Sánchez López, *Mujer española una sombra de destino en lo universal: Trayectoria histórica de sección Femenina de falange (1934–1977)* (Murcia: Universidad de Murcia, 1990); María Teresa Gallego, *Mujer, Falange y Franquismo* (Madrid: Taurus, 1983); Luis Suárez Fernández, *Crónica de la Sección Femenina y su tiempo* (Madrid: Asociación Nueva Andadura, 1993).

2. Juan J. Linz, "An Authoritarian Regime: Spain," in *Politics and Society in Twentieth-Century Spain,* edited by Stanley G. Payne (New York: New Viewpoints, 1976).

3. Joan Wallach Scott, *Gender and the Politics of History* (New York: Columbia University Press, 1988), 25–26. According to Foucault, there are two meanings to the word *subject.* First, it can mean being subject to someone else by control and dependence. Second, it can mean self-identity through conscious self-knowledge. Michel Foucault, "Subject and Power," quoted in Paul Rabinow, ed., *The Foucault Reader* (New York: Pantheon Books, 1984), 21.

4. Michel Foucault, "Discipline and Punish," quoted in Rabinow, ed., *Foucault Reader,* 17.

5. On National-Catholicism and education, see Gregorio Cámara Villar, *Nacional-Catolicismo y escuela: La socialización política del Franquismo (1936–1951)* (Madrid: Editorial Hesperia, 1984); Clotilde Navarro García, *La educación y el Nacional-Catolicismo* (Castilla la Mancha: Universidad de Castilla la Mancha, 1993); and Andrés Sopeña Monsalve, *El Florido Pensil: Memoria de la escuela nacionalcatólica* (Barcelona: Crítica, 1994).

6. Chris Weedon, *Feminist Practice and Poststructuralist Theory* (Oxford: Basil Blackwell, 1987), 24.

7. Luisa Passerini, "Oral History in Italy after the Second World War," *International Journal of Oral History* 9, no. 2 (1988): 121.

8. Jane Sherron de Hart, "Gender on the Right: Meanings behind the Existential Scream," *Gender and History* 3, no. 3 (1991): 246–67. On the subject of difference feminism, see Karen Offen, "Defining Feminism, a Comparative Historical Approach," *Signs* 14, no. 1 (1988): 119–57; Carole Pateman, *The Disorder of Women: Democracy, Feminism, and Political Theory* (Cambridge: Polity, 1989); Carole Pateman and Mary Lyndon Shanley, *Feminist Interpretations and Political Theory* (University Park: Pennsylvania State University Press, 1991); Jane Rendall, *The Origins of Modern Feminism: France, Britain and the United States, 1780–1860* (Houndwills: MacMillan, 1985); Nancy F. Cott, *The Grounding of*

Modern Feminism (New Haven, Conn.: Yale University Press, 1987); Wendy Sarvasy, "Beyond the Difference versus Equality Policy Debate: Postsuffrage Feminism, Citizenship, and the Quest for a Feminist Welfare State," *Signs* 17, no. 2 (1992): 329–62. Sherron de Hart, "Gender on the Right," 248.

1: MODERNITY AND THE WOMAN QUESTION

1. José María Jover Zamora, "Los años 80 y la consolidación del liberalismo," in Manuel Tuñón de Lara, Gabriel Tortella Casares, Casimiro Marti y Marti, José María Jover Zamora, José Luis García Delgado, and David Ruiz Gonzáles, *Revolución burguesa, oligarquía y Constitucionalismo (1834–1923)* (Barcelona: Labor, 1981), 324.

2. Mary Nash, *Defying Male Civilization: Women in the Civil War* (Denver: Arden Press, 1995), 7.

3. Andrés Ollero Tassara, *Universidad y política: Tradición y secularización en el siglo XIX español* (Madrid: Instituto de Estudios Políticos, 1972).

4. Teresa Rodríguez de Lecea, *Francisco Giner de los Ríos: Escritos sobre la universidad española* (Madrid: Espasa Calpe, Colección Austral, 1990); Vicente Cacho Viu, *La Institución Libre de Enseñanza* (Madrid: Ediciones Rialp, 1962); Juan Angel Blanco Carrascosa, *Un arquetipo pedagógico pequeño-burgués: Teoría y práxis de la Institución Libre de Enseñanza* (Valencia: Fernando Torres-Editor, S.A., 1980).

5. Ollero Tassara, *Universidad y política*, 20.

6. For the first ten years of Isabel II's rule, she was underage, and therefore her mother, María Cristina, ruled as regent queen. The constitutions enacted in Spain throughout the nineteenth century were the Constitution of 1812, the Royal Statute of 1834, the Constitution of 1837, the Constitution of 1845, the Constitution "nonnata" of 1856, the Constitution of 1869, and the Constitution of 1876, which continued in effect until the Second Republic's Constitution of 1931 was adopted.

7. Geraldine Scanlon, *La polémica feminista en la España contemporánea (1868–1974)* (Madrid: Siglo XXI, 1976), 15–57.

8. Casimiro Martí, "Afianzamiento y despegue del sistema liberal," in Tuñón de Lara et al., *Revolución burguesa*, 171. See Linda K. Kerber, *Women of the Republic: Intellect and Ideology in Revolutionary America* (New York: W. W. Norton, 1980).

9. José María Jover Zamora, "La época de la Restauración: Panorama político-social, 1875–1902," in Tuñón de Lara et al., *Revolución burguesa*, 278.

10. Ibid., 271.

11. Nash, *Defying Male Civilization*, 9. Emilia Pardo Bazán, quoted in Nash, *Defying Male Civilization*, 15.

12. Benjamin Martin, *The Agony of Modernization: Labor and Industrialization in Spain* (Ithaca, N.Y.: ILR Press, 1990), 149.

13. Alfonso Capitán Díaz, *Historia de la educación en España: Pedagogía contemporánea*, vol. 2 (Madrid: Dykinson, 1994).

14. Pedro Cuesta Escudero, *La escuela en la Restauración de la sociedad española (1900–1923)* (Madrid: Siglo XXI, 1994), 255. Unless otherwise noted, all translations from Spanish works are my own.

15. Nash, *Defying Male Civilization*, 21.

16. The American Board of Commissioners for Foreign Missions was founded in 1806. Carmen Zulueta, *Cien años de educación de la mujer española: Historia del Instituto Internacional* (Madrid: Editorial Castalia, 1992), 23. Joan Connelly Ullman, "La enseñanza superior de la mujer en España: Relaciones entre universitarias españolas y estadounidenses, 1877–1980," in *Nuevas perspectivas sobre la mujer*, edited by the Seminario de estudios de la Mujer (Madrid: Seminario de Estudios de la Mujer, Universidad Autónoma de Madrid, 1982), 196–205.

17. Rosa María Capel Martínez, "La apertura del horizonte cultural femenino: Fernando de Castro y los congresos pedagógicos del siglo XIX," in *Mujer y sociedad de España (1700–1975)*, edited by Rosa María Capel Martínez and María Angeles Durán (Madrid: Ministerio de Cultura, 1982), 121. Concepción Arenal, quoted in María Isabel Cabrera Bosch, "Las mujeres que lucharon solas: Concepción Arenal y Emilia Pardo Bazán," in *El feminismo en España: Dos siglos de historia*, edited by Pilar Folguera (Madrid: Editorial Pablo Iglesias, 1988), 38. Other works by Arenal include *La mujer del porvenir* (1868) and *La mujer de su casa* (1881). Emilia Pardo Bazán, quoted in Cabrera Bosch, "Las mujeres que lucharon solas," 39.

18. Scanlon, *La polémica feminista*, 72.

19. Quoted in Capel Martínez, *Mujer y sociedad de España*, 137.

20. Scanlon, *La polémica feminista*, 50. Pérez Galdós published *Fortunata y Jacinta* in 1886. Benito Pérez Galdós, *Fortunata and Jancita: Two Stories of Married Women*, translated and with an introduction by Agnes Moncy Gullón (Athens: University of Georgia Press, 1986), 259.

21. Scanlon, *La polémica feminista*, 50. Capel Martínez, *Mujer y sociedad de España*, 145.

22. See Francisco Ferrer y Guardia, *The Origin and Ideals of the Modern School* (London: Watts and Co., 1913); Buenaventura Delgado, *La Escuela Moderna de Ferrer i Guardia* (Barcelona: Ediciones CEAC, 1979). On the events of the Tragic Week, see Joan Connelly Ullman, *The Tragic Week: A Study of Anticlericalism in Spain, 1875–1912* (Cambridge, Mass.: Harvard University Press, 1968).

23. Scanlon, *La polémica feminista*, 52–55.

24. Capitán Díaz, *Historia de la educación*, 363. Andrés Manjón, quoted in Cuesta Escudero, *La escuela en la Restauración*, 220 (my emphasis).

25. Margarita Nelken, *La condición social de la mujer en España* (Madrid: CVS Ediciones, 1975), 62 (my emphasis). This book was first published in 1919 and re-edited by María Aurelia Capmany in 1975. Margarita Nelken was part of an active minority of left-wing European women; see on this subject Jane Slaughter and Robert Kern, eds., *European Women on the Left: Socialism, Feminism, and the Problems Faced by Political Women, 1880 to the Present* (Westport, Conn.: Greenwood Press, 1981). Gregorio Marañón, *Amor, conveniencia y eugenesia* (Madrid: Editorial Historia Nueva, 1929), 27.

26. José Ortega y Gasset, *Estudios sobre el amor* (Madrid: Alianza Editorial, 1981), 183.

27. Sebastián Balfour, "The Loss of Empire, Regenerationism, and the Forging of a Myth of National Identity," in *Spanish Cultural Studies: An Introduction*, edited by Helen Graham and Jo Labanyi (Oxford: Oxford University Press, 1995), 29.

28. On Spanish fascism and particularly on the Falange, see Stanley Payne, *Falange: A History of Spanish Fascism* (Stanford, Calif.: Stanford University Press, 1965); Stanley Payne, *Spain's First Democracy: The Second Republic, 1931–1936* (Madison: University of Wisconsin Press, 1993); Javier Jiménez Campo, *El fascismo en la crisis de la Segunda República* (Madrid: Centro de Investigaciones Sociológicas, 1982); Sheelagh Ellwood, *Spanish Fascism in the Franco Era: Falange Española de las JONS, 1936–1976* (Basingstoke: Macmillan, 1987).

29. Clara Campoamor, *El voto femenino y yo* (Barcelona: LaSal Edicions de les Dones, 1981), 107; see also Scanlon, *La polémica feminista.*

30. On Spanish women's suffrage, see also Campoamor, *El voto femenino y yo;* Concha Fagoaga, *Clara Campoamor, la sufragista española* (Madrid: Ministerio de Cultura, 1981); and Concha Fagoaga, *La voz y el voto de las mujeres: El sufragismo en España, 1877–1931* (Barcelona: Icaria, 1985). Left-wing republicans did not want to jeopardize the young republic by enfranchising an inexperienced segment of the population. Aurora Morcillo Gómez, "Feminismo y lucha política durante la II República y la Guerra Civil," in Folguera, *El feminismo en España,* 70.

31. Antonio Molero Pintado divides the Republican period into three stages of the educational reform: the first biennium, creation; the second, revision; and the rest, dissolution. *La reforma educativa en la Segunda República española* (Madrid: Aula XXI, Educación Abierta/Santillana, 1977), 16. Esther Cortada Andreu, *Escuela mixta y coeducación en Cataluña durante la II República* (Madrid: Instituto de la Mujer, 1988); Rosa María Capel Martínez, *El trabajo y la educación de la mujer en España (1900–1930)* (Madrid: Ministerio de Cultura, 1986); Connelly Ullman, "La enseñanza superior de la mujer en España," 196–205; María Carmen García Nieto and Esperanza Yllán, "La educación de la mujer," in *Historia de España (1808–1978),* edited by María Carmen García Nieto and Esperanza Yllán (Barcelona: Crítica, 1989); Geraldine Scanlon, "La mujer y la instrucción pública: De la Ley Moyano a la II República" *Historia de la Educación* 6 (1987): 193–208; María Luisa Barrera Peña and Ana López Peña, *Sociología de la mujer en la universidad: Análisis histórico-comparativo Galicia-España, 1900–1981* (Santiago de Compostela: Universidad de Santiago de Compostela, 1984).

32. Manuel Tuñón de Lara, Julio Aróstegui, Angel Viñas, Gabriel Cardona, and Josep M. Brical, eds., *La Guerra Civil Española 50 años después* (Madrid: Labor, 1986), 313.

33. Julio Aróstegui, "Los componentes sociales y políticos," in Tuñón de Lara et al., *La Guerra Civil Española,* 45–123. Tuñón de Lara et al., *La Guerra Civil Española,* 311, 317.

34. Initially, women participated in the militias created by the political parties and the trade unions, but the decree creating the Ejército Popular de la República in September of 1936 excluded them from this duty. On the participation of women in the Civil War, see Martha A. Ackelsberg, *Free Women of Spain: Anarchism and the Struggle for the Emancipation of Women* (Bloomington: Indiana University Press, 1991); Shirley Mangini, *Memories of Resistance: Women's Voices from the Spanish Civil War* (New Haven, Conn.: Yale University Press, 1995); María Teresa Gallego Méndez, *Mujer, Falange y Franquismo* (Madrid: Taurus, 1983); Carmen Alcalde, *La mujer en la guerra civil española* (Madrid: Cambio 16, 1976); Car-

lota O'Neill, *Una mujer en la guerra de España* (Madrid: Turner, 1979); Teresa Pamies, *Records de guerra i d'exili (Obres selectes i inedites)* (Barcelona: Dopesa, 1976); Mary Nash, *Mujer y movimiento obrero en España 1931–1939* (Barcelona: Editorial Fontamara, 1981); María Carmen García Nieto, "Las mujeres en la guerra civil de España: Nueva perspectiva," in *Nuevas perspectivas sobre la mujer,* edited by the Seminario de Estudios de la Mujer, 184–90.

35. On Mujeres Libres (Free Women), see Ackelsberg, *Free Women of Spain;* Mary Nash, *Mujeres Libres: España 1936–1939* (Barcelona: Tusquets, 1975); Mary Nash, "El neomaltusianismo anarquista y los conocimientos populares sobre control de la natalidad en España," in *Presencia y protagonismo: Aspectos de la historia de la mujer,* edited by Mary Nash (Barcelona: Ediciones del Serbal, 1984); Temma Kaplan, "Spanish Anarchism and Women's Liberation," *Journal of Contemporary History* 6, no. 2 (1971); and Temma Kaplan, "Other Scenarios: Women and Spanish Anarchism," in *Becoming Visible: Women in European History,* edited by Renate Bridenthal and Claudia Koonz (Boston: Houghton Mifflin, 1987). Lucia Sánchez Saornil, "Resumen al margen de la cuestión femenina," *Solidaridad Obrera,* 8 November 1935, quoted in Ackelsberg, *Free Women of Spain,* 117.

36. "Estatutos de la Agrupación de Mujeres Libres," quoted in Ackelsberg, *Free Women of Spain,* 115. Mercedes Comaposada, quoted in Ackelsberg, *Free Women of Spain,* 129.

37. Tuñón de Lara et al., *La Guerra Civil Española,* 288. "Los comunistas y anarquistas son los hijos de Caín." A pastoral letter by Pla i Daniel, 30 September 1936, entitled "Las dos ciudades," quoted in Tuñón de Lara et al., *La Guerra Civil Española,* 288. Fray Ignacio G. Menéndez Reigada, *La guerra nacional española ante la moral y el derecho* (Salamanca, 1937), quoted in Tuñón de Lara et al., *La Guerra Civil Española,* 289.

38. See Alicia Alted Vigil, "Notas para la configuración y el análisis de la política cultural del franquismo en sus comienzos: la labor del Ministerio de Educación Nacional durante la guerra," in *España bajo el franquismo,* edited by Josep Fontana (Barcelona: Editorial Crítica, 1986).

39. Gallego Méndez, *Mujer, Falange y Franquismo,* esp. 46. See also Elena Posa, "Una dona portadora de valors eterns: La Sección Femenina, 1934–1952," *Taula di Camvi* 5 (May–June 1977); Giuliana di Febo, "La política de la Secció Femenina de la Falange," *L'Avenç* 14 (March 1979); Victoria Enders, "Nationalism and Feminism: The Sección Femenina of the Falange," *History of European Ideas* 15 (1992). 673-80.

40. Tuñón de Lara et al., *La Guerra Civil Española,* 315. Decree of 7 October 1937, Sección Femenina, papers, Archivo General de la Administración, Alcalá de Henares, Spain (hereafter cited as SFP/AGA).

41. Gallego Méndez, *Mujer, Falange y Franquismo,* 90–99.

42. *Ideal,* 21 December 1936.

2: THE FRANCOIST RECOVERY OF TRADITION

1. Juan José Ruiz Rico, *El papel político de la iglesia católica en la España de Franco* (Madrid: Editorial Tecnos, 1977), 17.

2. William Callahan, *Church, Politics, and Society in Spain, 1750–1894* (Cambridge, Mass.: Harvard University Press, 1984), 183.

3. José Pemartín, *¿Qué es "lo nuevo"?: Consideraciones sobre el momento español actual* (Sevilla: Tip. Alvarez y Zambrano, 1937), quoted in Alejandro Mayordomo Pérez, *Nacional-catolicismo y educación en la España de la postguerra* (Madrid: Ministerio de Educación y Ciencia, Secretaría General Técnica, 1990), 22–23. Paul Preston, *Franco: A Biography* (New York: Basic Books, 1994), 323. Pius XII, *ABC* (Madrid), 2 April 1939, quoted in María Carmen García Nieto and Javier M. Donezar, *La España de Franco (1939–1973)* (Madrid: Guadiana, 1975).

4. As Raymond Carr has pointed out,

[t]he regime prided itself on its capacity for "institutional perfection" on the evolution of a constitution *sui generis,* completed by the Organic Law of 1967. This constitution embodied the principles of "Organic democracy," as opposed to the artificial "inorganic democracy" based on universal suffrage, the party system, and the responsibility of governments to an elected parliament.

Modern Spain, 1875–1980 (Oxford: Oxford University Press, 1990), 165. Once King Juan Carlos was raised to the throne, he favored the transition from an organic democracy to a democracy without adjectives. On the fascist nature of the regime, see Manuel Tuñón de Lara, ed., *Historia de España* (Barcelona: Labor, 1983); Manuel Tuñón de Lara, "El modelo franquista," *Historia* 16 (December 1982); Manuel Tuñón de Lara, "Algunas propuestas metodológicas para el análisis del Franquismo," in *Ideología y Sociedad en la España contemporánea: Por un análisis del Franquismo,* edited by Manuel Tuñón de Lara (Madrid: Edicusa, 1977); Manuel Ramírez Jiménez, ed. *Las fuentes ideológicas de un régimen (España 1939–1945)* (Zaragoza: Universidad de Zaragoza, Libros Pórtico, 1978); Benjamín Oltra and Amando de Miguel, "Bonapartismo y Catolicismo: Una hipótesis sobre los orígenes ideológicos del Franquismo," *Revista de Sociología "Papers"* 8 (1978); Daniel Sueiro and Bernardo Díaz Nosty, *Historia del Franquismo* (Madrid: Sarpe, 1986); Eduardo Pons Prades, *Guerrillas españolas (1936–1960)* (Barcelona: Espejo de España, 1978). Stanley G. Payne, *The Franco Regime: 1936–1975* (Madison: University of Wisconsin Press, 1987), 234. See Sheelagh M. Ellwood, "Falange y Franquismo," and Ricardo L. Chueca, "FET y de las JONS: La paradójica victoria de un fascismo fracasado," both in *España bajo el Franquismo,* edited by Josep Fontana (Barcelona: Editorial Crítica, 1986). See also Sheelagh M. Ellwood, *Prietas las filas: Historia de Falange Española, 1933–1983* (Barcelona: Crítica, 1984); and Sheelagh M. Ellwood, *Spanish Fascism in the Franco Era* (Basingstoke: Macmillan, 1987).

5. Alberto Reig Tapia, *Ideología e historia: Sobre la represión franquista en la guerra civil* (Madrid: Editorial Akal, 1984); Angel Suárez and Equipo 36, *Libro blanco de las cárceles franquistas* (París: Editions Ruedo Ibérico, 1976); Giuliana di Febo, *Resistencia y movimiento de mujeres en España, 1936–1976* (Barcelona: ICARIA Editorial, 1979); Shirley Mangini, "Memories of Resistance: Women Activists from the Spanish Civil War," *Signs* 17 (1991). These authors estimate that there were around ten thousand women in the prison of Ventas in Madrid, an institution built to house only five hundred inmates. Hence, the testimonies of women who were in prison are of extreme interest: Juana Doña, *Desde la noche y la niebla*

(Madrid: Ediciones la Torre, 1977); Angeles García Madrid, *Requien por la libertad* (Madrid: Copiasol, 1982).

6. On "political families," see Alexander de Grand, *Italian Fascism: Its Origins and Development* (Lincoln: University of Nebraska Press, 1989). The term "political families" refers to the different factions or interest groups that existed during the Franco regime and was used by Amando de Miguel in his book *Sociología del Franquismo: Análisis ideológico de los Ministros del Régimen* (Barcelona: Editorial Euros, 1975). De Miguel distinguishes the following groups: military men, *primorriveristas,* traditionalists, monarchists, Falangists, Catholics, *integristas,* and technocrats. Sheelagh Ellwood, *Franco* (London: Longman, 1994), 112–13. *Boletín Oficial del Estado,* 18 July 1945, cited in García Nieto and Donezar, *La España de Franco,* 194–98.

7. Juan J. Linz, "An Authoritarian Regime: Spain," 165.

8. See Gregorio Cámara Villar, *Nacional-Catolicismo y escuela: La socialización política del Franquismo (1936–1951)* (Madrid: Editorial Hesperia, 1984); Tuñón de Lara, "Algunas propuestas metodológicas"; Ramírez Jiménez et al., *Las fuentes ideológicas;* Oltra and de Miguel, "Bonapartismo y catolicismo"; and María A. Escudero, "The Image of Latin America Disseminated in Spain by the Franco Regime: Repercussions in the Configuration of National Identity," Ph.D. diss., University of California, San Diego, 1994.

9. Preston, *Franco,* xix. Juan Antonio Ansaldo, *¿Para qué . . . ? (de Alfonso XIII a Juan II)* (Buenos Aires, 1951), quoted in Preston, *Franco,* xix.

10. Decree of 28 November 1937, *SFP/AGA.*

11. Decree of 28 December 1939, *SFP/AGA.*

12. Decree of 28 November 1937, articles 12, 13, *Boletín Oficial del Estado* (hereafter cited as *BOE*), 30 November 1937.

13. Decree of 9 February 1944, *BOE,* 23 February 1944. Decree of 21 November 1944, *BOE,* 21 November 1944.

14. Geraldine Scanlon, *La polémica feminista en la España contemporánea (1868–1974)* (Madrid: Siglo XXI, 1976), 322. Law of 12 July 1941, *BOE,* 28 July 1941.

15. Law of 12 July 1941, article 15, *BOE,* 28 July 1941. Order of 20 December 1941, article 7, *BOE,* 21 December 1941.

16. Fuero del Trabajo (Labor charter), reissued by the decree of 20 December 1967, *BOE,* 21 December 1967.

17. Pius XI, *Quadragesimo Anno* (Rome: Typis polyglottis vaticanis, 1931), 26, 33.

18. Fuero del Trabajo, Decree of 20 April 1967, article 8, *BOE,* 21 April 1967. See Lourdes Benería, *Mujer, economía y patriarcado en la España de Franco* (Barcelona: Cuadernos Anagrama, 1977). Order of 27 December 1938, *BOE,* 31 December 1938.

19. Payne, *The Franco Regime,* 246–48.

20. Ibid., 250, 386.

21. Ibid., 388.

22. Ibid., 252. Vicente Enrique y Tarancón (obispo de Solsona), *El pan nuestro de cada día dánosle hoy . . .* (Madrid: Publicaciones HOAC, 1950).

23. Decree of 29 July 1948, ratified by the instrument of 12 June 1958, *BOE,* 21 August 1959.

24. Giuliana di Febo, *La santa de la raza: El culto barroco en la España franquista* (Barcelona: Icaria, 1988), 37–38. One of the biographers of Saint Teresa de Jesús, Father Silverio de Santa Teresa, wrote *Santa Teresa modelo de feminismo cristiano* (Burgos: Topografia del Monte Carmelo, 1931).

25. Di Febo, *La santa de la raza,* 68. Rosa Rossi, "Teresa de Jesús: La mujer y la Iglesia," *Mientras Tanto* 14 (1982): 63–79; and Rosa Rossi, "Teresa de Jesús: La mujer y la palabra," *Mientras Tanto* 15 (1983): 29–47.

26. Juan Luis Vives, *Instrucción de la mujer cristiana* (The instruction of the Christian woman) (1523; reprint, Buenos Aires: Espasa Calpe, 1940), 56.

27. Ibid., 30, 56.

28. Scanlon, *La polémica feminista,* 335. Fray Luis de León, *La perfecta casada* (The perfect married lady) (1583), in *Obras completas de Fray Luis de León,* edited by Felix García (Madrid: Biblioteca de Autores Españoles, 1944), 219–20, 226–27.

29. De León, *La perfecta casada,* 306.

30. Ibid., 276.

31. Mayordomo Pérez, *Nacional-catolicismo y educación,* 47.

32. Pius XI, "Divini Illius Magistri: Carta encíclica de Su Santidad Pio XI sobre la educación cristiana de la juventud," in *El Papa habla a los padres de familia* (Madrid: Confederación Católica de Padres de Familia, 1941), 103, 108.

33. Ibid., 122.

34. Pius XI, "Casti Connubii: Carta encíclica de Su Santidad Pio XI sobre la dignidad del matrimonio," in *El Papa habla a los padres de familia* (Madrid: Confederación Católica de Padres de Familia, 1941), 25 (my emphasis), 40.

35. Ibid., 42.

36. Ibid., 50.

37. The regime published two works against the spirit of FIL: E. Suñer, *Los intelectuales y la tragedia española* (San Sebastián: Biblioteca España Nueva, 1937); and a collective book under the title *Una poderosa fuerza secreta: La Institución Libre de Enseñanza* (San Sebastián: Editorial Española, 1940).

38. Manuel Puelles Benítez, *Educación e ideología en la España contemporánea* (Barcelona: Editorial Labor, 1980); Cámara Villar, *Nacional-catolicismo y escuela;* María Inmaculada Pastor, *La educación femenina en la postguerra (1939–1945): El caso de Mallorca* (Madrid: Instituto de la Mujer, 1984); Mayordomo Pérez, *Nacional-catolicismo y educación;* Clotilde Navarro García, *La educación y el Nacional-catolicismo* (Castilla la Mancha: Universidad de Castilla la Mancha, 1993); and Andrés Sopeña Monsalve, *El Florido Pensil: Memoria de la escuela nacionalcatólica* (Barcelona: Crítica, 1994). José Ibáñez Martín, inaugural speech for the academic year at the University of Madrid, October 1942, quoted in Mayordomo Pérez, *Nacional-catolicismo y educación,* 25. The order of 23 September 1936 and the order of 1 May 1939 prohibited coeducation. *Law of Elementary Education,* article 14, quoted in Mayordomo Pérez, *Nacional-catolicismo y educación,* 48.

39. Pastor, *La educación femenina,* 41. *BOE,* 26 August 1939.

40. See the following orders: order of 2 February 1943, *BOE,* 15 February 1943; order of 8 June 1943, *BOE,* 23 June 1943; and order of 2 November 1944, *BOE,* 2 December 1944. José Ibáñez Martín, speech, 16 July 1943, quoted in Mayordomo Pérez, *Nacional-catolicismo y educación,* 42.

41. The *Law of Elementary Education,* 17 July 1945, quoted in Pastor, *La educación femenina,* 48. José Pemartín, interview, *Signo,* 11 April 1942, quoted in Pastor, *La educación femenina,* 31.

42. *BOE,* 15 June 1941.

43. Sección Femenina de FET y de las JONS, "Historia de la Asociación de Enseñanza para la Mujer," Madrid, 1939, 2–6.

44. Alicia Alted Vigil, "La mujer en las coordenadas educativas del régimen franquista," in *Ordenamiento jurídico y realidad social de las mujeres,* edited by Seminario de Estudios de la Mujer, Universidad Autónoma de Madrid (Madrid, 1986). Decree of 2 March 1945, *Creación del Instituto de Enseñanzas Profesionales de la Mujer, BOE,* 17 March 1945.

45. Elena Posa "Una dona portadora de valors eterns: La Sección Femenina, 1934–1952," *Taula de Camvi* 5 (May–June 1977): 127.

3: CATHOLIC WOMANHOOD AND CONSUMERISM

1. According to Payne, the system that Franco developed was more like the one proposed by Calvo Sotelo and the Acción Española theorists for the establishment of an authoritarian monarchy, rather than a system based strongly on the fascist formulas of the Falange.

> All seven points of *Acción Española* had been met: the legislation of 1947 had converted the system into an authoritarian monarchist state; a controlled corporative parliamentary system had been in place since 1943; economic policy was based on state *dirigiste* neo-capitalism; labor relations were administered through state corporative syndicalism; since 1945 the Movimiento had been deemphasized; the system relied on the ultimate support of the military, who had initiated it; and religious, cultural, and educational policy had developed an elaborate structure of "national Catholicism" that provided more effective support than did any remaining fervor for the Falangist program.

Stanley Payne, *The Franco Regime,* 413, 434.

2. On gender and consumption, see Victoria de Grazia and Ellen Furlough, eds., *The Sex of Things: Gender and Consumption in Historical Perspective* (Berkeley: University of California Press, 1996)—the selected bibliography in this volume is most helpful; Carol Siegel and Ann Kibbey, eds., *Forming and Reforming Identity* (New York: New York University Press, 1995); Barbara Einhorn, *Cinderella Goes to Market: Citizenship, Gender and Women's Movements in East Central Europe* (London: Verso, 1993); John Hartley, *Popular Reality: Journalism, Modernity, Popular Culture* (London: Arnold, 1996); Timothy Burke, *Lifebuoy Men, Lux Women: Commodification, Consumption, and Cleanliness in Modern Zimbabwe* (Durham, N.C.: Duke University Press, 1996); Mary Louise Roberts, "Gender, Consumption and Commodity Culture," *American Historical Review* 103, no. 3 (June 1998): 817–44—this is a great review essay on the topic.

3. Geraldine Scanlon, *La polémica feminista,* 337.

4. Paul Preston, *Franco,* 594–624.

5. José Antonio Biescas and Manuel Tuñón de Lara, *España bajo la dictadura franquista (1939–1975),* vol. 10 of *Historia de España,* edited by

Manuel Tuñón de Lara (Barcelona: Editorial Labor, 1980), 260.

6. Payne, *The Franco Regime*, 414. *Time*, 20 December 1948, quoted in Carlton J. H. Hayes, *The United States and Spain: An Interpretation* (New York: Sheed and Ward, 1951), 184.

7. Spain entered the World Health Organization in 1951, UNESCO in 1952, and the International Labor Organization in 1953. Payne, *The Franco Regime*, 418. Hayes, *The United States and Spain*, 181 (my emphasis).

8. Juan Pablo Fusi, *Franco: Autoritarismo y poder personal* (Madrid: Ediciones El País, 1985), 120. Payne says the "official American figures place the value of all forms of American aid (including credits) over the next ten years at 1,688 million dollars, to which was added 521 million in military assistance." *The Franco Regime*, 418, 419.

9. "The best thing that Americans did for us," Franco said in private to Camilo Alonso Vega, "was to empty the bars and cabarets of whores, since they almost all marry American sergeants and GI's." Quoted in Preston, *Franco*, 627.

10. Preston, *Franco*, 619–22. Biescas and Tuñón de Lara, *España bajo la dictadura franquista*, 265.

11. See Tuñón de Lara, *Historia de España;* Payne, *The Franco Regime;* Preston, *Franco;* and Ellwood, *Franco.*

12. Payne, *The Franco Regime*, 431.

13. The NACP was founded in 1909 with the support of the Jesuit Order, which wanted to extend the social influence of the "Congregaciones Marianas," better known as "Los Luises." These were groups of elite students of the Jesuits who wanted to incorporate their religious zeal into everyday life. Father Ayala was the founder, and the lawyer Angel Herrera was the president for twenty years. The NACP dominated Catholic Action. Most Spanish Catholic Action leaders were also Propagandists. The NACP aspired to contribute to the formation of an active elite to direct the political and social Spanish order, which could be nothing but Catholic. About the NACP, see A. Saez Alba, *La Asociación Católica Nacional de propagandistas y el caso del Correo de Andalucía* (París: Ruedo Ibérico, 1974). The *New Catholic Encyclopedia* (1st ed., 1967) defines "secular institutes" as "societies whose members, whether clerical or not, in order to attain Christian perfection and to exercise a full apostolate, profess the evangelical counsels in the world, but do not practice the religious life in common." About the Opus Dei, see Daniel Artigues, *El Opus Dei en España* (París: Ruedo Ibérico, 1971); María Angustias Moreno, *El Opus Dei anexo a una historia* (Barcelona: Editorial Planeta, 1976); Peter Berglar, *Opus Dei: Vida y obra del fundador José María Escrivá de Balaguer* (Madrid: Rialp Ediciones, 1987); Luis Carandell, *Vida y milagros de monseñor Escrivá de Balaguer: Fundador del Opus Dei* (Barcelona: Deriva, 1992); Amadeo de Fuenmayor, *Escritos sobre prelaturas personales* (Pamplona: Universidad de Navarra, 1992); Amadeo Fuenmayor, ed., *El itinerario jurídico del Opus Dei: Historia y defensa de un carisma* (Pamplona: Colección Canónica de la Universidad de Navarra, 1990); Dominique Le Tourneau, *What Is Opus Dei?* (Dublin: Mercier Press, 1987); Yvon Le Vaillant, *La Santa Mafia: El expediente secreto del Opus Dei* (Mexico: Edamex, 1985); Gaetano Locastro, *Las prelaturas personales: Perfiles jurídicos* (Pamplona: Ediciones Universidad de Navarra, 1991); Alberto Moncada, *Historia oral de Opus Dei* (Barcelona: Plaza y Janes, 1987); Michael Walsh, *The Secret World of Opus*

Dei (London: Crafton, 1989); William O'Connor, *Opus Dei: An Open Book: A Reply to* The Secret World of Opus Dei *by Michael Walsh* (Dublin: Mercier Press, 1991); Michael Walsh, *Opus Dei: An Investigation into the Secret Society Struggling for Power within the Catholic Church* (San Francisco: Harper San Francisco, 1992); Jaime Escobar, *Opus Dei: Génesis y expansión en el mundo: Antecedentes sobre el polémico proceso de beatificación de su fundador* (Santiago: LOM Ediciones, 1992); Juan Estruch, *L'Opus Dei i les seves paradoxes: Un estudi sociologic* (Barcelona: Col Leccio Estudis i Documents, 1993). The quotation is from Artigues, *El Opus Dei en España*, 74. Estruch, *L'Opus Dei i les seves paradoxes*, 319. Payne, *The Franco Regime*, 438. The "Generación del 48" revolved around the ideas spelled out by Calvo Serer in *España sin problema* (1949), which he wrote in response to Laín Entralgo's work *España como problema*. Calvo Serer opposed this thesis, claiming that the uniqueness of Spain resided in its Catholicism forged in the "Reconquista." Only Catholicism could give cohesion to Spain, being the only guarantee of unity. Calvo Serer proposed the establishment of a "Catholic culture" under the protection of a genuinely antiparliamentary monarchy. *España sin problema* made it clear that any conflict or historical dilemma had been settled in the Civil War. Artigues, *El Opus Dei en España*, 148.

14. Payne, *The Franco Regime*, 416. Preston, *Franco*, 615.

15. The postwar economic legislation followed previous economic norms of the turn-of-the-century Regeneracionismo. Hence, the 24 October 1939 *Law of New Industries of National Interest* emulated other legislation on the nationalization of the country's industry, such as the law of 14 February 1907, the law of 2 March 1917, or the law-decree of 30 April 1924. José Luis García Delgado, "Notas sobre el intervencionismo económico del primer Franquismo," *Revista de Historia Económica* 1 (1985): 136. See on this subject Pedro Tedde de Lorca, "Economía y Franquismo: A propósito de una biografía," *Revista de Historia Económica* 3 (1986): 627–37; Fusi, *Franco;* Manuel Jesús González, *La economía política del Franquismo (1940–1970)* (Madrid: Tecnos, 1979); Jacinto Ros Hombravella, ed., *Capitalismo español: De la autarquia a la estabilización (1939–1959)* (Madrid: Alianza, 1973); Angel Viñas, "De la autarquia a la liberalización: Veinte aniversario del plan de estabilización," *El País*, 21 July 1979. García Delgado, "Notas sobre el intervencionismo económico," 135–45.

16. Payne, *The Franco Regime*, 465.

17. Ellwood, *Spanish Fascism*, 113. The quotations from the Church hierarchy are in Payne, *The Franco Regime*, 448. "Leyes Fundamentales: Jefatura del Estado," *BOE* (Madrid, 19 May 1958), 4511.

18. "Leyes Fundamentales: Jefatura del Estado," *BOE* (Madrid, 19 May 1958), 4511, 4512. Linz, "An Authoritarian Regime: Spain."

19. Ellwood, *Prietas las filas*, 186–87. Near the end of 1957, Carrero proposed a "coordinated plan to increase national production," which recommended an intensification of autarchist policies. It meant the avoidance of the international market and of the need to export, and solving the balance of payments deficit by a drastic reduction in imports. Payne, *The Franco Regime*, 468.

20. It was of little use to produce increasing quantities of goods if the mass of the population could not afford to buy them. Wage increases were thus granted not only as a response to disruptive strikes but also to enable demand to absorb supply,

and the effect of this was to attract people from the rural areas to the cities. Ellwood, *Franco*, 179.

21. Fusi, *Franco*, 144–47.

22. Concha Borreguero, Elena Carena, Consuelo de la Sándara, and María Salas, *La mujer española: De la tradición a la modernidad (1960–1980)* (Madrid: Tecnos, 1986); Scanlon, *La polémica feminista.*

23. Maria Laffitte, *La mujer en España: Cien años de historia (1860–1960)* (Madrid: Aguilar, 1963), 274, 275.

24. Ellwood, *Franco*, 169. On domesticity and cleanliness, see Roberts, "Gender, Consumption, and Commodity Culture," a great review of two studies that address this subject: Burke, *Lifebuoy Men, Lux Women*, and Kristin Ross, *Fast Cars, Clean Bodies: Decolonization and the Reordering of French Culture* (Cambridge: MIT Press, 1995).

25. Laffitte, *La mujer en España*, 277. De León, *La perfecta casada*, 276.

26. Barbara J. Coleman, "Maidenform(ed): Images of American Women in the 1950s," in Siegel and Kibbey, *Forming and Reforming Identity*, 10. On this topic, see also Elaine Tyler May, *Homeward Bound: American Families in the Cold War Era* (New York: Basic Books, 1988). Victoria de Grazia, "Nationalizing Women: The Competition between Fascist and Commercial Cultural Models in Mussolini's Italy," in Grazia and Furlough, eds., *The Sex of Things*, 344.

27. Carmen Martín Gaite, *Usos amorosos de la postguerra española* (Madrid: Anagrama, 1987), 69, 104. See also Rafael Abella, *La vida cotidiana bajo el régimen de Franco* (Madrid: Ediciones Temas de Hoy, 1996); Rafael Torres, *La vida amorosa en tiempos de Franco* (Madrid: Ediciones Temas de Hoy, 1996); and Richard Wright, *Pagan Spain* (New York: Harper, 1957). On the code of courtship and sexuality in the American context during the 1950s, see Brett Harvey, *The Fifties: A Women's Oral History* (New York: Harper Collins, 1993); May, *Homeward Bound;* Eugenia Kaledin, *Mothers and More: American Women in the 1950s* (Boston: Twayne, 1984); John D'Emilio and Estelle B. Freedman, *Intimate Matters: A History of Sexuality in America* (New York: Harper and Row, 1988). Abella, *La vida cotidiana*, 223.

28. There had been Catholic pressure to push a new press censorship law through Arias Salgado's Ministry of Information and Tourism, which had been in charge of state censorship since 1951. Arias Salgado was in poor health and was criticized from within the regime for the continuing rigidity of the censorship. In November 1960, a petition was signed by many leading Spanish writers and intellectuals asking for more careful regulation of the censorship. Payne, *The Franco Regime*, 437, 503. José Luis Berlanga and Antonio Bardem were influenced by Italian neorealism, and with movies such as *Bienvenido Mister Marshall* (Welcome Mister Marshall, 1952) or *Calle mayor* (Main Street, 1956), they initiated a sardonic criticism of American economic help in the first case and of provincial life and Catholic conventions in the latter. J. M. Caparrós Lera and Rafael de España, *The Spanish Cinema: An Historical Approach* (Madrid: Centre for Cinematic Research, "Film Historia," 1987), 53–54; Franco himself, under the pseudonym Jaime de Andrade, wrote the script for a movie *(Raza)* that featured a model family by the name of Churrucas. The strong Catholic mother figure was fashioned after Franco's own mother. Payne, *The Franco Regime*, 402.

29. Martín Gaite, *Usos amorosos*, 213. See Abigail Solomon-Godeau, "The

Other Side of Venus: The Visual Economy of Feminine Display," in de Grazia and
Furlough, eds., *The Sex of Things*. Roberts, "Gender, Consumption, and Commodity Culture," 829.

30. Payne, *The Franco Regime*, 476.

31. By 1969, the number of foreign visitors increased to 21.7 million; by 1973,
it was 34.6 million. Biescas and Tuñón de Lara, *España bajo la dictadura franquista*, 89. Manuel Fraga Iribarne, *Horizonte español* (Madrid, 1966), quoted in
Rafael Esteve Sedall, "El turismo y la reinserción de España en la cadena imperialista,"
Cuadernos de Ciencias Económicas y Empresariales 4 (1979): 35. The concentration of the tourist industry in certain regions favored the unfolding of a sort of neocolonialism and an unequal regional development and distribution of the per capita
income. Biescas and Tuñón de Lara, *España bajo la dictadura franquista*, 88.

32. Fraga Iribarne, quoted in Esteve Sedall, "El turismo y la reinserción," 45.

33. Preston, *Franco*, 596.

34. The *Penal Code* of 1870 condemned the "blood crimes" (rape, abduction, adultery, abortion, infanticide). The wife's adultery was always punished,
whereas that of the husband became a crime only if he had a mistress living in the
conjugal home. Maria Telo, "La evolución de los derechos de la mujer en España,"
in Borreguero et al., *La mujer española*, 82–84.

35. Laffitte, *La mujer en España*, 367.

36. Ley de 24 de Abril de 1958 por la que se reforma el Código Civil, *BOE*,
Madrid, 1958. Rosario Sainz Jackson, *Los derechos de la mujer* (Madrid: Publicaciones Españolas, 1968), 20–21.

37. Ley de derechos políticos, profesionales y del trabajo de la mujer, 15 July
1961, *BOE*, Madrid, 24 July 1961. See Lourdes Benería, *Mujer, economía y patriarcado en la España de Franco* (Barcelona: Cuadernos Anagrama, 1977).

38. "Discurso del Excmo. Sr Fernando Herrero Tejedor," in *Derechos políticos, profesionales y del trabajo de la mujer* (Madrid: Imprenta Nacional del Boletín
Oficial del Estado, 1961), 12, 13.

39. Ibid., 15.

40. "Discurso de la Excma. Sra. Dª Pilar Primo de Rivera y Saenz de Heredia," in *Derechos políticos*, 31.

41. "Ley de derechos políticos," *BOE*, 24 July 1961, 11004.

42. Ibid.

43. Ibid., 11005. Women's access to the legal profession continued to be limited until 1966, when the restrictions posed by section c of article 3 were repealed.

44. "La mujer española," [1959?], 40, SFP/AGA.

45. Ibid., [1960?], 4, 37.

46. Ibid., 11. "Vital Statistics: Rates per 1000 population," in *International
Historical Statistics: Europe 1750–1988*, edited by B. R. Mitchell (New York:
Stockton Press, 1989), 112.

47. "La mujer española," 26, 30, SFP/AGA.

48. The Women's Section gathered this data from several sources: *Anuario
estadístico de España*, statistical publications of the Falangist syndicate organization, statistical publications of the Ministries of Education and Industry, and inquiries in different provinces by the delegates and members of the Women's Section
in various companies with ten to fifty employees. "Realidad laboral de la mujer,"
esp. 19, SFP/AGA.

49. "Realidad laboral de la mujer," 4, SFP/AGA. The report does not provide statistical data about the marital status of women before 1960. The quotations are from pp. 6 and 15.

50. Benería, *Mujer, economía y patriarcado*, 38–43. José Montero Alonso, "El salario femenino," *Teresa*, March 1954, 11–12. Abella, *La vida contidiana*, 221.

51. "Las mujeres quieren trabajar: La Escuela de Auxiliares de Investigación," *Teresa*, March 1956, 38–39. "Las mujeres quieren trabajar: La formación técnica de archiveros, bibliotecarios y arqueólogos," *Teresa*, March 1957, 40–41.

52. "Las mujeres quieren trabajar: El periodismo," *Teresa*, November 1956, 38–39.

53. "Se ha celebrado en Madrid la I Asamblea Nacional de Enfermeras," *Teresa*, May 1959, 39–41 (my emphasis).

54. "Escuela de Servicio Doméstico: Jueves por la tarde cursos de orientación profesional para cocineras y doncellas," *Teresa*, May 1960, 35.

55. Rosario Sánchez López, *Mujer española, una sombra de destino en lo universal: Trayectoria histórica de Sección Femenina de Falange (1934–1977)* (Murcia: Universidad de Murcia, 1990), 61.

56. Pilar Primo de Rivera, Circular 54, ser. A, Madrid, 1 December 1955, SFP/AGA. Luis Suárez Fernández, *Crónica de la Sección Femenina y su tiempo* (Madrid: Asociación Nueva Andadura, 1993), 297.

57. The law of 20 December 1952, *Reorganization of the Board for the Protection of Women*, articles 1, 4, 8, BOE, 22 December 1952. Decree of 3 March 1956, *Abolition of the Brothels* ("Abolición de centros de tolerancia y otras medidas relativas a la prostitución"), BOE, 10 March 1956.

58. Laffitte, *La mujer en España*, 293.

4: KNOWLEDGE AND POWER IN THE FRANCOIST UNIVERSITY

1. For more on the notion of building consensus as part of right-wing regimes, see Renzo de Felice, *Mussolini Il duce: Gli anni del conseso, 1929–1936* (Torino: Einaudi, 1974). De Felice points out the existence of a period of material and moral consensus. Part of the regime's appeal was its claim to a revolution that was, first of all, a restoration of the traditional culture and a fulfillment of the *Resorgimento*. Material consensus arose from the security that the regime offered to Italians (including working-class), and moral consensus grew out of the fascist call for change and a new society that appealed particularly to the young. Fascism, according to de Felice, had a genuinely "revolutionary" component in its desire to incorporate the mass of the population into the life of the state and the nation. This element of mass culture is certainly traceable also in Francoist Spain from the 1950s on. On mass culture, see Victoria de Grazia, *The Culture of Consent: Mass Organization of Leisure in Fascist Italy* (New York: Cambridge University Press, 1981).

2. On National-Catholicism and education, see Gregorio Cámara Villar, *Nacional-Catolicismo y escuela: La socialización política del Franquismo (1936–1951)* (Madrid: Editorial Hesperia, 1984); Clotilde Navarro García, *La educación y el Nacional-Catolicismo* (Castilla la Mancha: Universidad de Castilla la Mancha, 1993); and Andrés Sopeña Monsalve, *El Florido Pensil: Memoria de la escuela nacionalcatólica* (Barcelona: Crítica, 1994).

3. Shirley Mangini, *Rojos y rebeldes: La cultura de la disidencia durante el Franquismo* (Barcelona: Anthropos, 1987).

4. Michel Foucault, *The History of Sexuality,* vol. 1, *An Introduction* (Harmondsworth: Pelican, 1981), quoted in Chris Weedon, *Feminist Practice and Poststructuralist Theory* (New York: Basil Blackwell, 1987).

5. Victoria de Grazia, "Nationalizing Women," in Grazia and Furlough, eds., *The Sex of Things,* 337–58. The quotation is on p. 338.

6. Rabinow, ed., *The Foucault Reader,* 22.

7. Enders, "Nationalism and Feminism," 673-80; Sánchez López, *Mujer española;* Gallego Méndez, *Mujer, Falange y Franquismo;* and Suárez Fernández, *Crónica de la Sección Femenina.*

8. Alberto Jiménez, *Historia de la universidad española* (Madrid: Alianza Editorial, 1971); Carlos Paris, *La universidad española actual: Posibilidades y frustraciones* (Madrid: Edicusa, 1974).

9. On the nature and goals of the Spanish university, see José Ortega y Gasset, *La misión de la universidad* (Madrid: Revista de Occidente, 1930); Pedro Laín Entralgo, *La Universidad, el intelectual y Europa* (Madrid: Editorial Cultura Hispánica, 1950); Juan José López Ibor, *Discurso a los universitarios españoles* (Madrid: Rialp, 1964); J. López Méndez, *La universidad por dentro* (Barcelona: Juan Flors, 1959); A. D'ors, *Papeles del oficio universitario* (Madrid: Rialp, 1961); Angel Latorre, *Universidad y sociedad* (Barcelona: Ediciones Ariel, 1964); París, *La universidad española actual;* Antonio Tovar, *Universidad y educación de masas* (Barcelona: Ediciones Ariel, 1968).

10. Latorre, *Universidad y sociedad,* 29. Napoleon, quoted in Latorre, *Universidad y sociedad,* 29. Paris, *La universidad española,* 56. Also see José Orlandis, *La crisis de la universidad en España* (Madrid: Ediciones Rialp, 1966); Amando de Miguel, *Reformar la universidad* (Barcelona: Editorial Euros, 1976); Joaquín Tena Artigas, Cordero Pascual, Luis Díaz Jares, and José Luis, *La universidad española datos para un problema* (Madrid: Confederación Española de Cajas de Ahorros, 1976). The Ministry of Education published the "Libro Blanco," proposing a new educational policy in *La educación en España: Bases para una política educativa* (Madrid: MEC, 1969).

11. Tovar, *Universidad y educación de masas,* 25–29. The quotation is on p. 28. Latorre, *Universidad y Sociedad,* 45.

12. Latorre, *Universidad y Sociedad,* 48.

13. *URL, BOE,* 31 July 1943, 7408.

14. Michel Foucault, *Discipline and Punish* (New York: Vintage Books, 1975), 198. Foucault defines "bio-power" as the disciplinary control of a population. Normative, serialized order is an integral component of bio-power in which surveillance is the key to achieving the desired control. Franco's regime articulated a system of normalization to sustain his grip on the power structures. This system clearly delineated what was marginal, that is, outside the center or the norm. Paul Rabinow defines Foucauldian normalization as "a system finely arranged in measurable intervals in which individuals can be distributed around a norm; a norm which both organizes and is the result of this controlled distribution." Rabinow, introduction to *The Foucault Reader,* 20. Also see Michel Foucault, *The History of Sexuality,* vol. 1 (New York: Pantheon Books, 1978); and Colin Gordon, ed., *Power/Knowledge* (New York: Pantheon Books, 1980).

15. *URL, BOE,* 31 July 1943, 7406.

16. José Antonio Biescas and Manuel Tuñón de Lara, *España bajo la dictadura franquista (1939–1975),* vol. 10 of *Historia de España,* edited by Manuel Tuñón de Lara (Barcelona: Editorial Labor, 1980), 174–79.

17. *URL, BOE,* 31 July 1943, 7407.

18. Ibid.

19. Ibid., 7424 (my emphasis). By the decree of 2 March 1943, the Institute for the Professional Training of Women was created in Madrid. Alted Vigil, "Las coordenadas educativas del régimen franquista." José Pemartín *¿Qué es lo nuevo?* (1940), quoted in Alted Vigil, "Las coordenadas educativas del régimen franquista," 435. Pilar Primo de Rivera, *Discursos, Circulares, Escritos* (Madrid, n.d.), 172–73.

20. On right-wing women in other contexts, see Claudia Koonz, *Mothers in the Fatherland: Women, the Family, and Nazi Politics* (New York: Saint Martin's, 1987); Rebecca Klatch, *Women of the New Right* (Philadelphia, Pa.: Temple University Press, 1987); Jane Sherron de Hart, *Sex, Gender, and the Politics of ERA: A State and the Nation* (New York: Oxford University Press, 1990); Jane Sherron de Hart, "Gender on the Right: Meanings behind the Existential Scream," *Gender and History* 3, no. 3 (1991): 246–67.

21. Mangini, *Rojos y Rebeldes,* 58.

22. Ibid., 102. See also Carmen Martín Gaite, *Esperando el porvenir: Homenaje a Ignacio Aldecoa* (Madrid: Siruela, 1994).

23. Mangini, *Rojos y rebeldes,* 78; J. M. Caparrós Lera and Rafael de España, *The Spanish Cinema: An Historical Approach* (Madrid: Centre for Cinematic Research, "Film Historia," 1987), 53.

24. Martín Gaite, *Esperando el porvenir,* 41.

25. Joan L. Brown, "Women Writers in Spain: An Historical Perspective," in *Women Writers of Contemporary Spain: Exiles in the Homeland,* edited by Joan L. Brown (Newark: University of Delaware Press, 1991), 13, 14, 20. Mangini, *Rojos y Rebeldes,* 134. Joan L. Brown, "Carmen Martín Gaite: Reaffirming the Pact between Reader and Writer," in Brown, *Women Writers,* 72.

26. In the last few years, several doctoral dissertations have focused on the novels of Spanish women writers. See María Elena Solino, "Women and Children First: The Novels of Ana María Matute, Carmen Martín Gaite, Ana María Moix, and Esther Tusquets," Ph.D. diss., Yale University, 1993; Francisca López, "Myth and Discourse in the Postwar Spanish Novel by Women," Ph.D. diss., University of Connecticut, 1992; and Margaret Carmell González, "Literature of Protest: The Franco Years," Ph.D. diss., Louisiana State University and Agricultural and Mechanical College, 1994. See also María Jesús Mayans Natal, *Narrativa feminista española de postguerra* (Madrid: Editorial Pliegos, 1991); Carmen Martín Gaite, *Desde la ventana: Enfoque femenino de la literatura española* (Madrid: Espasa Calpe, 1987); Elizabeth J. Ordóñez, *Voices of Their Own: Contemporary Spanish Narrative by Women* (Lewisburg, Penn.: Buckwell University Press, 1991). Brown, *Women Writers,* 21. Gustavo Pérez Firmat, "Carmen Laforet: The Dilemma of Artistic Vocation," in Brown, *Women Writers,* 27–39.

27. Alvaro Santamarina, *Joaquín Ruiz Giménez: Perfil humano y político* (Madrid: Editorial Cambio 16, 1977), 15–35. Payne, *The Franco Regime,* 435.

28. Jacques Maritain was much influenced by the philosophy of Henry Bergson. Originally a Protestant, he converted to Catholicism and devoted himself to

the study of Thomism. Maritain urged Christian involvement in secular affairs, a view that greatly influenced members of the Second Vatican Council. See Saez Alba, *La Asociación Católica Nacional.* Pedro Laín Entralgo, *Descargo de conciencia (1930–1960)* (Barcelona: Barral Editores, 1976). Other former supporters of Francoism wrote about their disenchantment with the regime: Dionisio Ridruejo, *Casi unas memorias* (Barcelona, 1976); Tovar, *Universidad y educación de masas.*

    29. Payne, *The Franco Regime,* 437.

    30. Ibid., 439. On the student movement, see José María Maravall, *Dictadura y disentimiento político: Obreros y estudiantes bajo el Franquismo* (Madrid: Alfaguara, 1978); París, *La universidad española actual.*

    31. Santamarina, *Joaquín Ruiz Giménez,* 21–22; Mangini, *Rojos y rebeldes,* 84–85; Maravall, *Dictadura y disentimiento,* 120.

    32. Ellwood, *Spanish Fascism in the Franco Era,* 108–9.

    33. Alted Vigil, "Las coordenadas educativas del régimen franquista," 326. *Professional Industrial Training Act, BOE,* 21 July 1955, 4442–53.

    34. *Secondary Education Regulatory Law, BOE,* 27 February 1953, 1119–31. The quotations are on p. 1119.

    35. Ibid., 1120, 1121.

    36. Ibid., 1125.

    37. Ibid., 1127. Some of the textbook titles included Magdalena Santiago Fuentes, *La escuela y la patria: Lecturas para niñas* (Burgos: Hijos de Santiago Rodríguez, 1940); Agustín Serrano de Haro, *Yo soy español* (Madrid: Escuela Española, 1953); Agustín Serrano de Haro, *Hemos visto al Señor* (Madrid: Escuela Española, 1963); Antonio Onieva, *Escudo imperial* (Burgos: Hijos de Santiago Rodríguez, 1957). For more information on Francoist textbooks, see María Escudero," The Image of Latin America Disseminated in Spain by the Franco Regime: Repercussions in the Configuration of a National Identity," Ph.D. diss., University of California, San Diego, 1994; and Sopeña Monsalve, *El Florido Pensil.*

    38. Order of 9 February 1955, "Cuestionarios de Formación del Espíritu Nacional, educación física y escuelas del hogar, que han de cursar las alumnas de bachilllerato," *BOE,* 28 July 1955, 4622.

    39. Order of 9 February 1955, regulating male instruction in the national spirit and political indoctrination. Ibid., 4622–23.

    40. Ibid., 4627.

    41. Ibid., 4625–27.

    42. Ibid., 4624–25.

    43. Ibid., 4627.

    44. Ibid., 4629.

    45. Ibid., 4627. The Women's Section's magazine *Teresa* initiated in 1954 a section entitled "Women Want to Work" (Las mujeres quieren trabajar), in which several careers and professions appropriate for women were discussed. See chapter 2 on this subject. Remigio Vilariño, *Amor,* quoted in Amando de Miguel, *Carta abierta a una universitaria* (Madrid: Ediciones 99, 1973), 22.

    46. My own elaboration, *Anuario Estadístico de España* (Madrid: Instituto Nacional de Estadística, 1957, 1958, 1966).

    47. My own elaboration, María Luisa Barrera Peña and Ana López Peña, *Sociología de la Mujer en la Universidad: Análisis histórico comparativo*

Galicia-España, 1900-1981 (Santiago de Compostela: Universidad de Santiago de Compostela, 1984), 357–58, 177–80.

48. Amando de Miguel, *Manual de estructura social de España* (Madrid: Editorial Tecnos, 1974), 233, 239.

49. My own elaboration, Barrera Peña and López Peña, *Sociología de la Mujer en la Universidad*, 177–78; My own elaboration, *Anuario Estadístico de España* (Madrid: Instituto Nacional de Estadística, 1957, 1958, 1966).

50. My own elaboration, *Estadística de Enseñanza en España* (Madrid: Instituto Nacional de Estadística, 1966).

51. Rosario Sainz Jackson, *Los derechos de la mujer* (Madrid: Publicaciones Españolas, 1968), 8. The average income of a full professor was about 130,000 pesetas. If he agreed to devote his full time to university work, he received an additional annual allowance of 87,500 pesetas. See United Nations Scientific and Cultural Organization, *World Survey of Education*, vol. 4, *Higher Education* (New York: Unesco Publications Center, 1966), 1021. Ricardo Montoro Romero, *La universidad en la España de Franco (1939–1970): Un análisis sociológico* (Madrid: Centro de Investigaciones Sociológicas, 1981), 72–73. The discontinuity in numbers of professors appeared for the following academic years also: 1948–49, 1949–50, 1962–63, 1963–64, and 1964–65. From 1965 on, the total number goes back to the gradual growth of 1959. Montoro Romero, *La universidad en la España de Franco,* 77.

52. My own elaboration, *Estadística de Enseñanza en España* (Madrid: Instituto Nacional de Estadística, 1966).

5: THE WOMEN'S SECTION OF THE FALANGE

1. Suárez Fernández, *Crónica de la Sección Femenina*, 28. On the origins of the Women's Section from a feminist perspective, see Posa, "Una dona portadora de valors eterns," 121–33; di Febo, "La política de la Secció Femenina," 56–60; Gallego, *Mujer, Falange y Franquismo;* Sánchez López, *Mujer española, una sombra de destino en lo Universal;* Enders, "Nationalism and Feminism," 673–80. See chapter 1 on the foundation of the Women's Section.

2. By 1959 the main schools were the José Antonio National School for Commands; the Isabel la Católica National School of General Instructors for the Youth; the Onésimo Redondo National School of Agriculture; the Julio Ruíz de Alda Specialties School; the Santa Teresa National School for Social Service; and the Ramiro Ledesma Ramos National School of Social Service. "La Sección Femenina de FET y de las JONS: Síntesis de una organización," *Teresa*, October 1959.

3. Ibid.

4. On gender and modernization, see Mary Nolan, *Visions of Modernity: American Business and the Modernization of Germany* (New York: Oxford University Press, 1994); Atina Grossman, *Reforming Sex: The German Movement for Birth Control and Abortion Reform, 1920–1950* (New York: Oxford University Press, 1995); and Victoria de Grazia, *How Fascism Ruled Women: Italy, 1922–1945* (Berkeley: University of California Press, 1992). "Realidad laboral de la mujer," [n.d.], 9, 15, SFP/AGA.

5. Pilar Primo de Rivera, Circular Letter 54, Madrid, 1 December 1955, SFP/AGA (my emphasis).

6. Pilar Primo de Rivera, Circular Letter, Madrid, 8 March 1957, SFP/AGA.

7. Pilar Primo de Rivera, Circular Letter 44, ser. A, Madrid, 29 February 1952, SFP/AGA (my emphasis).

8. Pilar Primo de Rivera, Circular Letter, Madrid, 22 November 1958, SFP/AGA.

9. Ibid.

10. Pilar Primo de Rivera, Circular Memorandum, 15 November 1956, SFP/AGA. Pilar Primo de Rivera, Circular Letter, Madrid, 9 February 1959, SFP/AGA.

11. By law all Spanish women had to render social service to the state as a prerequisite for everything from a passport to a driving license. On social service legislation, see previous chapters.

12. "Las profesiones creadas por la Sección Femenina de FET y JONS," Madrid, Delegación Nacional de Asociaciones y Comisión Nacional Española del Instituto Internacional de Estudios de Clases Medias, n.d., SFP/AGA. The quotation is on p. 1.

13. Suárez Fernández, *Crónica de la Sección Femenina*, 293–303.

14. Inaugural speech of Pilar Primo de Rivera, quoted in ibid., 322.

15. Pilar Primo de Rivera, *Recuerdos de una vida* (Madrid: Ediciones Dyrsa, 1983), 261–62.

16. Closing speech of Raimundo Fernández Cuesta, minister secretariat general of the movement, to the Seventeenth National Council in 1952, quoted in Suárez Fernández, *Crónica de la Sección Femenina*, 273. The statutes of the SEU were approved by a decree of 21 November 1937. Article 1 defined the Falangist syndicate as follows: "Under the name of Spanish University Student Union is created a student association whose goals are (a) to exalt professional intellectuality in a profound Catholic and Spanish sense. . . . (b) to promote syndical spirit among students tending to the single and mandatory unionization." *BOE,* 23 November 1937, 4474.

17. General secretary of the movement, Order of 10 November 1951, "por la que se establece el plan nacional de formación política del Sindicato Español Universitario," 1, SFP/AGA.

18. Ibid., 4.

19. Servicio universitario de extensión cultural, "Reunión nacional de mandos del SEU: Conclusiones, Tema VIII," Madrid, 12–19, 1, September 1952, SFP/AGA.

20. "Orden de 18 de octubre de 1958 por la que se reorganiza el Sindicato Español Universitario," *BOE,* 20 October 1958, 1771.

21. Ibid.

22. The national head of SEU counted on the assistance of the Representative National Council of SEU, where the Women's Section was represented. Ricardo Montoro Romero, *La universidad en la España de Franco (1939–1970)* (Madrid: Centro de Investigaciones sociológicas, 1981), 99–105.

23. On the Spanish university movement, see José María Maravall, *Dictadura y disentimiento político: Obreros y estudiantes bajo el Franquismo* (Madrid: Editorial Alfaguara, 1978); Montoro Romero, *La universidad en la España de Franco;* and Enrique Palazuelos, *Movimiento estudiantil y democratización de la universidad* (Madrid: Manifiesto Editorial, 1977).

24. Syra Manteola, Circular Letter, Madrid, 6 March 1950, SFP/AGA. "Informe de la Regiduría Central de Estudiantes y Graduadas: XXIII Consejo Nacional de la Sección Femenina," Gerona, 12–20 January 1966, 12–13, SFP/AGA.

25. Sección Femenina Delegatión Nacional de Educación, "Normas sobre la misión de la Sección Femenina en las Juntes Municipales le conseps provinciales de Educación y consejos de Distrito Universitario," Circular Letter, 27 September 1954, SFP/AGA.

26. María Dolores Bermúdez Cañete, central secretary of the WS/SEU, Circular Letter 11, November 1963, SFP/AGA. During the 1960s, María Dolores Bermúdez Cañete was the national head of the WS/SEU. Primo de Rivera, *Recuerdos de una vida,* 262.

27. "Sección Femenina," [1952?], 1, SFP/AGA.

28. Syra Manteola, Circular Letter, Madrid, 29 September 1950, SFP/AGA.

29. National Delegation of Education, Circular Letter 6, Madrid, 13 November 1956, SFP/AGA.

30. "Servicio Social Universitario," [1952?], 1, SFP/AGA.

31. Syra Manteola, Circular Letter, Madrid, 9 June 1949, SFP/AGA.

32. Pilar Primo de Rivera, Circular Letter, Madrid, 3 April 1957, 7, SFP/AGA.

33. Ibid., 15.

34. "Formación de cursos y albergues: Regiduria central del SEU," Madrid, 1 June 1962, 2, SFP/AGA.

35. Ibid., 12, 6.

36. "Informe de la Regiduría Central de Estudiantes y Graduadas: XXIII Consejo Nacional de la Sección Femenina," Gerona, January 1966, 24, SFP/AGA. Gabinete de Estudiantes Graduadas de la Sección Femenina, "La juventud universitaria femenina en España (Female university youth in Spain): Análisis sociológico," Madrid, [1967?], SFP/AGA. The final project was published by María Angeles Durán Heras and Juan Antonio Peredo Linacero, *Los universitarios opinan* (Madrid: Departamento de Estudiantes y Graduados, Sección Femenina del Movimiento, 1970).

37. Gabinete de Estudiantes Graduadas de la Sección Femenina, "La juventud universitaria femenina en España: Análisis sociológico," Madrid, [1967?], 10–20, SFP/AGA. The quotation is on p. 20.

38. Ibid., 15, 16.

39. Ibid., 19.

40. Ibid., 14, 23.

41. In the American context on this subject, see Dorothy C. Holland and Margaret Eisenhart, *Educated in Romance: Women, Achievement, and College Culture* (Chicago: University of Chicago Press, 1990). Gabinete de Estudiantes Graduadas de la Sección Femenina, "La juventud universitaria femenina en España: Análisis sociológico," Madrid, [1967?], 37, SFP/AGA.

42. Clara González, interview by author, tape recording, Granada, 6 June 1989. A pseudonym is used to protect her privacy.

43. María Leiva, interview by author, tape recording, Granada, 6 June 1989. A pseudonym is used to protect her privacy.

44. Clara González, interview.

45. María Leiva, interview.

46. Clara González, interview.
47. María Leiva, interview.
48. Clara González, interview.
49. Ibid.
50. Ibid.
51. Ibid.
52. María Leiva, interview.
53. Ibid.
54. Ibid.
55. Kathleen M. Blee, *Women of the Klan: Racism and Gender in the 1920s* (Berkeley: University of California Press, 1991), 1.
56. Claudia Koonz, *Mothers in the Fatherland,* 55. See Gisela Bock's review of Koonz's book in *Geschichte und Gasellschaft: Zeitschrift für Historische Sozialwissenschaft* 15 (1989): 563-79. See also Atina Grossmann, "Feminist Debates about Women and National Socialism," *Gender and History* 3, no. 3 (1991): 350-58.

6: IN THEIR OWN WORDS: WOMEN IN HIGHER EDUCATION

1. On oral historiography, see David Henige, *Oral Historiography* (London: Longman, 1982); Paul Richard Thompson, *The Voice of the Past,* 2d ed. (Oxford: Oxford University Press, 1988); Trevor Lummis, *Listening to History: The Authenticity of Oral Evidence* (London: Hutchinson, 1987); Luisa Passerini, "Work, Ideology, and Consensus under Italian Fascism," *History Workshop Journal* 8 (1979): 82-108; Luisa Passerini, *Fascism in Popular Memory: The Cultural Experience of the Turin Working Class* (London: Cambridge University Press, 1977); Luisa Passerini, "Oral History in Italy after the Second World War: From Populism to Subjectivity," *International Journal of Oral History* 9, no. 2 (1988): 114-24; Luisa Passerini, ed., *Memory and Totalitarianism* (Oxford: Oxford University Press, 1992).
2. Passerini emphasizes the subjective aspects of oral sources and their historical value if used in combination with written sources. Her sophisticated analysis of Turin's working class under fascism represents more than an attempt to give voice to an oppressed minority. She points out that previous studies of the working class ignored issues such as whether the worker's needs were met and the relationship between the individual and power. Passerini, "Work, Ideology, and Consensus," 85. Passerini, "Oral History in Italy," 121.
3. Pedro Poveda, "A las universitarias: Nuestro programa" (1930?), in *Pedro Poveda: Itinerario pedagógico,* edited by Angeles Galino (Madrid: Consejo Superior de Investigaciones Científicas, Instituto de Pedagogía, 1964), 333.
4. There are numerous biographies of Pedro Poveda: Mercedes Gómez del Manzano, *Pedro Poveda. Dinamismo profético* (Madrid: Narcea, 1991); *Pedro Poveda, hombre interior* (1971); *Interpelado por la palabra* (1975); *Un prete scómodo, Dom Pietro Poveda Castroverde fondatore della Istituzione Teresiana* (1961); *Una figura del pensamiento español* (1974). There are two series entitled *Cuadernos biográficos,* the first one by Father Silverio de Santa Teresa (1942) and the second by Flavia Paz Velázquez (1986); both series were published by the Teresian Institute. Teresa Barrenechea, interview by author, tape recording, Madrid, 11 April 1994.

5. Barrenechea, interview. Gómez del Manzano, *Pedro Poveda,* 109; Galino, *Pedro Poveda,* 86–87. See also Pedro Poveda, *Folletos* (Madrid: Publicaciones del Archivo de la Institución Teresiana, 1989). Between 1907 and 1912, Poveda wrote *Pedagogical Essay for the Foundation of a Catholic Institution of Education, Journal of a Foundation, The Academies, About a Project,* and *For the Children.*

6. *Ensayo de Proyectos Pedagógicos para la fundación de una Institución Católica de Enseñanza* (Pedagogical essay for the foundation of a Catholic institution of education) was edited four times, and only in the last edition (1921) does Poveda appear as the author. Angeles Galino, *Pedro Poveda,* 88–89. Barrenechea, interview.

7. Pedro Poveda, *Avisos espirituales de Santa Teresa de Jesús* (Spiritual warnings of Saint Teresa de Jesús) (1912), quoted in Gómez del Manzano, *Pedro Poveda,* 140.

8. Barrenechea, interview.

9. Gómez del Manzano, *Pedro Poveda,* 203. Barrenechea, interview.

10. Quoted in Galino, *Pedro Poveda,* 70.

11. Galino, *Pedro Poveda,* 72.

12. Ibid., 72–79.

13. Barrenechea, interview.

14. Jo Ann Kay McNamara, *Sisters in Arms: Catholic Nuns through Two Millennia* (Cambridge, Mass.: Harvard University Press, 1996), 2, 3. On celibacy and women, see also Jo Ann Mcnamara, *A New Song: Celibate Women in the First Three Christian Centuries* (New York: Institute for Research in History/Haworth Press, 1983). On celibacy and women in other religions, see Sally L. Kitch, *Chaste Liberation: Celibacy and Female Cultural Status* (Urbana: University of Illinois Press, 1989).

15. McNamara, *Sisters in Arms,* 6.

16. "Estatutos de la Institución Teresiana: Parte II. Los miembros de la Institución Teresiana" and "Parte III. Organización y Gobierno de la Institución Teresiana" (Archivo Histórico de la Institución Teresiana, Madrid, 1990). The statutes that I was able to consult are the current ones. I was denied access to those that were in effect during the 1950s. The institute fought for forty years to regain its canonical status as a "Pious Union," after having been a secular institute like Opus Dei under the consideration of *Provida Mater* (1947), which created the canonical figure of the secular institutes.

17. Barrenechea, interview.

18. Josefa Segovia, *Eidos,* July–December 1954. Some of the issues discussed in *Eidos* dealt with the professional promotion of women: Ana María López Díaz-Otazu, "Formación profesional de la mujer," *Eidos,* July–December 1958; and Ana María López Díaz-Otazu, "Problemas morales y jurídicos del mundo laboral femenino," *Eidos,* January–June 1961.

19. Rafaela Rodríguez, "Hacia qué mujer vamos," *Eidos,* July–December 1955, 53. Pius XII, "Discurso a las mujeres católicas de Italia," 21 October 1945, quoted in Rodríguez, "Hacia qué mujer vamos," 56.

20. Rodríguez, "Hacia qué mujer vamos," 70.

21. Ibid., 74.

22. *La Revista* was first issued in 1913 under the title *Boletín Oficial de la*

Institución Teresiana; in the 1950s its name was changed to *La Revista de la Institución Teresiana.* Angeles Galino, "A las universitarias," *La Revista,* January 1959. Ana María Macias, "La mujer cara al tiempo," *La Revista,* January 1962, 16–17 (my emphasis).

23. Macias, "La mujer cara al tiempo," 17. M. A. Pascual, "La mujer: Dignidad semejante, misión complementaria," *La Revista,* May 1962, 8, 9.

24. "Hemos preguntado," interview with Angeles Galino, *La Revista,* May 1962, 12–13.

25. Ibid., 13 (my emphasis).

26. López Díaz-Otazu, "Problemas morales y jurídicos," 13–33. The quotation is on p. 14.

27. Barrenechea, interview.

28. Rafael González Moralejo, *El magisterio pontificio y jerárquico en la evolución histórica de la Acción Católica Española* (Madrid: Ediciones Marova S. L., 1967), 45.

29. Pius XI to the Presidency of the International Union of Female Catholic Associations (1928), quoted in ibid., 51.

30. Pius XI to the Argentinean Episcopate (1931), quoted in González Moralejo, *El magisterio pontificio jerárquico,* 52.

31. Pius XI set the principles of Catholic Action in his encyclical "Urbi arcano" issued in December 1922. González Moralejo, *El magisterio pontificio y jerárquico,* 71.

32. Alberto Bonet, *Manual de Acción Católica* (Madrid: Ediciones Acción Católica, 1960), 214, 217.

33. Pius XII was alarmed by the resurgence of Communism in Italy after World War II and fostered the growth of Catholic Action groups to strengthen the Christian Democratic Party. He excommunicated Italian Catholics who joined the Communist Party. Pius XII, Christmas radio speech, 24 December 1952, in Consejo Superior de Mujeres de Acción Católica, *La personalidad de la mujer: Documentos pontificios* (Madrid: Maribel, Artes Gráficas, Tomás Bretón, 1953), 50, 51.

34. Dirección General de la Acción Católica Española, *Reglamento General de la Asociación de las Mujeres de Acción Católica* (Toledo: Editorial Católica Toledana, 1940), 42. See Bonet, *Manual de Acción Católica.*

35. Dirección General de la Acción Católica Española, *Reglamento General,* 8.

36. Consejo Superior de Mujeres de Acción Católica, *La personalidad de la mujer.* "El Papa se preocupa de la familia," *Senda,* March 1950, 6–7.

37. "El Papa se preocupa de la familia," *Senda,* March 1950, 6.

38. Nicolás González Ruiz, "Familias numerosas: Escenas de hogar: I. Leyes fundamentales," *Senda,* January 1951, 7. "Decálogo de la alegría en el hogar cristiano," *Senda,* January 1951, 2. "La mujer española," *Senda,* January 1953, 1.

39. "Más hijos, o menos hijos," *Senda,* March 1953, 6. "La madre santa," *Senda,* May 1951, 1. "Pio XII y la mujer," *Senda,* March 1956, 6–7.

40. In November 1952, Pilar Bellosillo, vice president at the time, was elected president of the High Board of Catholic Action Women. The members and the heads of the different secretaries were reshuffled. A new secretary of university graduates and writers was created to reach the women's professional world and influence science and literature with a Christian spirit. *Senda,* November 1952. "Las mujeres se reunen en París, Londres y Dublín," *Senda,* July–August 1956. "Una interviú a

través del Atlántico con Pilar Bellosillo," *Senda,* November 1956, 17.

41. María Sabater, quoted in Juanita Espinos Orlando, "¿Puede formarse el sentido social?" *Senda,* March 1957, 16–17. Some of the companies were "Bressel S.A., Standard Eléctrica, Aeronaútica Industrial, Gas Madrid, Editorial Católica, Cervezas el Aguila, Telefumken, Agroman, Galerias Preciados, Empresa Nacional Bazan, Hijos de Fournier." Espinos Orlando, "¿Puede formarse el sentido social?" 16–17.

42. Margarita Sánchez Brito, "Protagonista: La joven: Como ven las azafatas su propia vida," *Senda,* January 1959, 17–18.

43. Sánchez Brito, "Protagonista: La joven: Las policias sanitarias una profesión que no pueden hacer ellos," *Senda,* July 1959, 22–23.

44. "Universitarios: Las estudiantes se examinan . . . y os examinan," *Senda,* February 1960, 18–19.

45. Purificación Prieto, interview by author, tape recording, Madrid, 20 October 1994.

46. Ibid.

47. Ibid.

48. Ibid. In the early 1960s, there were several workers' strikes in Asturias supported by the student movement. Initiated with the miners' strike of 1958, they reoccurred in 1962, 1963, and 1964.

49. Biescas and Tuñón de Lara, *España bajo la dictadura franquista,* 354–55, 301.

50. Prieto, interview.

51. Ibid.

52. "Asociación de Universitarias Españolas," Archivo de la Asociación de Universitarias Españolas, ASUW Papers, ASUW Archive, Madrid.

53. In 1953, Teresa Bermejo Luaza was president and Pilar Lago Couceiro de Lapesa was vice president. The Spanish Association of University Women is still alive. M. Luisa Maillard, *Asociación Española de Mujeres Universitarias: 1920–1990* (Madrid: AEMU Instituto de la Mujer, 1990), 37–41.

54. Letter from Asunción Ibarra to author, Madrid, 12 December 1994. ("Asunción Ibarra" is a pseudonym, to protect the privacy of the informant.)

55. Asunción Ibarra's written comments about two interviews we held in Madrid on 16 April 1994 and 7 November 1994. Also, a written document entitled "Asociación de Universitarias Españolas" declares that the association of university women created around the International Institute served as a stimulus to ASUW's emergence in 1954 (Madrid, ASUW Papers, 14 August 1957).

56. Carmen Gayarre, interview by author, tape recording, Madrid, 6 November 1994.

57. Ibid.

58. Ibid.

59. Carmen Gayarre, interview by author, tape recording, Madrid, 16 April 1994.

60. Gayarre considers the Fundación Centro de Enseñanza Especial her best contribution to society. The institution not only teaches but also trains retarded adolescents and adults to learn a trade. In the 1960s the foundation helped 325 individuals, and by 1991 the number increased to 500. *Fundación Centro de Enseñanza Especial* (Madrid: Fundación Centro Enseñanza Especial, 1991), 3.

61. Gayarre, interview by author, tape recording, 6 November 1994.

62. "Asociación de Universitarias Españolas," Madrid, 14 August 1957, ASUW Papers, ASUW Archive, Madrid. Asociación de Universitarias Españolas, *Estatutos,* Madrid, 1957, ASUW Papers, ASUW Archive, Madrid. Asunción Ibarra, interview by author, tape recording, Madrid, 7 November 1994.

63. Ibarra, interview, 7 November 1994.

64. Ibarra's written comments on interviews, 12 December 1994, in the author's possession.

65. Gayarre, interview by author, tape recording, Madrid, 7 November 1994.

66. "Ejercicios espirituales para universitarias," 13–17, April 1957, flyer issued by ASUW, in ASUW Papers.

67. Minutes of the Asociación de Universitarias Españolas, Madrid, 14 August 1957, ASUW Papers. See also Asociación de Universitarias Españolas, *Estatutos,* chapter 4, Madrid, 1957, ASUW Papers. "Graduadas y estudiantes universitarias, actividades," November 1957, leaflet issued by ASUW, in ASUW Papers.

68. "Ciclo de Conferencias de Orientación de Estudios Universitarios," Madrid, 15 March to 9 April 1958, leaflet issued by ASUW, in ASUW Papers.

69. Minutes of the ASUW, 1957, ASUW Papers. Ibarra, interview, 7 November 1994.

70. Ibarra, interview, 7 November 1994.

71. Gayarre, interview, 6 November 1994.

CONCLUSION

1. Koonz, *Mothers in the Fatherland;* De Grazia, *How Fascism Rules Women.*

2. Koonz, *Mothers in the Fatherland,* 388.

3. Françoise Navailh, "The Soviet Model" in *A History of Women in the West: Toward a Cultural Identity in the Twentieth Century,* edited by Françoise ThéBaud (Cambridge, Mass.: Harvard University Press, 1994), 248.

4. Glen Jeansonne, *Women of the Far Right: The Mothers' Movement and World War II* (Chicago: The University of Chicago Press, 1996), 10.

5. Jeansonne, *Women of the Far Right,* 11.

6. Jeansonne, *Women of the Far Right,* 13.

7. Later on she produced a film that showed Franco's soldiers rebuilding Spain and children greeting Dilling with the fascist salute. Jeansonne, *Women of the Far Right,* 73.

8. See the various works of Luisa Passerini, "Work, Ideology, and Consensus under Italian Fascism"; *Fascism in Popular Memory;* "Oral History in Italy"; and *Memory and Totalitarianism.*

9. Sandra F. McGee, "Right-Wing Female Activists in Buenos Aires, 1900–1932," in *Women and the Structure of Society,* edited by Barbara J. Harris and JoAnn K. McNamara (Durham, N.C.: Duke University Press, 1984), 85–97; Sandra McGee Deutsch, *Counter Revolution in Argentina, 1900–1932: The Argentine Patriotic League* (Lincoln: University of Nebraska Press, 1986).

10. Ronald Dolkart, "The Right in the Década Infame, 1930–1943," in *The Argentine Right: Its History and Intellectual Origins, 1910 to the Present,* edited by Sandra McGee Deutsch and Ronald H. Dolkart (Wilmington: SR Books, 1993), 78.

11. Kenneth Maxwell, "Spain's Transition to Democracy: A Model for Eastern Europe?" *Proceedings of the Academy of Political Science* 38, no. 1 (1991): 35–49. The quotation is from p. 40.

12. Geoffrey Pridham, "Democratic Transitions in Theory and Practice: Southern European Lessons for Eastern Europe," in *Democratization in Eastern Europe: Domestic and International Perspectives,* edited by Geoffrey Pridham and Tatu Vanhanen (New York: Routledge, 1994), 20. See also Victor Pérez Díaz, "La emergencia de la España Democrática: La 'invención' de una tradición y la dudosa institucionalización de una democracia" (Centro de Estudios Avanzados en Ciencias Sociales, Abril, 1991).

13. Barbara Einhorn, *Cinderella Goes to Market: Citizenship, Gender, and Women's Movements in East Central Europe* (London: Verso, 1993).

14. Victoria de Grazia, "Nationalizing Women: The Competition between Fascist and Commercial Cultural Models in Mussolini's Italy," in Grazia and Furlough, eds., *The Sex of Things,* 356.

GLOSSARY

ASUW Association of Spanish University Women (Asoçiación de Universitarias Españolas, ADUE). Catholic organization of university women, founded in 1953.

CEDA Coalición Española de Derechas Autónomas. Right-wing coalition that won the republican elections of 1933.

CSIC Consejo Superior de Investigaciones Científicas (National Research Council). Founded in 1939.

FET de las JONS Falange Española Tradicionalista y de las JONS. Francoist single party, founded in 1933 by José Antonio Primo de Rivera.

FIL Free Institution of Learning (Institución Libre de Enseñanza, ILE). Founded in 1876 by the initiative of Julián Sanz del Rio, follower of the German philosopher Federico Krause.

JAC Juventud Agrana Católica (Rural Catholic Action Youth).

JEC Juventud de Estudiantes Catolicos. Acción Católica Española (Catholic Student Youth). Part of the specialized movements that flourished in the 1950s.

JIC Independent Catholic Youth.

JOC Juventudes Obreras Católicas (Catholic Workers Youth).

JONS Juntas de Ofensiva Nacional Sindicalista. The first Spanish fascist political organization, founded in 1931.

Krausismo Educational movement introduced in Spain in the late nineteenth century by Julián Sanz del Río, follower of Federico Krause, German philosopher and pedagogue.

NACP National Association of Catholic Propagandists (Asociación Católica Nacional de Propagandistas, ACNP). Founded in 1909 by Father Ayala. The lawyer Angel Herrera was the president for twenty years. Most Spanish Catholic Action leaders were also Propagandists. The Association aspired to contribute to the formation of an active elite to direct the political and social Spanish order to be nothing but Catholic.

Opus Dei Religious lay order founded by Monseñor Javier Escrivá de Balaguer in 1928. It was declared a secular institute by the papal constitution *Provida Mater* in 1947.

RTVE Radio Televisión Española. National broadcasting company, inaugurated in 1956.

SAUW Spanish Association of University Women (Asociación Española de Mujeres Universitarias, AEMU). Liberal organization founded in 1953.

SCA Spanish Catholic Action.

SEU Sindicato Español Universitario (Spanish University Student Union). Falangist student union, founded in 1934. SEU became the only Francoist student union after the Civil War. It was reformed in 1958 and eliminated in 1965.

TI Teresian Institute (Institución Teresiana, IT). Female lay order founded in 1911 by Father Pedro Poveda Castroverde.

URL *University Regulatory Law* (Ley de Ordenación Universitaria, LOU). Law regulating the Spanish university until 1970.

USS University Social Service (Servicio Social Universitario, SSU). Social service rendered to the state by university women. Mandatory service required for Spanish women to receive a school diploma, a passport, or a driving license.

WS The Women's Section (Sección Femenina de Falange). Falangist women's section founded in 1934 within SEU. It became the official Francoist women's organization by decree of 28 December 1939.

WS/SEU Women's Falangist section at the university level.

WUCWO World Union of Catholic Women's Organizations (Unión Mundial de Organizaciones Católicas Femeninas, UMOCF). International forum for women's Catholic organizations to which Spanish women of Catholic Action belonged.

BIBLIOGRAPHY

MANUSCRIPT COLLECTIONS

ASUW. Papers. Archivo de la Asociación de Universitarias Españolas, Madrid.
Centro de Documentación del Instituto de la Mujer, Ministerio de Asuntos Sociales, Madrid.
Hemeroteca Municipal de Madrid.
History Archives. Universidad de Granada.
Hoover Institution, Stanford University.
Institución Teresiana, Manuscript Collection.
Sección Femenina. Papers. Archivo General de la Administración, Alcalá de Henares, Spain (SFP/AGA).
Seminario Conciliar de Madrid.

JOURNALS

Blanco y Negro, 1954–1964.
Consigna, 1947–1948.
Eidos: Revista de la Institución Teresiana, 1954–1961.
Ideal, 21 December 1936.
La Revista de la Institución Teresiana, 1959–1964.
Senda, 1950–1961.
Teresa: Revista para todas las mujeres, 1954–1961.

INTERVIEWS

Barrenechea, Teresa. Interview by author. Tape recording. Madrid, 11 April 1994.
Gayarre, Carmen. Interview by author. Tape recording. Madrid, 6 November 1994.
Gayarre, Carmen, Amalia Sarriá, and Consolación Morales. Interview by author. Tape recording. Madrid, 16 April 1994.
González, Clara [pseud.], and María Leiva [pseud.]. Interview by author. Tape recording. Granada, 6 June 1989.
Guindo, Carmen, and Pilar López. Interview by author. Tape recording. Granada, 6 June 1989.
Ibarra, Asunción [pseud.], and Carmen Gayarre. Interview by author. Tape recording. Madrid, 7 November 1994.
Prieto, Purificación. Interview by author. Tape recording. Madrid, 20 October 1994.
Sarriá, Amalia. Interview by author. Tape recording. Madrid, 7 November 1994.

BOOKS AND ARTICLES

Abella, Rafael. *La vida cotidiana bajo el régimen de Franco*. Madrid: Ediciones Temas de Hoy, 1996.

Ackelsberg, Martha A. *Free Women of Spain: Anarchism and the Struggle for the Emancipation of Women*. Bloomington: Indiana University Press, 1991.

Alcalde, Carmen. *La mujer en la guerra civil española*. Madrid: Cambio 16, 1976.

Alted Vigil, Alicia. "La mujer en las coordenadas educativas del régimen franquista." In Seminario de Estudios de la Mujer, *Ordenamiento jurídico y realidad social de las mujeres*. Madrid: Seminario de Estudios de la Mujer, Universidad Autónoma de Madrid, 1986.

Ariés, Philippe, and Georges Duby, eds. *A History of Private Life: Riddles of Identity in Modern Times*. Cambridge, Mass.: Harvard University Press, 1991.

Artigues, Daniel. *El Opus Dei en España*. París: Ruedo Ibérico, 1971.

Artola, Miguel. *Antiguo Régimen y Revolución Liberal*. Barcelona: Ariel, 1978.

———. *La burguesía revolucionaria (1808–1869)*. Madrid: Alfaguara, 1973.

Barrera Peña, María Luisa, and Ana López Peña. *Sociología de la mujer en la universidad: Análisis histórico-comparativo Galicia-España, 1900–1981*. Santiago de Compostela: Universidad de Santiago de Compostela, 1984.

Benería, Lourdes. *Mujer, economía y patriarcado en la España de Franco*. Barcelona: Cuadernos Anagrama, 1977.

Berglar, Peter. *Opus Dei: Vida y obra del fundador José María Escrivá de Balaguer*. Madrid: Rialp Ediciones, 1987.

Bernal, Antonio M. *La lucha por la tierra y la crisis del Antiguo Régimen*. Madrid: Taurus, 1979.

Biescas, José Antonio, and Manuel Tuñón de Lara. *España bajo la dictadura franquista (1939–1975)*. Vol. 10 of *Historia de España*, edited by Manuel Tuñón de Lara. Barcelona: Editorial Labor, 1980.

Blanco Carrascosa, Juan Angel. *Un arquetipo pedagógico pequeño-burgués: Teoría y práxis de la Institución Libre de Enseñanza*. Valencia: Fernando Torres-Editor, S.A., 1980.

Blee, Kathleen M. *Women of the Klan: Racism and Gender in the 1920s*. Berkeley: University of California Press, 1991.

Bonet, Alberto. *Manual de Acción Católica*. Madrid: Ediciones Acción Católica, 1960.

Borreguero, Concha, Elena Carena, Consuelo de la Sándara, and María Salas. *La mujer española: De la tradición a la modernidad (1960–1980)*. Madrid: Tecnos, 1986.

Boxer, Marilyn, and Jean Quataert, eds. *Connecting Spheres: Women in the Western World, 1500 to the Present*. New York: Oxford University Press, 1987.

Breines, Wini. *Young, White and Miserable: Growing Up Female in the Fifties*. Boston: Beacon Press, 1992.

Bridenthal, Renate, Anita Grossmann, and Marion A. Kaplan. *When Biology Became Destiny*. New York: Monthly Review, 1984.

Brown, Joan L., ed. *Women Writers of Contemporary Spain: Exiles in the Homeland*. Newark: University of Delaware Press, 1991.

Brown, Wendy. "Finding the Man in the State." *Feminist Studies* 18, no. 1 (spring 1992): 7–34.

———. *Manhood and Politics: A Feminist Reading in Political Theory.* Totowa, N.J.: Rowman and Littlefield, 1988.

Cabrera Bosch, María Isabel. "Las mujeres que lucharon solas: Concepción Arenal y Emilia Pardo Bazán." In *El feminismo en España: Dos siglos de historia,* edited by Pilar Folguera. Madrid: Editorial Pablo Iglesias, 1988.

Cacho Viu, Vicente. *La Institución Libre de Enseñanza.* Madrid: Ediciones Rialp, 1962.

Callahan, William. *Church, Politics, and Society in Spain, 1750–1894.* Cambridge, Mass.: Harvard University Press, 1984.

Cámara Villar, Gregorio. *Nacional-Catolicismo y escuela: La socialización política del Franquismo (1936–1951).* Madrid: Editorial Hesperia, 1984.

Campoamor, Clara. *El voto femenino y yo.* Barcelona: LaSal Edicions de les Dones, 1981.

Cancio, Miguel. *Funciones sociales de la universidad: De 1939 a la retirada de la LAU.* Santiago de Compostela: Universidad de Santiago de Compostela, 1986.

Caparrós Lera, J. M., and Rafael de España. *The Spanish Cinema: An Historical Approach.* Madrid: Centre for Cinematic Research, "Film Historia," 1987.

Capel Martínez, Rosa María, and María Angeles Durán. *Mujer y sociedad de España (1700–1975).* Madrid: Ministerio de Cultura, 1982.

———. *El trabajo y la educación de la mujer en España (1900–1930).* Madrid: Ministerio de Cultura, 1986.

Capitán Díaz, Alfonso. *Historia de la educación en España: Pedagogía contemporánea.* Madrid: Dykinson, 1994.

Carandell, Luis. *Vida y milagros de monseñor Escrivá de Balaguer: Fundador del Opus Dei.* Barcelona: Deriva, 1992.

Carr, Raymond. *Modern Spain, 1875–1980.* Oxford: Oxford University Press, 1990.

Castillo Castillo, José. *La Universidad en Galicia: Una aproximación sociológica.* Santiago de Compostela: Universidad de Santiago de Compostela, 1978.

Coleman, Barbara J. "Maidenform(ed): Images of American Women in the 1950s." In Siegel and Kibbey, eds., *Forming and Reforming Identity.*

Colomer i Calsina, Josep M. *Els estudiants de Barcelona sota el Franquisme.* Barcelona: Curial, 1978.

Connelly Ullman, Joan. "La enseñanza superior de la mujer en España: Relaciones entre universitarias españolas y estadounidenses, 1877–1980." In *Nuevas perspectivas sobre la mujer,* edited by the Seminario de Estudios de la Mujer. Madrid: Seminario de Estudios de la Mujer, Universidad Autónoma de Madrid, 1982.

———. *The Tragic Week: A Study of Anticlericalism in Spain, 1875–1912.* Cambridge, Mass.: Harvard University Press, 1968.

Consejo Superior de Mujeres de Acción Católica. *La personalidad de la mujer: Documentos pontificios.* Madrid: Maribel, Artes Gráficas, Tomás Bretón, 1953.

Cornejo-Parriego, Rosalía. *La escritura posmoderna del poder.* Madrid: Editorial Fundamentos, 1993.

Cortada Andreu, Esther. *Escuela mixta y coeducación en Cataluña durante la II República.* Madrid: Instituto de la Mujer, 1988.

Cuesta Escudero, Pedro. *La escuela en la Restauración de la sociedad española (1900–1923).* Madrid: Siglo XXI, 1994.

"Decálogo de la alegría en el hogar cristiano." *Senda,* January 1951.

De Fuenmayor, Amadeo. *Escritos sobre prelaturas personales.* Pamplona: Universidad de Navarra, 1992.

———, ed. *El itinerario jurídico del Opus Dei: Historia y defensa de un carisma.* Pamplona: Colección Canónica de la Universidad de Navarra, 1990.

De Grand, Alexander. *Italian Fascism: Its Origins and Development.* Lincoln: University of Nebraska Press, 1989.

De Grazia, Victoria. *How Fascism Ruled Women: Italy, 1922–1945.* Berkeley: University of California Press, 1992.

De Grazia, Victoria, and Ellen Furlough, eds. *The Sex of Things: Gender and Consumption in Historical Perspective.* Berkeley: University of California Press, 1996.

De Hart, Jane Sherron. "Gender on the Right: Meanings behind the Existential Scream." *Gender and History* 3, no. 3 (1991): 246–67.

———. *Sex, Gender, and the Politics of ERA: A State and the Nation.* New York: Oxford University Press, 1990.

De León, Fray Luis. *La perfecta casada.* In *Obras completas de Fray Luis de León,* edited by Felix García. Madrid: Biblioteca de Autores Españoles, 1944.

Delgado, Buenaventura. *La escuela moderna de ferrer i guardia.* Barcelona: Ediciones CEAC, 1979.

Delibes, Miguel. *Cinco horas con Mario.* Barcelona: Ediciones Destino, 1969.

De Miguel, Amando. *Carta abierta a una universitaria.* Madrid: Ediciones 99, 1973.

———. *Diagnóstico de la universidad.* Madrid: Ediciones Guadarrama, 1973.

———. *Manual de estructura social de España.* Madrid: Editorial Tecnos, 1974.

———. *Miedo a la igualdad varones y mujeres en una sociedad machista.* Barcelona: Grijalbo, 1975.

———. *Sociología del Franquismo: Análisis ideológico de los ministros del régimen.* Barcelona: Editorial Euros, 1975.

D'Emilio, John, and Estelle B. Freedman. *Intimate Matters: A History of Sexuality in America.* New York: Harper and Row, 1988.

Derechos políticos, profesionales y del trabajo de la mujer. Madrid: Imprenta Nacional del Boletín Oficial del Estado, 1961.

Di Febo, Giuliana. "La política de la Secció Femenina de la Falange." *L'Avenç* 14 (March 1979): 56–60.

———. *Resistencia y movimiento de mujeres en España, 1936–1976.* Barcelona: Icaria Editorial, 1979.

———. *La santa de la raza: El culto barroco en la España franquista.* Barcelona: Icaria, 1988.

Dirección General de la Acción Católica Española. *Reglamento General de la Asociación de las Mujeres de Acción Católica.* Toledo: Editorial Católica Toledana, 1940.

Dolkart, Ronald. "The Right in the Década Infame, 1930–1943." In *The Argentine Right: Its History and Intellectual Origins, 1910 to the Present,* edited by Sandra McGee Deutsch and Ronald H. Dolkart. Wilmington, Del.: SR Books, 1993.

Dona, Juana. *Desde la noche y la niebla.* Madrid: Ediciones la Torre, 1977.

Duran, María Angeles. *Liberación y utopía.* Madrid: Akal/Universitaria, 1982.

Ellwood, Sheelagh M. *Franco.* London: Longman, 1994.

———. *Prietas las filas: Historia de Falange Española, 1933–1983.* Barcelona: Crítica, 1984.

———. *Spanish Fascism in the Franco Era: Falange Española de las JONS, 1936–1976.* Basingstoke, N.H.: Macmillan, 1987.

Enders, Victoria. "Nationalism and Feminism: The Sección Femenina of the Falange." *History of European Ideas* 15 (1992): 673–80.

Enrique y Tarancón, Vicente. *El pan nuestro de cada día dánosle hoy* . . . Madrid: Publicaciones HOAC, 1950.

Escobar, Jaime. *Opus Dei: Génesis y expansión en el mundo: Antecedentes sobre el polémico proceso de beatificación de su fundador.* Santiago: LOM Ediciones, 1992.

Escudero, María A. "The Image of Latin America Disseminated in Spain by the Franco Regime: Repercussions in the Configuration of a National Identity." Ph.D. diss., University of California, San Diego, 1994.

"Escuela de Servicio Doméstico: Jueves por la tarde cursos de orientación profesional para cocineras y doncellas." *Teresa,* May 1960.

Espinos Orlando, Juanita. "¿Puede formarse el sentido social?" *Senda,* March 1957.

Estadística de Enseñanza en España. Madrid: Instituto Nacional de Estadística, 1966.

Estatutos de la Institución Teresiana. Madrid: Archivo Histórico Institucion Teresiana, 1990.

Esteve Sedall, Rafael. "El turismo y la reinserción de españa en la cadena imperialista." *Cuadernos de Ciencias Económicas y Empresariales* 4 (1979).

Estruch, Juan. *L'Opus Dei i les seves paradoxes: Un estudi sociologic.* Barcelona: Col Leccio Estudis i Documents, 1993.

Fagoaga, Concha. *Clara Campoamor, la sufragista española.* Madrid: Ministerio de Cultura, 1981.

———. *La voz y el voto de las mujeres: El sufragismo en España, 1877–1931.* Barcelona: Icaria, 1985.

Ferrer y Guardia, Francisco. *The Origin and Ideals of the Modern School.* London: Watts and Co., 1913.

Folguera, Pilar, ed. *El feminismo en España: Dos siglos de historia.* Madrid: Editorial Pablo Iglesias, 1988.

Fontana, Josep, ed. *España bajo el Franquismo.* Barcelona: Editorial Crítica, 1986.

Foucault, Michel. *Historia de la sexualidad.* Madrid: Siglo XXI, 1980.

———. *Microfísica del poder.* Madrid: Las Ediciones de la Piqueta, 1980.

Friedan, Betty. *La mística de la feminidad.* Madrid: Ediciones Jucar, 1974.

Fundación Centro de Enseñanza Especial. Madrid: Fundación Centro Enseñanza Especial, 1991.

Fusi, Juan Pablo. *Franco: Autoritarismo y poder personal.* Madrid: El País, 1985.

Galino, Angeles. "A las universitarias." *La Revista,* January 1959.

———, ed. *Pedro Poveda: Itinerario pedagógico.* Madrid: Consejo Superior de Investigaciones Científicas, Instituto de Pedagogía, 1964.

Gallego Méndez, María Teresa. *Mujer, Falange y Franquismo.* Madrid: Taurus, 1983.

García Delgado, José Luis. "Notas sobre el intervencionismo económico del primer Franquismo." *Revista de Historia Económica* 1 (1985): 135–45.

García Madrid, Angeles. *Requien por la libertad.* Madrid: Copiasol, 1982.

García Nieto, María Carmen. "Las mujeres en la guerra civil de España: Nueva perspectiva." In *Nuevas perspectivas sobre la mujer,* edited by the Seminario de

Estudios de la Mujer. Madrid: Universidad Autónoma de Madrid, 1982.

García Nieto, María Carmen, and Javier M. Donezar. *La España de Franco (1939–1973)*. Madrid: Guadiana, 1975.

García Nieto, María Carmen, and Esperanza Yllán, eds. *Historia de España (1808–1978)*. Barcelona: Crítica, 1989.

Garreta, Nuria, and Pilar Coreaga. *Modelos masculino y femenino en los textos de EGB*. Madrid: Instituto de la Mujer, Ministerio de Cultura, 1987.

Gómez del Manzano, Mercedes. *Pedro Poveda: Dinamismo profético*. Madrid: Narcea, 1991.

González, Manuel Jesús. *La economía política del Franquismo (1940–1970)*. Madrid: Editorial Tecnos, 1979.

González, Margaret Carmell. "Literature of Protest: The Franco Years." Ph.D. diss., Louisiana State University and Agricultural and Mechanical College, 1994.

González Moralejo, Rafael. *El magisterio pontificio y jerárquico en la evolución histórica de la Acción Católica Española*. Madrid: Ediciones Marova S.L., 1967.

González Ruiz, Nicolás. "Familias numerosas: Escenas de hogar: I. Leyes fundamentales." *Senda*, January 1951.

Graham, Helen, and Jo Labanyi, eds. *Spanish Cultural Studies: An Introduction*. Oxford: Oxford University Press, 1995.

Grossmann, Atina. "Feminist Debates about Women and National Socialism." *Gender and History* 3, no. 3 (1991): 350–58.

———. *Reforming Sex: The German Movement for Birth Control and Abortion Reform, 1920–1950*. New York: Oxford University Press, 1995.

Halberstam, David. *The Fifties*. New York: Villard Books, 1993.

Hartley, John. *Popular Reality: Journalism, Modernity, Popular Culture*. London: Arnold, 1996.

Harvey, Brett. *The Fifties: A Women's Oral History*. New York: Harper Collins, 1993.

Hayes, Carlton J. H. *The United States and Spain: An Interpretation*. New York: Sheed and Ward, 1951.

"Hemos preguntado." Interview with Angeles Galino. *La Revista*, May 1962.

Henige, David. *Oral Historiography*. London: Longmans, 1982.

Herr, Richard. *Rural Change and Royal Finances in Spain at the End of the Old Regime*. Berkeley: University of California Press, 1989.

Higonnet, Margaret, ed. *Behind the Lines: Gender and the Two World Wars*. New Haven, Conn.: Yale University Press, 1987.

Holland, Dorothy C., and Margaret A. Eisenhart. *Educated in Romance: Women, Achievement, and College Culture*. Chicago: University of Chicago Press, 1990.

Horowitz, Morris. *Manpower and Education in Franco Spain*. Hamden, Conn.: Archon Books, 1974.

Instituto de la Mujer. *La presencia de las mujeres en el sistema educativo*. Madrid: Instituto de la Mujer, Ministerio de Cultura, 1988.

Jeansonne, Glen. *Women of the Far Right: The Mothers' Movement and World War II*. Chicago: The University of Chicago Press, 1996.

Jiménez, Alberto. *Historia de la universidad española*. Madrid: Alianza Editorial, 1971.

Jiménez Campo, Javier. *El fascismo en la crisis de la Segunda República*. Madrid: Centro de Investigaciones Sociológicas, 1982.

Kaledin, Eugenia. *Mothers and More: American Women in the 1950s.* Boston: Twayne, 1984.

Kaplan, Temma. "Other Scenarios: Women and Spanish Anarchism." In *Becoming Visible: Women in European History,* edited by Renate Bridenthal and Claudia Koonz. Boston: Houghton Mifflin, 1987.

———. "Spanish Anarchism and Women's Liberation." *Journal of Contemporary History* 6, no. 2 (1971).

Kerber, Linda K. "Separate Spheres, Female Worlds, Woman's Place: The Rhetoric of Women's History." *Journal of American History* 75, no. 1 (June 1988).

———. *Women of the Republic: Intellect and Ideology in Revolutionary America.* New York: Norton, 1986.

Kern, Robert. *Liberals, Reformers, and Caciques in Restoration Spain, 1875–1909.* Albuquerque: University of New Mexico Press, 1974.

Klatch, Rebecca. *Women of the New Right.* Philadelphia: Temple University Press, 1987.

Koonz, Claudia. *Mothers in the Fatherland: Women, the Family, and Nazi Politics.* New York: Saint Martin's, 1987.

Laffitte, María. *La mujer en España: Cien años de historia.* Madrid: Aguilar, 1963.

Laín Entralgo, Pedro. *Descargo de conciencia (1930–1960).* Barcelona: Barral Editores, 1976.

———. *Sobre la cultura española.* Madrid: Editora Nacional, 1953.

Latorre, Angel. *Universidad y sociedad.* Barcelona: Ediciones Ariel, 1964.

Le Tourneau, Dominique. *What Is Opus Dei?* Dublin: Mercier Press, 1987.

Le Vaillant, Yvon. *La Santa Mafia: El expediente secreto del Opus Dei.* Mexico: Edamex, 1985.

Linz, Juan J. "An Authoritarian Regime: Spain." In *Politics and Society in Twentieth-Century Spain,* edited by Stanley G. Payne. New York: New Viewpoints, 1976.

Locastro, Gaetano. *Las prelaturas personales: Perfiles jurídicos.* Pamplona: Ediciones Universidad de Navarra, 1991.

López, Francisca. "Myth and Discourse in the Postwar Spanish Novel by Women." Ph.D. diss., University of Connecticut, 1992.

López Díaz-Otazu, Ana María. "Formación profesional de la mujer." *Eidos,* July–December 1958.

———. "Problemas morales y jurídicos del mundo laboral femenino." *Eidos,* January–June 1961.

López Ibor, Juan José. *Discurso a los universitarios españoles.* Madrid: Ediciones Rialp, 1964.

Lummis, Trevor. *Listening to History: The Authenticity of Oral Evidence.* London: Hutchinson, 1987.

Macciocchi, Maria Antonietta. "Female Sexuality in Fascist Ideology." *Feminist Review* 1 (1979): 67–82.

Macias, Ana María. "La mujer cara al tiempo." *La Revista,* January 1962.

"La madre santa." *Senda,* May 1951.

Maillard, M. Luisa. *Asociación Española de Mujeres Universitarias: 1920–1990.* Madrid: AEMU Instituto de la Mujer, 1990.

Mangini, Shirley. "Memories of Resistance: Women Activists from the Spanish Civil War." *Signs* 17 (1991).

———. *Memories of Resistance: Women's Voices from the Spanish Civil War.* New

Haven, Conn.: Yale University Press, 1995.

———. *Rojos y rebeldes: La cultura de la disidencia durante el Franquismo.* Barcelona: Anthropos, 1987.

Marañón, Gregorio. *Amor, conveniencia y eugenesia.* Madrid: Editorial Historia Nueva, 1929.

Maravall, José María. *Dictadura y disentimiento político: Obreros y estudiantes bajo el Franquismo.* Madrid: Editorial Alfaguara, 1978.

Martin, Benjamin. *The Agony of Modernization: Labor and Industrialization in Spain.* Ithaca, N.Y.: ILR Press, 1990.

Martín Gaite, Carmen. *Desde la ventana: Enfoque femenino de la literatura española.* Madrid: Espasa Calpe, 1987.

———. *Esperando el porvenir: Homenaje a Ignacio Aldecoa.* Madrid: Siruela, 1994.

———. *Usos amorosos de la postguerra española.* Madrid: Anagrama, 1987.

"Más hijos, o menos hijos." *Senda,* March 1953.

Maxwell, Kenneth. "Spain's Transition to Democracy: A Model for Eastern Europe?" *Proceedings of the Academy of Political Science* 38, no. 1 (1991): 35–49.

May, Elaine Tyler. *Homeward Bound: American Families in the Cold War Era.* New York: Basic Books, 1988.

Mayans Natal, María Jesús. *Narrativa feminista española de postguerra.* Madrid: Editorial Pliegos, 1991.

Mayordomo Pérez, Alejandro. *Nacional-catolicismo y educación en la España de la postguerra.* Madrid: Ministerio de Educación y Ciencia, Secretaría General Técnica, 1990.

McNamara, Jo Ann Kay. *Sisters in Arms: Catholic Nuns through Two Millennia.* Cambridge, Mass.: Harvard University Press, 1996.

Mitchell, B. R., ed. *International Historical Statistics: Europe 1750–1988.* New York: Stockton Press, 1989.

Molero Pintado, Antonio. *La reforma educativa en la Segunda República española.* Madrid: Aula XXI, Educación Abierta/Santillana, 1977.

Moncada, Alberto. *Historia oral de Opus Dei.* Barcelona: Plaza y Janes, 1987.

Montero Alonso, José. "El salario femenino." *Teresa,* March 1954.

Montoro Romero, Ricardo. *La universidad en la España de Franco (1939–1970): Un análisis sociológico.* Madrid: Centro de Investigaciones Sociológicas, 1981.

Moreno, María Angustias. *El Opus Dei anexo a una historia.* Barcelona: Editorial Planeta, 1976.

"La mujer española." *Senda,* January 1953.

"Las mujeres quieren trabajar: La Escuela de Auxiliares de Investigación." *Teresa,* March 1956.

"Las mujeres quieren trabajar: La formación técnica de archiveros, bibliotecarios y arqueólogos." *Teresa,* March 1957.

"Las mujeres quieren trabajar: El periodismo." *Teresa,* November 1956.

"Las mujeres se reunen en París, Londres y Dublín." *Senda,* July–August 1956.

Nadal, Jordi. *El fracaso de la Revolución Industrial en España.* Barcelona: Ariel, 1975.

———. *La población española (siglos XVI a XX).* Barcelona: Ariel, 1974.

Nash, Mary. *Defying Male Civilization: Women in the Civil War.* Denver: Arden Press, 1995.

————. *Mujeres Libres: España, 1936–1939*. Barcelona: Tusquets, 1975.

————. *Mujer y movimiento obrero en España, 1931–1939*. Barcelona: Editorial Fontamara, 1981.

————. "El neomaltusianismo anarquista y los conocimientos populares sobre control de la natalidad en España." In *Presencia y protagonismo: Aspectos de la historia de la mujer,* edited by Mary Nash. Barcelona: Ediciones del Serbal, 1984.

Navarro García, Clotilde. *La educación y el Nacional-Catolicismo.* Castilla La Mancha: Universidad de Castilla la Mancha, 1993.

Nelken, Margarita. *La condición social de la mujer en España.* Madrid: CVS Ediciones, 1975.

Nolan, Mary. *Visions of Modernity: American Business and the Modernization of Germany.* New York: Oxford University Press, 1994.

O'Connor, William. *Opus Dei: An Open Book: A Reply to* The Secret World of Opus Dei, *by Michael Walsh.* Dublin: Mercier Press, 1991.

Ollero Tassara, Andrés. *Universidad y política: Tradición y secularización en el siglo XIX español.* Madrid: Instituto de Estudios Políticos, 1972.

Oltra, Benjamín, and Amando de Miguel. "Bonapartismo y Catolicismo: Una hipótesis sobre los orígenes ideológicos del Franquismo." *Revista de Sociología "Papers"* 8 (1978).

O'Neill, Carlota. *Una mujer en la guerra de España.* Madrid: Turner, 1979.

Ordóñez, Elizabeth J. *Voices of Their Own: Contemporary Spanish Narrative by Women.* Lewisburg, Penn.: Buckwell University Press, 1991.

Ortega y Gasset, José. *Estudios sobre el amor.* Madrid: Alianza Editorial, 1981.

————. *La misión de la universidad.* Madrid: Revista de Occidente, 1930.

————. *La rebelión de las masas.* Madrid: Revista de Occidente, 1930.

Palazuelos, Enrique. *Movimiento estudiantil y democratización de la Universidad.* Madrid: Manifiesto Editorial, 1977.

Pamies, Teresa. *Records de guerra i d'exili (Obres selectes i inedites).* Barcelona: Dopesa, 1976.

El Papa habla a los padres de familia. Madrid: Confederación Católica de Padres de Familia, 1941.

"El Papa se preocupa de la familia." *Senda,* March 1950.

París, Carlos. *La universidad española actual: Posibilidades y frustraciones.* Madrid: Edicusa, 1974.

Pascual, M. A. "La mujer: Dignidad semejante, misión complementaria." *La Revista,* May 1962.

Passerini, Luisa. *Fascism in Popular Memory: The Cultural Experience of the Turin Working Class.* London: Cambridge University Press, 1977.

————. "Oral History in Italy after the Second World War: From Populism to Subjectivity." *International Journal of Oral History* 9, no. 2 (1988): 114–24.

————. "Work, Ideology, and Consensus under Italian Fascism." *History Workshop Journal* 8 (1979): 82–108.

————, ed. *Memory and Totalitarianism: International Yearbook of Oral History and Life Stories.* Vol. 1. Oxford: Oxford University Press, 1992.

Pastor, María Inmaculada. *La educación femenina en la postguerra (1939–1945): El caso de Mallorca.* Madrid: Instituto de la Mujer, 1984.

Payne, Stanley G. *Falange: A History of Spanish Fascism.* Stanford, Calif.: Stanford University Press, 1965.

———. *The Franco Regime: 1936–1975.* Madison: University of Wisconsin Press, 1987.

———. *Spain's First Democracy: The Second Republic, 1931–1936.* Madison: University of Wisconsin Press, 1993.

Pemartín, José. *Qué es "lo nuevo": Consideraciones sobre el momento español actual.* Sevilla: Tip. Alvarez y Zambrano, 1937.

Pérez Galdós, Benito. *Fortunata and Jancita: Two Stories of Married Women.* Translated and with an introduction by Agnes Moncy Gullón. Athens: University of Georgia Press, 1986.

"Pio XII y la mujer." *Senda,* March 1956.

Pius XI. "Casti Connubii: Carta encíclica de Su Santidad Pio XI sobre la dignidad del matrimonio." In *El Papa habla a los padres de familia.* Madrid: Confederación Católica de Padres de Familia, 1941.

———. "Divini Illius Magistri: Carta encíclica de Su Santidad Pio XI sobre la educación cristiana de la juventud." In *El Papa habla a los padres de familia.* Madrid: Confederación Católica de Padres de Familia, 1941.

———. *Quadragesimo Anno.* Rome: Typis Polyglottis Vaticanis, 1931.

Pons Prades, Eduardo. *Guerrillas españolas (1936–1960).* Barcelona: Espejo de España, 1978.

Posa, Elena. "Una dona portadora de valors eterns: La Sección Femenina, 1934–1952." *Taula di Camvi* 5 (May–June 1977): 121–33.

Poveda, Pedro. *Folletos.* Madrid: Publicaciones del Archivo de la Institución Teresiana, 1989.

Preston, Paul. *Franco: A Biography.* New York: Basic Books, 1994.

Pridhamm, Geoffrey. "Democratic Transitions in Theory and Practice: Southern European Lessons for Eastern Europe." In *Democratization in Eastern Europe: Domestic and International Perspectives,* edited by Geoffrey Pridham and Tatu Vanhanen. New York: Routledge, 1994.

Primo de Rivera, Pilar. *Discursos, Circulares, Escritos.* Madrid, n.d.

———. *Recuerdos de una vida.* Madrid: Ediciones Dyrsa, 1983.

Puelles Benítez, Manuel. *Educación e ideología en la España contemporánea.* Barcelona: Editorial Labor, 1980.

Rabinow, Paul, ed. *The Foucault Reader.* New York: Pantheon Books, 1984.

Reig Tapia, Alberto. *Ideologia e historia: Sobre la represión franquista en la guerra civil.* Madrid: Editorial Akal, 1984.

Río Cisneros, Agustín del. *Revolución Nacional (Puntos de Falange).* Madrid: Ediciones Prensa del Movimiento, 1949.

Roberts, Mary Louise. "Gender, Consumption, and Commodity Culture." *American Historical Review* 103, no. 3 (June 1998): 817–44.

Rodríguez, Rafaela. "Hacia qué mujer vamos." *Eidos,* July–December 1955.

Rodríguez de Lecea, Teresa. *Francisco Giner de los Ríos: Escritos sobre la universidad española.* Madrid: Espasa Calpe, Colección Austral, 1990.

Rosenberg, Rosalind. *Beyond Separate Spheres: Intellectual Roots of Modern Feminism.* New Haven, Conn.: Yale University Press, 1982.

Ros Hombravella, Jacinto, ed. *Capitalismo español: De la autarquia a la estabilización (1939–1959).* Madrid: Alianza, 1973.

Rossi, Rosa. "Teresa de Jesús: La mujer y la Iglesia." *Mientras Tanto* 14 (1982):

63–79.

———. "Teresa de Jesús: La mujer y la palabra." *Mientras Tanto* 15 (1983): 29–47.

Ruiz Rico, Juan José. *El papel político de la iglesia católica en la España de Franco.* Madrid: Editorial Tecnos, 1977.

Saez Alba, A. *La Asociación Católica Nacional de propagandistas y el caso del Correo de Andalucía.* París: Ruedo Ibérico, 1974.

Sainz Jackson, Rosario. *Los derechos de la mujer.* Madrid: Publicaciones Españolas, 1968.

Sánchez Brito, Margarita. "Protagonista: La joven: Como ven las azafatas su propia vida." *Senda,* January 1959.

———. "Protagonista: La joven: Las policias sanitarias una profesión que no pueden hacer ellos." *Senda,* July 1959.

Sánchez López, Rosario. *Mujer española, una sombra de destino en lo universal: Trayectoria histórica de Sección Femenina de Falange (1934–1977).* Murcia: Universidad de Murcia, 1990.

Santamarina, Alvaro. *Joaquín Ruiz Giménez: Perfil humano y político.* Madrid: Editorial Cambio 16, 1977.

Santa Teresa, Silverio de. *Santa Teresa modelo de feminismo cristiano.* Burgos: Topografía del Monte Carmelo, 1931.

Scanlon, Geraldine. "La mujer y la instrucción pública: De la Ley Moyano a la II República." *Historia de la Educación* 6 (1987).

———. *La polémica feminista en la España contemporánea (1868–1974).* Madrid: Siglo XXI, 1976.

Scott, Joan Wallach. *Gender and the Politics of History.* New York: Columbia University Press, 1988.

Seage, Julio, and Pedro de Blas. "La administración educativa en España (1900–1971)." *Revista de Educación* 240 (September–October 1975).

"Se ha celebrado en Madrid la I Asamblea Nacional de Enfermeras." *Teresa,* May 1959.

La Sección Femenina de FET y de las JONS. "Síntesis de una organización." *Teresa,* October 1959.

Shubert, Adrian. *A Social History of Modern Spain.* London: Routledge, 1990.

Siegel, Carol, and Ann Kibbey, eds. *Forming and Reforming Identity.* New York: New York University Press, 1995.

Slaughter, Jane, and Robert Kern, eds. *European Women on the Left: Socialism, Feminism, and the Problems Faced by Political Women, 1880 to the Present.* Westport, Conn.: Greenwood Press, 1981.

Smith, Bonnie. *Changing Lives: Women in European History since 1700.* London: Heath, 1989.

Solino, María Elena. "Women and Children First: The Novels of Ana María Matute, Carmen Martín Gaite, Ana María Moix, and Esther Tusquets." Ph.D. diss., Yale University, 1993.

Sopeña Monsalve, Andrés. *El Florido Pensil: Memoria de la escuela nacionalcatólica.* Barcelona: Crítica, 1994.

Suárez, Angel, and Equipo 36. *Libro blanco de las cárceles franquistas.* París: Editions Ruedo Ibérico, 1976.

Suárez Fernández, Luis. *Crónica de la Sección Femenina y su tiempo.* Madrid: Asociación Nueva Andadura, 1993.

Subirats, Marina, and Cristina Brullet. *Rosa y azul: La transmisión de los géneros en la escuela mixta*. Madrid: Instituto de la Mujer, Ministerio de Cultura, 1988.

Sueiro, Daniel, and Bernardo Díaz Nosty. *Historia del Franquismo*. Madrid: Sarpe, 1986.

Tedde de Lorca, Pedro. "Economía y Franquismo: A propósito de una biografía." *Revista de Historia Económica* 3 (1986): 627–37.

Thébaud, Françoise, ed. *A History of Women in the West: Toward a Cultural Identity in the Twentieth Century*. Cambridge, Mass.: Harvard University Press, 1994.

Thompson, Paul Richard. *The Voice of the Past*. 2d ed. Oxford: Oxford University Press, 1988.

Torres, Rafael. *La vida amorosa en tiempos de Franco*. Madrid: Ediciones Temas de Hoy, 1996.

Tovar, Antonio. *Universidad y educación de masas*. Barcelona: Ediciones Ariel, 1968.

Tuñón de Lara, Manuel. "Algunas propuestas metodológicas para el análisis del Franquismo." In *Ideología y Sociedad en la España contemporánea: Por un análisis del Franquismo*, edited by Manuel Tuñón de Lara. Madrid: Edicusa, 1977.

———. *Estudios sobre el Siglo XIX Español*. Madrid, 1971.

Tuñón de Lara, Manuel, José María Jover Zamora, José Luis García Delgado, and David Ruiz Gonzáles. *Revolución burguesa, oligarquía y Constitucionalismo (1834–1923)*. Barcelona: Labor, 1981.

Tuñón de Lara, Manuel, Julio Aróstegui, Angel Viñas, Gabriel Cardone, and Josep M. Brical, eds. *La Guerra Civil Española 50 años después*. Madrid: Labor, 1986.

"Una interviú a través del Atlántico con Pilar Bellosillo." *Senda*, November 1956.

United Nations Scientific and Cultural Organization. *World Survey of Education*. Vol. 4, *Higher Education*. New York: Unesco Publications Center, 1966.

"Universitarios: Las estudiantes se examinan . . . y os examinan." *Senda*, February 1960.

Viñas, Angel. "De la autarquia a la liberalización: Veinte aniversario del plan de estabilización." *El País*, 21 July 1979.

Vives, Juan Luis. *Instrucción de la mujer cristiana*. Buenos Aires: Espasa Calpe, 1940.

Walsh, Michael. *Opus Dei: An Investigation into the Secret Society Struggling for Power within the Catholic Church*. San Francisco: Harper San Francisco, 1992.

———. *The Secret World of Opus Dei*. London: Crafton, 1989.

Weedon, Chris. *Feminist Practice and Poststructuralist Theory*. Oxford: Basil Blackwell, 1987.

Yetano, Ana. *La enseñanza religiosa en la España de la Restauración (1900–1920)*. Barcelona: Anthropos, 1988.

Zulueta, Carmen. *Cien años de educación de la mujer española: Historia del Instituto Internacional*. Madrid: Editorial Castalia, 1992.

INDEX

CPSIA information can be obtained
at www.ICGtesting.com
Printed in the USA
LVHW021712291121
704745LV00003B/531